Lessons from Europe?

For Tasha and Zara

Lessons from Europe?

What Americans Can Learn from European Public Policies

R. Daniel Kelemen

Rutgers University

Editor

Los Angeles | London | New Delhi
Singapore | Washington DC

Los Angeles | London | New Delhi
Singapore | Washington DC

FOR INFORMATION:

CQ Press

An Imprint of SAGE Publications, Inc.

2455 Teller Road

Thousand Oaks, California 91320

E-mail: order@sagepub.com

SAGE Publications Ltd.

1 Oliver's Yard

55 City Road

London EC1Y 1SP

United Kingdom

SAGE Publications India Pvt. Ltd.

B 1/I 1 Mohan Cooperative Industrial Area

Mathura Road, New Delhi 110 044

India

SAGE Publications Asia-Pacific Pte. Ltd.

3 Church Street

#10-04 Samsung Hub

Singapore 049483

Printed in the United States of America

Library of Congress Cataloging-in-Publication Data

Lessons from Europe? : what can Americans learn from European
public policies / R. Daniel Kenelmen, Rutgers University, editor.

p. cm.

Includes bibliographical references and index.

ISBN 978-1-4833-4375-4 (pbk. : alk. paper)

1. European Union countries—Politics and government—21st century.
2. Policy sciences—European Union countries. 3. Public
administration—European Union countries. I. Kenelmen,
R. Daniel, editor of compilation.

JN30.L465 2014
320.6094--dc23   2013032505

This book is printed on acid-free paper.

Acquisitions Editor: Charisse Kiino

Editorial Assistant: Davia Grant

Production Editor: Laura Barrett

Copy Editor: Diane DiMura

Typesetter: C&M Digitals (P) Ltd.

Proofreader: Ellen Howard

Indexer: Ellen Slavitz

Cover Designer: Glenn Vogel

Marketing Manager: Erica DeLuca

14 15 16 17 18 10 9 8 7 6 5 4 3 2 1

Contents

Preface

The United States is facing a number of major policy challenges, from an unaffordable health care system, to failing schools, to a fractured social safety net and rising inequality, to a mounting climate crisis, to high long-term unemployment, to a massive government debt. The economically advanced democracies of Europe face many of the same policy challenges we do, and they have confronted them in a variety of ways—some successful, some not. This book explores what US policymakers can learn from the experiences—both successes and failures—of European democracies in confronting our common policy challenges.

Too often, public policy debates and even scholarly research on public policy in the United States fail to take into account European experiences where these might offer useful lessons. Where public discussions do invoke comparisons with European policies, these are often based on misleading rhetoric and caricatures that have little to do with the realities of contemporary European public policies. On the Left, some idealize European social democracies ignoring the many problems and policy failings that countries across the continent are contending with today. On the Right, many treat *Europe* as a synonym for high taxes, big government, and economic stagnation, ignoring the impressive successes of many European countries in many policy domains. This book seeks to move beyond rhetoric and simplistic understandings to examine in detail what Americans can actually learn from the experiences of European democracies in confronting our common challenges across a wide range of policy areas.

The book has been crafted with an undergraduate audience in mind, with the aim that the book would be adopted in undergraduate courses on comparative public policy, comparative politics, European politics, and—for those who wish to bring in a comparative perspective—courses on American politics and public policy. I wrote this book because no book quite like it existed. Of course, there are a number of fine books that focus on transatlantic comparisons relating to public policy, some exploring the scale, nature, and causes of transatlantic differences, others making arguments about whose policies are superior and why. There are also general texts on comparative public policy and lesson drawing in public policy that touch on themes related to those explored here. However, none of these books do precisely what *Lessons from Europe?* does: bring together leading experts in their fields to offer even-handed comparisons of what American policymakers and citizens might learn from European experiences across a wide range of policy areas.

The book begins with my introduction, which explores why contemporary discussions of Europe in the American political arena are so often plagued by distortion and misunderstanding and makes the case that Americans can benefit by drawing lessons from Europe. The eight policy area case-study chapters focus on public policies in a range of salient fields: work–family reconciliation, health care, pensions, labor markets, immigration, climate change, transportation, and political reform. In each chapter, the authors explore what US citizens and policymakers can learn from a variety of European policies in that field. In the conclusion, Kent Weaver takes an overarching view, reflecting on the many obstacles to applying lessons from Europe in the United States and examining how and when—despite these obstacles—American policymakers might still use lessons from Europe in crafting policy. As I discuss in the introduction, the policy areas covered in this book are only a sampling of the many fields where Americans might usefully draw lessons from Europe. The book aims to open a discussion, not to close it. I hope the book will serve as an invitation to a way of thinking, inspiring readers to explore lessons from Europe in other policy areas of interest to them.

Acknowledgments

This book is the culmination of a three-year series of events I organized as director of Rutgers University's Center for European Studies. The center hosted a number of guest speakers and a Jean Monnet Research Workshop on the theme of "Lessons from Europe," bringing together the authors who eventually contributed to this volume. We benefited from the generous funding of the European Commission's Life Long Learning Programme through the Jean Monnet Chair I held here at Rutgers. We benefited also from funding from Rutgers School of Arts and Sciences, Office of Undergraduate Education's Signature Course program, which helped bring outside speakers to visit the new Lessons from Europe course I developed around the themes explored in this book.

I thank all of the contributors to the volume for their commitment to the project and for the outstanding chapters they have produced. Thanks goes also to a range of scholars and policymakers who contributed to the project in various ways, including Erik Bleich, Mark Blyth, Heather Boushey, James Bradbury, Thomas Brewer, Martin Bunzl, Sir Alan Collins, Rafaela Dancygier, Derek DeLia,

Christian Egenhofer, Denny Ellerman, Frank Felder, Alexandra Filindra, Arne Jungjohann, Nathaniel Keohane, Julia Lynch, Per Kongshøj Madsen, Ambassador Jarl Frijs-Madsen, David Mechanic, Michael Mehling, Bruce Mizrach, Xavier Prats Monné, Kimberly Morgan, Robert Noland, Olivier Pairault, William Rodgers, Patricia Roos, Pasi Sahlberg, Joseph Seneca, Friedo Sielemann, Carl Van Horn, Jane Waldfogel, and Thomas Zeltner. Special thanks also to the staff of the Center for European Studies, Susanna Treesh, Amanda Marziliano, and Erin Heidt-Forsythe, who organized events in connection with the project, and to Alexander Jakubow who provided extensive editorial assistance on the book. Thanks also to the scholars who took such great care in reviewing the manuscript for CQ Press: Daniel Allen, Anderson University; Mark Ferguson, University of Alabama; Maria Garcia-Acevedo, California State University, Northridge; Marianne Githens, Goucher College, and two anonymous reviewers; and to my editor at CQ Press, Charisse Kiino, who shared my enthusiasm for the manuscript and offered helpful advice in crafting the final version. Finally, a great thanks to the hundreds of students who have taken my Lessons from Europe course in recent years; their enthusiasm for learning from Europe provided a constant source of inspiration as we completed this project.

R. Daniel Kelemen
Philadelphia, July 20, 2013

Note: This project has been funded with support from the European Commission. This publication reflects the views only of the author, and the commission cannot be held responsible for any use that may be made of the information contained therein.

Education and Culture DG

Lifelong Learning Programme

About the Contributors

Lawrence D. Brown is Professor of Health Policy and Management in the Mailman School of Public Health at Columbia University. A political scientist, he got a Ph.D. in government at Harvard University in 1973. After positions at Harvard, the Brookings Institution, and the University of Michigan, in 1988 he came to Columbia, where he chaired the Department of Health Policy and Management for ten years and the university's Public Policy Consortium for three years. He is the author of Politics and Health Care Organizations: HMOs as Federal Policy (Brookings Institution, 1983) and of articles on the political dimensions of community cost containment, expansion of coverage for the uninsured, national health reform, the role of analysis in the formation of health policy, and cross-national health policy. Mr. Brown edited the Journal of Health Politics, Policy and Law for five years, has served on several national advisory committees for the Robert Wood Johnson Foundation, has an RWJ Investigators in Health Policy award, and is a member of the Institute of Medicine.

Ralph Buehler is an Associate Professor in the Urban Affairs & Planning at Virginia Tech's Alexandria Center. Most of his research has an international comparative perspective, contrasting transport and land-use policies, transport systems, and travel behavior in Western Europe and North America. His research interests fall into three areas: (1) the influence of transport policy, land use, socio-demographics on travel behavior; (2) bicycling, active travel, and public health; and (3) and public transport demand, supply, financial efficiency, and policy

Frank J. Convery is Senior Fellow and chairman of the board of the UCD Earth Institute, University College, Dublin. He was educated at University College Dublin and the State University of New York and has degrees in forestry and resource economics. Prior to taking up his post at UCD, he was Assistant and then Associate Professor of Natural Resource Economics at Duke University, USA and Research Professor at the Economic and Social Research Institute, Ireland. Frank

Convery has been active on a number of EU wide investigations and bodies, including membership of the Science Committee of the European Environment Agency and Honorary President of the European Association of Environmental and Resource Economists. He has written extensively on resource and environmental economics issues with particular reference to the use of market based instruments for environmental policy.

Janet C. Gornick is Professor of Political Science and Sociology at the Graduate Center of the City University of New York. She is also Director of LIS (formerly, the Luxembourg Income Study), a cross-national data archive and research center located in Luxembourg. Most of her research is comparative, across the industrialized countries, and concerns social welfare policies and their impact on family wellbeing and gender equality. She is co-author or co-editor of three books: *Families That Work: Policies for Reconciling Parenthood and Employment* (Russell Sage Foundation 2003); *Gender Equality: Transforming Family Divisions of Labor* (Verso Press 2009); and *Income Inequality: Economic Disparities and the Middle Class in Affluent Countries* (Stanford University Press 2013). She has published articles on gender, employment, and social policy in several journals, including the *American Sociological Review;* the *Annual Review of Sociology;* the *Socio-Economic Review;* the *Journal of European Social Policy;* the *European Sociological Review; Social Science Quarterly; Monthly Labor Review;* and *Feminist Economics.*

Ariane Hegewisch is a Study Director with responsibility for issues of workplace discrimination, workforce development and work-life reconciliation, at the Institute for Women's Policy Research in Washington, DC. She is a specialist in comparative human resource management, with a focus on policies and legislative approaches to facilitate greater work life reconciliation and gender equality, in the US and internationally. Prior to coming to the USA she taught comparative European human resource management at Cranfield School of Management in the UK where she was a founding researcher of the Cranet Survey of International HRM, the largest independent survey of human resource management policies and practices, covering 40 countries worldwide. She has published many papers and articles and co-edited several books, including *Women, Work and Inequality: The Challenge of Equal Pay in a Deregulated Labour Market.*

Steven Hill is a writer, columnist and political professional based in the United States with two decades of experience in politics. He is a frequent speaker at academic, government, NGO and business events, speaking on a wide range of topics related to politics, economics, climate change, global complexity, geo-strategy and trends. Mr. Hill is the author, most recently, of *Europe's Promise: Why the European Way Is the Best Hope for an Insecure Age* (www.EuropesPromise.org), published in January 2010. His previous books include *10 Steps to Repair American Democracy, Whose Vote Counts* (with Rob Richie) and *Fixing Elections: The Failure of America's Winner Take All Politics*. Mr. Hill is a prolific writer and commentator who has been widely published and quoted in media around the world. Mr Hill has also appeared on international, national and local radio and television programs, and he has lectured widely in the United States and Europe. His website is www.Steven-Hill.com.

R. Daniel Kelemen is Professor of Political Science and Jean Monnet Chair at Rutgers University. His research interests include the politics of the European Union, law and politics, comparative political economy, and comparative public policy. He is author of two books — *Eurolegalism: The Transformation of Law and Regulation in the European Union* (Harvard University Press, 2011) and *The Rules of Federalism: Institutions and Regulatory Politics in the EU and Beyond* (Harvard University Press, 2004), as well as over forty book chapters and articles, and he is co-editor of the *Oxford Handbook of Law and Politics* (Oxford University Press, 2008). He serves on the editorial boards of the *Journal of European Public Policy and West European Politics* and is a former member of the Executive Committee of the European Union Studies Association. Prior to Rutgers, Kelemen was Fellow in Politics, Lincoln College, University of Oxford. He has been a Member of the Institute for Advanced Study at Princeton, a Fulbright Fellow in European Union Studies at the Centre for European Policy Studies in Brussels, and he is currently a Fellow of the Program in Law and Public Affairs at the Woodrow Wilson School of Public and International Affairs at Princeton University.

Mitchell A. Orenstein is Professor and Chair of Political Science at Northeastern University in Boston, MA. A scholar of international affairs and European politics, Orenstein is best known for his work on the political economy of policy reform in Central and Eastern Europe after 1989, pension privatization globally since the 1990s, and the diffusion of neoliberalism. He is the author of *Out of the Red: Building Capitalism and Democracy in Postcommunist Europe* (Michigan, 2001), *Roma in an Expanding Europe: Breaking the Poverty Cycle* (World Bank 2005; coauthors Dena Ringold and Erika Wilkens), and *Pension Privatization: The Transnational Campaign for Social Security Reform* (Princeton 2008). His articles have appeared in *Governance, Comparative Political Studies, Journal of Democracy, Post-Soviet Affairs*, and *International Social Security Review*. He is also Chair of the Executive Committee of the new Center for International Affairs and World Cultures at Northeastern University.

John Pucher is a Professor in the Bloustein School of Planning and Public Policy at Rutgers University. Pucher has conducted research on a wide range of topics in transport economics and finance, including numerous projects for the U.S. Department of Transportation, the Canadian government, and various European ministries of transport. For almost three decades, he has examined differences in travel behavior, transport systems, and transport policies in Europe, Canada, and the USA. Over the past twelve years, Pucher's research has focused on walking and bicycling. His international comparative analysis has included Australia, Canada, the USA, Germany, the Netherlands, Denmark and several other European countries. He has published 35 articles and book chapters on walking and cycling and given over a hundred featured talks, keynote addresses, and conference talks on this subject.

Martin Schain is Professor of Politics at New York University. Among other books, he is the author of *The Politics of Immigration in France, Britain and the United States: A Comparative Study*, second edition (Palgrave, 2012), French Communism and Local Power (St. Martin's, 1985), and co-author of Politics in France (Harper-Collins, 1992). He is co-editor and author of Comparative Federalism: *The US and EU in Comparative Perspective* (Oxford, 2006) and *Shadows Over Europe: The Development and Impact of the Extreme Right in Europe* (Palgrave, 2002). Professor Schain is the founder and former director of the Center for European Studis at NYU and former chair of the European Union Studies Association. He is co-editor of the transatlantic scholarly journal, *Comparative European Politics*.

Tobias Schulze-Cleven is Assistant Professor of Labor Studies and Employment Relations at Rutgers University. He specializes in the comparative political economy of labor market and education reforms in advanced democracies, studying both the drivers and the consequences of contemporary institutional changes. His current book project analyzes changes in labor market policy in Europe, focusing in particular on the role of unions in shaping national processes of adaptation in Germany and Denmark. Professor Schulze-Cleven's research has been published in journal articles, book chapters, and newspapers. His work has been supported by fellowships from Harvard's Labor and Worklife Program, Germany's Max Planck Society, and the University of California's Labor and Employment Research Fund.

R. Kent Weaver joined the Georgetown Public Policy Institute as Professor of Public Policy in the fall of 2002, after 19 years at the Brookings Institution. Weaver's major fields of interest are American and comparative social policy, comparative political institutions, and the politics of expertise. He is particularly interested in understanding how political institutions, past policy choices, and the motivations of politicians interact to shape public policy choices. Much of his work has attempted to understand when and why politicians undertake actions that appear to offer more political risks than rewards, and how they attempt to avoid blame when they do so. He is currently completing a book on what the United States can learn from the experiences of other advanced industrial countries in reforming their public pension systems. He is also writing another book on how states have implemented welfare reform legislation in the United States.

Chapter 1

Introduction: Why Look to Europe for Lessons?

R. Daniel Kelemen

Americans are looking for solutions to major policy challenges. The United States faces high unemployment, an unaffordable health care system that leaves millions uninsured, failing urban schools, a mounting climate crisis, a broken immigration system, rising inequality, a fractured social safety net, an aging population generating rising pension costs, and a massive and growing government debt, to name just a few challenges. In these areas and many more, American policymakers and citizens are engaged in heated debates about how our policies should be reformed. To understand which policies are likely to be effective in meeting our challenges and which are not, we must of course look to the lessons of our history and to the wealth of policy ideas circulating in our public sphere—among political parties, think tanks, academics, state and local governments, and citizens.

But this book is dedicated to another proposition—namely, that Americans should also look abroad for policy lessons. We should examine how other advanced democracies have addressed challenges similar to those we face, understand which policies have proved successful and which have failed, and consider whether these experiences might inform our own choices. In particular, the contributors to this book argue that the varied experiences of economically advanced European democracies offer a rich source of policy lessons—both negative and positive lessons—that provide valuable insights for policymaking in the United States.

We recognize the challenges in drawing meaningful lessons from European experiences and the even greater political and cultural barriers to applying any such lessons in the United States. But, difficult as it is, lesson drawing is inevitable. As discussed below, American citizens and policymakers draw lessons from Europe all the time, but they often do so based on misinformation and prejudice. This book seeks to move beyond the misleading rhetoric and distorted understandings that have characterized recent discussions of Europe in the United States and to explore what Americans can actually learn from the experiences of European democracies in confronting our common twenty-first-century policy challenges.

Why Europe? Why Now?

It might strike many readers as an odd moment in time to look to Europe for anything but the most negative lessons. Much of the continent is mired in recession and record unemployment. Greece, Ireland, Portugal, and Spain are struggling with profound debt crises. Ineffective handling of the eurozone crisis by European leaders has sparked fears that the common currency may collapse. The US media is full of gloomy stories about Europe, such as *Time* magazine's August 2011 cover story on "The End of Europe" (Foroohar 2011). Titles of recent books, such as *After the Fall: The End of the European Dream and the Decline of a Continent* (Lacquer 2012), *The Decline and Fall of Europe* (Bongiovanni 2012), *The End of the West: The Once and Future Europe* (Marquand 2011) reflect the widespread view that Europe is an *old* continent in terminal decline, fading into irrelevance in the face of the rise of Brazil, Russia, India, and China, the *BRIC* economies.

Negative references to Europe have become a regular staple of national political discourse in America in recent years. Mitt Romney and other candidates in the 2012 Republican primary accused President Obama of seeking to transform the United States into a European-style social welfare state and said he must be stopped. As Romney put it in his New Hampshire primary victory speech, "He [Obama] wants to turn America into a European-style social welfare state. We want to make sure that we remain a free and prosperous land of opportunity." Or as primary candidate and former Pennsylvania Senator Rick Santorum stated repeatedly on the campaign trail, "You want to see America after the Obama administration is through, just read up on Greece" (Fischer 2012).

Democrats talk far less about Europe than Republicans. Some prominent public intellectuals on the American Left do argue that we can learn valuable lessons from European public policies. Paul Krugman, for instance, has argued that the United States can draw positive lessons from European social democracies on how to achieve both social justice and economic growth, and he has argued that we can draw negative lessons about austerity policies from their failure in Europe (Krugman 2010, 2011). Though many Democratic politicians surely agree, they are generally reluctant to admit as much publicly. There are exceptions—such as when President Obama called for the United States to draw lessons from Germany's successful youth vocational training programs in his 2013 State of the Union address (Hill 2013). But generally Democratic politicians avoid mentioning lessons from European experiences when discussing public policy reform, even where

European experiences are clearly relevant to the proposals they are advocating, in areas such as health care, climate change, public transportation, or work–life balance. The reluctance of Democrats to publicly highlight positive lessons from Europe is understandable. In a political environment that often treats European ideas with skepticism or outright hostility, suggesting that a reform proposal is inspired by a policy in Europe would be a good way to kill it.

Recent discussions of Europe in the American political arena have produced more heat than light. Much has been said; almost nothing has been learned. Most discussions of Europe are based on inaccurate caricatures, not analysis of actual European policies. Consider for instance how comparisons with Europe were invoked in the context of the debate over health care reform in 2009 and 2010. Opponents of health care reform in Congress and town hall meetings across America regularly equated proposals for universal health insurance coverage in the United States with the specter of *socialized medicine* and a British-style state-run health bureaucracy. Our public debates rarely recognized that in fact most European countries achieve universal coverage while leaving health care provision and even insurance in private hands. There was little discussion of whether we might draw lessons from the most successful European models, such as those found in Switzerland, the Netherlands, or Germany.[1]

The recession that has plagued much of Europe in recent years has provided fodder for simplistic, blanket attacks on European economic models. Critics of European social democracy—particularly those on the Right—treat *Europe* as a synonym for big government, high taxes, crushing debt, and economic stagnation. They have interpreted the recent crisis as proof of their claims that the European social model leads to ruin. In short: Europe = Socialism = Greece. This line of argument ignores some inconvenient truths about the current crisis and about the divergent experiences of various European economies throughout the crisis. First, this view ignores the fact that a number of countries in the European Union (EU) have weathered the global recession with lower unemployment rates than those in the United States. Second, this view ignores the fact that the more prosperous European countries funding the euro zone bailout, above all Germany, have larger social welfare states than the struggling countries (Greece, Ireland, Portugal, and Spain) who have received the bailouts. In short, the crisis has not demonstrated the failure of social market economies (some of which are performing well). Rather, the crisis has demonstrated the flaws in the design of the governance system for the euro zone currency and the failings of the economic policies of some European countries that have lost competitiveness within the bloc. More generally, the bogus depictions of Europe from the Right ignore the impressive achievements of many European social democracies. European countries continue to dominate the top twenty in international rankings of most conceivable measures of success, from gross domestic product (GDP) per capita, to standard of living, to economic competitiveness, to good governance,[2] and they stand out as leaders in specific fields, such as health, education, worker training, social welfare, transportation, and many more.

While distorted views of Europe may be most common on the Right, many on the American Left also hold biased views of Europe. Many Europhiles on the left view Europe through rose-colored glasses (Geoghegan 2011; Rifkin 2004).[3] Some imagine a community of social-democratic nirvanas that happily balance capitalism, social justice, and sustainable development. But such rosy depictions ignore the great variations in the policies that European countries have pursued, the successes and failures they have experienced, and the many profound challenges they face today. It is important to recognize that though the European Union is encouraging the convergence of public policies in many domains, significant national differences remain in all of the areas discussed in this book. There is no single *European model*, there are many. US Supreme Court Justice Brandeis famously said that US states served as "laboratories of democracy" where one could observe the effects of various social and economic policies. The same is clearly true of the member states of the European Union, whose diversity of approaches to important public policy challenges—their successes and their failures—can yield powerful lessons.

This book seeks to offer a balanced approach, neither idealizing nor demonizing European public policies but asking what the United States can learn from their achievements and shortcomings. Certainly, there are many negative lessons today, including cautionary tales about excessive deficits, rigid labor market regulations, and poorly regulated banking sectors and real estate markets. But there are many positive lessons as well—lessons about successful work–life balance policies; about the design of sustainable urban transport systems; about active labor market policies that produce a skilled workforce and combat unemployment; about health care systems that achieve universal, high-quality coverage at a far lower cost than in the United States.

In recent decades, the transatlantic flow of policy learning has moved mostly from the new world to the old: European countries and the EU itself took many lessons from US experience as they worked to liberalize their economies (Djelic 2001). But there is also an older tradition of US policymakers studying and drawing lessons from Europe. As Daniel Rodgers (1998) shows in his brilliant book, *Atlantic Crossings*, US Progressives in the late nineteenth and early twentieth centuries borrowed extensively from European models in developing the American welfare state. Again today, the economically advanced democracies of Europe provide a rich potential source of lessons for US policymakers.

With pundits speaking of the decline of the west and the rise of the rest, it may be tempting to look to the BRICs and other emerging economies, rather than to Europe, for policy lessons. And indeed, the United States may draw useful policy lessons from a range of countries around the world. However, the United States has more in common with and is more likely to find applicable lessons in wealthy democracies than in developing countries or authoritarian regimes. And most of the world's wealthy democracies are in Europe and are members of the European Union.[4] With twenty-eight member states, the EU comprises the largest group of democracies in the world. Collectively, the EU is the world's largest economy and the United States' biggest trade and investment partner (Hamilton and Quinlan 2013).

Our European partners face many of the same policy challenges that we do. They too must address issues surrounding increasing international economic competition, rising health care and pension costs, school reform, climate change, large scale immigration, financial market regulation, and child care and work–life balance, to name just a few common challenges. Various European democracies have taken different approaches to address these challenges—and seen different results. We can benefit greatly from studying European experiences, learning lessons both from policies that have proved successful and from approaches that have failed.

Of course, as Kent Weaver describes in the concluding chapter of this book, there are many profound obstacles—cultural, institutional, and political ones— to transplanting lessons from successful policies in Europe. And likewise, approaches that fail in Europe may succeed in the United States. One of the crucial tasks of comparative public policy analysis is to determine—given cross-national differences in culture, institutions, and existing constellations of power and interests—which policy lessons from one country may be applied in another. This book takes up this challenge, exploring not only which policies have proved effective in Europe, but asking whether or not such policies might prove effective in the US context.

American Exceptionalism?

It might seem obvious to many readers that we should look abroad for lessons that might be applicable in the United States. And as Rodgers's *Atlantic Crossings* reminds us, there is a long tradition of drawing lessons from Europe for US policymaking. However, despite this history, a powerful stream in US political thought—*American exceptionalism*—largely rejects the notion that we can draw lessons from abroad. The concept of American exceptionalism has a long pedigree in American political life, and there has been a dramatic increase in public discussion of the term in recent years, particularly in the context of the 2012 Presidential Election (see Figure 1.1). Generally, American exceptionalism is the notion that the United States is unique among all other nations, and that because of its distinctive history, culture, and values the normal rules and historical forces that apply in other countries do not apply in America.

FIGURE 1.1   Discussions of "American Exceptionalism" in Print Media (frequency)

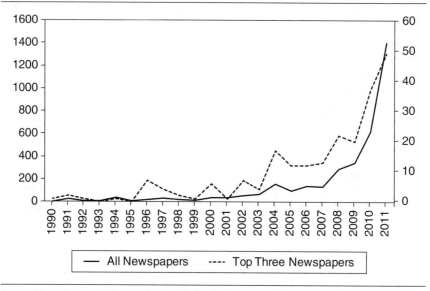

Source: Data from Westlaw and Alliance for Audited Media (2013).

Note: Top three newspapers (by circulation): 1. *The Wall Street Journal,* 2. *The New York Times,* 3. *USA Today.*

American exceptionalism has taken on different meanings over the years. The term itself can be traced to two sources—a French aristocrat and a Soviet dictator. In *Democracy in America,* Alexis de Tocqueville's brilliant study of early nineteenth-century American democracy, he wrote, "The position of the Americans is therefore quite exceptional, and it may be believed that no democratic people will ever be placed in a similar one" (1990, 36 [originally published in 1840]). De Tocqueville highlighted Americans' Puritan ethos, their commercial culture, their geographic position, and their class structure as factors that make the United States exceptional. While de Tocqueville argued that the position of Americans was exceptional, it was Joseph Stalin who first used the actual term *American exceptionalism.* In 1929, Stalin chastised American Communist leader Jay Lovestone, who had explained the absence of proletarian revolution in the United States arguing that America was exempt from the historical forces described by Marxist-Leninist orthodoxy. Stalin demanded that Lovestone and his followers recant the "heresy of American exception" (McCoy 2012; Pease 2009, 10).

Understandably, American politicians invoking the term *American exceptionalism* prefer not to cite a communist dictator. Some do reference de Tocqueville, but as a Frenchman, he, too, is suspect. Therefore, American politicians from both sides of the aisle—from John F. Kennedy and Barack Obama to Ronald Reagan, George W. Bush, and Mitt Romney—often link the notion of American exceptionalism to a deeper, home-grown source, John Winthrop's 1630 sermon, "A Model of Christian Charity." In that sermon, Winthrop invoked Jesus's Sermon on the Mount and told his fellow Massachusetts Bay Colonists that their new community would be "a city upon a hill"; the world's eyes would be upon them and therefore they had a special duty to embody the Christian virtues they held so dear and to set an example for other nations.

For some, American exceptionalism and the city-upon-a-hill metaphor imply that the United States has a special set of obligations and a special destiny—to set an example of democratic virtue and to lead other nations. For others, these ideas mean not only that America is unique but that it is better than other countries—the greatest nation on Earth. Though politicians across the spectrum have invoked the notion of American exceptionalism, the idea has been embraced more forcefully on the Right. Reagan made use of the term regularly as a candidate and as president, as did President George W. Bush. American exceptionalism became a catchphrase in the 2012 Republican presidential primaries, with Newt Gingrich, Rick Santorum, and the eventual Republican nominee Mitt Romney regularly incorporating the term into their stump speeches. Newt Gingrich (2011) wrote a book on the subject, *A Nation Like No Other: Why American Exceptionalism Matters*. Mitt Romney made the concept a centerpiece of his general election campaign, attacking President Obama for his supposed lack of belief in American exceptionalism. As he put to a crowd of supporters in Wisconsin, "Our president doesn't have the same feelings about American exceptionalism that we do." Romney went on to implore them to take the opportunity "to restore to this country the principles that made this nation the greatest nation in the history of the Earth" (Mehta 2012).

Discussion of American exceptionalism is not confined to the political realm. There is a large academic literature on American exceptionalism as well.[5] The concept is invoked in studies examining the distinctiveness of American culture and values (Hartz 1955; Lipset 1996; D. Madsen 1998), American political institutions (Kingdon 1999), the history of the American labor movement and the failure of socialism in America (Voss 1994; Lipset and Marks 2011), domestic social policies (Hacker 2002; Morgan and Campbell 2011), foreign policy (Ignatieff 2005; Kagan 2004; Koh 2002; Lepgold and McKeown 1995), and even sports (Markovitz and Hellerman 2001).

American exceptionalism makes a global claim—that the United States is fundamentally different from all other nations. But in fact, many of the politicians and scholars who invoke American exceptionalism have a more specific target of comparison in mind: Europe. The origins of the concept, whether you trace it to Winthrop, de Tocqueville, or Stalin, always had Europe in mind as the comparative reference point. And today, Republican politicians who espouse American exceptionalism regularly warn that their Democratic opponents want to undermine American exceptionalism by turning the United States into a European-style social democracy.

Ultimately, the concept of American exceptionalism rests on the belief that America is different from Europe and that policies, institutions, and values found in Europe cannot or should not take root in the United States. Those who espouse American exceptionalism draw lessons from Europe all the time, but these are often false lessons based on inaccurate views of European policies. Those who believe that America is exceptional should be interested in actual comparisons of European and American public policies—if only to understand better what is truly exceptional about the United States. For as the great social scientist Seymour Martin Lipset (1996) put it in his book, *American Exceptionalism*, "Those who know only one country, know no country" (17).[6]

A Roadmap for Lesson Drawing

Lesson drawing is as old as the study of politics. Richard Rose begins his 2005 book on lesson learning in public policy, *Learning from Comparative Public Policy*, with a quote from Plato's *Laws*: "It is always right for one who dwells in a well-ordered state to go forth on a voyage of enquiry by land and sea so as to confirm thereby such of his native laws as are rightly enacted and to amend any that are deficient." Today, there is a rich academic literature on lesson learning in public policy— sometimes framed as policy transfer or policy diffusion. Most of that literature focuses on how and under what conditions policymakers learn lessons from other jurisdictions; what impact if any that learning has; and ultimately when, how, and why policies spread across jurisdictions.[7] The contributors to this volume engage some those questions, and in his concluding chapter, Kent Weaver examines in detail the potential for European policy lessons to influence US policymaking. But this book is not designed to provide a contribution to the academic literature on policy diffusion. The primary aim of the case studies in this book is not to assess whether, or under what conditions, US policymakers *will* learn and apply lessons from Europe. Instead, their main aim is simply to enrich our policy debates by offering an analysis of what US citizens and policymakers *could* learn from Europe.

Richard Rose (1993), perhaps more than any other contemporary scholar of comparative public policy, has worked to offer advice on how policy makers can effectively draw lessons from other countries and apply them at home. As he puts it, "A lesson is more than a symbol invoked to sway opinion . . . A lesson is a detailed cause and effect description of a set of actions that a government can consider in the light of experience elsewhere, including a prospective evaluation of whether what is done elsewhere could someday become effective here" (27). He provides a rich set of guidelines to those who would draw lessons effectively, emphasizing the importance of taking into account local culture, politics, and institutions and of adapting policies from other jurisdictions to local conditions. The contributors to this volume follow the spirit of that advice, identifying nuanced, contextualized lessons from Europe for the United States.

This volume brings together a group of policy-area experts with extensive knowledge of both US and European policies in their fields. While each chapter explores a different policy area, each asks a similar set of questions: In confronting major contemporary policy challenges, what can US policymakers learn from European experiences? Might successful policies adopted in European countries be applied in the United States? Can the United States avoid the pitfalls associated with failed policies in European cases?

In Chapter 2, Janet Gornick and Ariane Hegewisch explore lessons for the United States from European work–family reconciliation policies—policies that help workers balance the demands of employment and parenthood. They examine policies at the EU and national levels in three main fields: parental leave, working time regulations, and publicly supported child care. They demonstrate that US provisions in each of these fields is remarkably limited compared to the various provisions found in European countries and explore the impact of these differences on women's employment. They suggest that while immediate expansion of such policies in the United States is highly unlikely, the longer-term prospects for developing European-style work–family policy in the United States may be greater than many assume.

In Chapter 3, Lawrence Brown compares the strategies the United States and various European countries use to regulate different aspects of their health care systems, including funding, governance and content of coverage, and payment of providers, and he explores how the Affordable Care Act (ACA, commonly known as Obamacare) will influence US regulation. In drawing lessons from several models of regulation in Europe, Brown emphasizes that where European systems seek uniformity and equity in their approaches to regulation, the US system is highly particularistic and fragmented, characterized by a variety of often uncoordinated funding, governance, and payment regimes. Compared to the more uniform approaches to regulation that prevail in European countries, the *regulatory particularism* of the US system is highly costly and the ACA—whatever its merits in expanding coverage and containing costs—only adds to this fragmentation and particularism.

In Chapter 4, Mitchell Orenstein casts a skeptical eye on the lessons from Europe in the field of pensions. First, he notes that in recent years, generous European pension systems have proven financially unsustainable, and governments have been forced to scale them back in the face of the economic crisis. European governments have drawn lessons from the United States and moved closer to the

US approach of combining modest public pensions with a system of individual savings accounts. The experience of pension crisis and reform in Europe offers important lessons for the United States. First, comparison of the state of the US Social Security system with European pension systems shows that—contrary to the fears of many Americans—Social Security is relatively healthy. Second, the experiences of European governments in reforming their private workplace pension systems provide important lessons on microlevel program design as American policymakers seek to improve on our workplace pension system, which suffers from high fees and low coverage.

In Chapter 5, Tobias Schulze-Cleven explores potential lessons for the United States from labor market policies in Denmark and Germany. Schulze-Cleven argues that in an era of economic globalization, advanced industrialized democracies need labor market policies that both encourage flexibility and help workers adapt to economic dislocation by investing in training and education schemes that help unemployed workers rejoin the labor force and maximize their productive potential. He notes that while many European countries with disastrously high unemployment rates have negative policy lessons to offer, the high average rates of unemployment in Europe lead US policymakers to ignore positive lessons from successful economies such as Denmark and Germany. He notes that the success of Denmark's *flexicurity* approach to labor market policy—which combines the promotion of labor market flexibility with the guarantee of social security—shows that the combination of flexible labor market rules, social protection mechanisms, and public–private job-training schemes for unemployed workers can help maintain a highly skilled, competitive workforce. Schulze-Cleven also draws lessons from Germany for the process of reforming labor market policies. Germany's success in reforming labor market policy over the past decade shows how a strategy of *layering*—grafting *new* elements onto *old* policies rather than attempting direct, systemic reform—can overcome legislative gridlock and lead to incremental but transformative changes. He suggests that a similar reform strategy, built around the expansion of US Trade Adjustment Assistance programs, might eventually yield broad changes in American labor market policies.

In Chapter 6, Martin Schain compares US and European immigration policies and finds that US policies have been far more successful in most respects. He examines policies on immigrant entry, immigrant integration, and border control, and considers the potential impact of immigration reform currently pending in Congress. Whatever the shortcomings of existing US policies in these domains, he finds that on the whole, US immigration policy has been better defined, more consistent—and has found greater social and political support—than policies in Europe. Many European countries have maintained vague, inconsistent policies on immigrant entry and integration, which have heightened political discord over immigration and bolstered support for xenophobic political parties. While there is far more consistent support for legal immigration in the United States, policies introduced because of mounting concern over undocumented immigration are negatively affecting legal migrants as well. Some European countries may have lessons to offer the United States on more effective tools to control undocumented migration, but these tools, often relying on identification cards and labor market controls. seem to be politically unacceptable in America.

In Chapter 7, Frank Convery provides an overview of the EU's far-reaching climate-change policies, including its policies on emissions trading, renewable energy, and energy efficiency. Convery highlights the importance of sustained public support for these policies and committed leadership from the EU and large member states. He offers a set of tentative lessons for the United States from the EU's experience in pursuing climate change policy. He draws specific lessons from the tumultuous history of the EU's emissions trading scheme for those who would craft a cap-and-trade scheme in the United States, as well as more general lessons about the economic impact of climate change policies. In particular, he notes that the countries in the EU that have pursued the most ambitious climate change policies (Germany and the Nordics) have not suffered economically as a result.

In Chapter 8 on sustainable urban transport, Ralph Buehler and John Pucher compare public policies in Germany and the United States that affect transportation behaviors and patterns of land use. They begin with a broad comparison of patterns of transportation in the United States and Western Europe, which highlights just how car dependent America is relative to European countries. They then turn their focus to a detailed comparison of transportation policy in the United States and Germany, a country that is comparable to the United States in many relevant respects but which has a far more sustainable transport system. To illustrate the impact of sustainable transport policy at the local level, they offer a detailed case study of Freiburg, Germany, a leading innovator in sustainable transport. Finally, they conclude by drawing seven specific lessons for the United States from the German experience. They emphasize that while it is unlikely that the United States will adopt German-style transport-sustainability policies at a national level, many American municipalities have adopted some of these policies at a local level.

In Chapter 9, Steven Hill turns the focus from public policy to the political process itself—the very process that may determine whether any of the policies discussed in this book are successfully reformed. Hill offers vigorous critiques of many American political institutions—from the system of campaign finance, to the winner-take-all electoral system, to the antimajoritarian Senate, to political media institutions—arguing that they increasingly undermine the quality of the democratic process in the United States. He points out important shortcomings of European democracies but maintains that many of them are "better adapted than America's democracy for the demands of representation, consensus seeking and policy formation in the twenty-first century." Hill recognizes that US and European democratic institutions are rooted in distinctive histories and cultures and that profound reforms of US political institutions, such as moving from first-past-the-post to proportional representation voting or relying on public financing of campaigns, are political nonstarters. Nevertheless, he argues that the United States might feasibly introduce and benefit from a number of microlevel democratic institutions that have proven effective in European countries, including automatic voter registration, Question Time before Congress, or more free media time for candidates.

In his concluding chapter, Kent Weaver draws on existing literatures on the policymaking process and on policy diffusion and learning to explore how and under what conditions American policymakers might effectively use lessons from Europe in crafting policy. Weaver begins by emphasizing the diversity of public policy across European democracies. There is never a single *lesson from Europe*: in any policy domain, various European countries will offer examples of effective and ineffective policies, ones that might be emulated and ones to be avoided. Weaver then emphasizes that in the United States, there are high political and institutional barriers to adopting policy lessons from Europe, even when European experiences offer clear and potentially transferable lessons. Weaver argues that those who would see the United States draw lessons—positive or negative ones—from Europe must craft strategies designed to overcome those barriers. He discusses a few such strategies: focusing on how policy reforms should be framed and how reform advocates might take advantage of *policy windows* to push for incremental reforms, sometimes at the state or local rather than the federal level.

Conclusion

The policy areas explored in this book—on work–family reconciliation, health care, pensions, labor markets, immigration, climate change, transportation, and political reform—are only a small sampling of the many policy areas where the United States might usefully draw lessons from Europe. Many other policy areas are ripe for such analysis. For example, we might look to Europe for lessons for education reform, investigating why it is that the United States lags behind European countries in the Organisation for Economic Co-operation and Development (OECD) comparative assessment of student achievement in math and science[8] and why some European countries, such as Finland, regularly score at or near the top of the pack (Sahlberg 2011). We might investigate the role that cooperative industrial relations institutions such as *codetermination* played in helping Germany avoid a spike in unemployment during the global economic downturn and achieve tremendous success as an exporter (Panknin 2012; Rattner 2011; Schulz 2012). We might compare US and European criminal justice policies to better understand why the US rate of incarceration is so much higher than that of any west European country and to consider whether there may be more effective (and far less costly) alternatives to mass incarceration (Hartney 2006; Mauer 2003; Tonry 2009). Likewise, we might usefully draw lessons from policy areas ranging all the way from antipoverty policies (Alesina and Glaeser 2007; Waldfogel 2010), to policies designed to prevent teen pregnancy (Darroch et al. 2001), to drug control policies (MacCoun and Reuter 2001), to counterterrorism policies (Art and Richardson 2007; Crenshaw 2010), to policies designed to combat racism while preserving freedom of speech (Bleich 2011), to policies to respond to banking crises (Jackson 2008), to the impact of austerity policies (Blyth 2013).

We make no claim that the case studies presented here are a representative sample of policymaking across Europe. Though the authors analyze policy in a number of European countries and at the EU level, the focus is clearly weighted to northern and western Europe, with less emphasis on lessons from southern or eastern Europe (though Orenstein's chapter is an exception). Finally, though Schain's and Orenstein's chapters consider clear negative lessons from Europe (mistakes to be avoided) and though other chapters also explore cautionary lessons, on the whole the case studies presented in this book focus on positive lessons.

Our emphasis on positive lessons from northern and western Europe is deliberate. Of course, European countries have many negative policy lessons to offer—from labor market regulation in Spain, to fiscal policy in Greece, to banking regulation in Ireland, to governance of a monetary union at the EU level. But given all the negative press coverage of Europe in recent years, these stories are relatively well known, while the many successes of European policymaking are less well recognized. Thus, our emphasis on the positive serves as a corrective and a reminder that—for all the serious problems facing the EU and its member states today—the United States still has many positive lessons to learn from European public policies.

Endnotes

1. There were of course important exceptions such as the analyses by T. R. Reid in his book, *The Healing of America* (2009), and the 2008 PBS *Frontline* documentary "Sick Around the World," and by Princeton economist Uwe Reinhardt in his *New York Times Economix* blog posts (http://economix.blogs.nytimes.com). But such analyses received little attention in the broader public debates over health care reform.

2. On standard of living see the United Nations Human Development Program's Human Development Index (http://hdr.undp.org/en/humandev); on economic competitiveness see the World Economic Forum's Global Competitiveness index (www.weforum.org/issues/global-competitiveness); on the quality of governance see the World Bank's Worldwide Governance Indicators (http://info.worldbank.org/governance/wgi/index.asp).

3. For more nuanced analyses of the European Social Model see Baldwin 2009; Hill 2010.

4. Twenty-five of the thirty-four member countries of the Organization for Economic Cooperation and Development (OECD), the *club* of the world's wealthy democracies, are European countries; twenty-one of them are members of the EU.

5. For overviews of this literature see Schafer 1991; Lipset 1996; Koh 2002; Pease 2009.

6. Lipset was echoing a sentiment expressed earlier by Rudyard Kipling in a very different context. In his 1891 poem, "The English Flag," Kipling wrote, "And what should they know of England who only England know?" Students of British policymaking often invoke that phrase as a justification for comparative studies.

7. For examples of this literature see Waltman 1980; Rose 1991, 1993, 2002, 2005; Bennett and Howlett 1992; Haas 1992; Hall 1993; Dolowitz and Marsh 1996, 2000; Stone 1999; Evans and Davies 1999; Weyland 2006; James and Lodge 2003; Freeman 2007; Volden, Ting, and Carpenter 2008; Dunlop 2009; Dwyer and Ellison 2009; Gilardi, Fuglister, and Luyet 2009; Gilardi 2010.

8. The United States regularly scores at the bottom on math and science on the OECD's PISA (Programme for International Student Assessment) tests. (See www.oecd.org/pisa)

References

Alesina, A., and N. Glaeser. *Fighting poverty in the US and Europe: A world of difference.* Oxford: Oxford University Press, 2007.

Art, R. J., and L. Richardson, eds. *Democracy and counterterrorism: Lessons from the past.* Washington, DC: United States Institute of Peace Press, 2007.

Baldwin, P. *The narcissism of minor differences: How Europe and America are alike.* Oxford: Oxford University Press, 2009.

Bennett, C. J. "What is policy convergence and what causes it?" *British Journal of Political Science* 21, no. 2 (1991): 215–33.

Bennett, C. J., and M. Howlett. "The lessons of learning: Reconciling theories of policy learning and policy change." *Policy Sciences* 25, no. 3 (1992): 275–94.

Bleich, E. *The freedom to be racist? How the United States and Europe struggle to preserve freedom and combat racism.* New York: Oxford University Press, 2011.

Blyth, M. *Austerity: The history of a dangerous idea.* New York: Oxford University Press, 2013.

Bongiovanni, F. *The decline and fall of Europe.* Basingstoke: Palgrave MacMillan, 2012.

Casey, B. H. "Learning across borders: Labour market and social policies." *International Social Security Review* 62, no. 4 (2009): 3–20.

Crenshaw, M., ed. *The consequences of counterterrorism.* New York: Russell Sage Foundation, 2010.

Darroch, J., S. Singh, J. Frost, and the Study Team. "Differences in teenage pregnancy rates among five developed countries: The roles of sexual activity and contraceptive use." *Family Planning Perspectives* 33, no. 6 (2001): 244–50.

Djelic, M. L. *Exporting the American model: The postwar transformation of European business.* Oxford: Oxford University Press, 2001.

Dobbin, F., B. Simmons, and G. Garrett. "The global diffusion of public policies: Social construction, coercion, competition, or learning?" *Annual Review of Sociology* 33, no. 1 (2007): 449–72.

Dolowitz, D. P., and D. Marsh. "Learning from abroad: The role of policy transfer in contemporary policy-making." *Governance* 13, no. 1 (2000): 5–24.

———. "Who learns what from whom: A review of the policy transfer literature." *Political Studies* 44, no. 2 (1996): 343–57.

Dunlop, C. A. "Policy transfer as learning: Capturing variation in what decision-makers learn from epistemic communities." *Policy Studies* 30, no. 3 (2009): 289–311.

Dwyer, P., and N. Ellison. "'We nicked stuff from all over the place': Policy transfer or muddling through?" *Policy & Politics* 37, no. 3 (2009): 389–407.

Evans, M., and J. Davies. "Understanding policy transfer: A multi-level, multi-disciplinary perspective." *Public Administration* 77, no. 2 (1999): 361–85.

Fischer, Sebastian. "Socialism and welfare: Republicans bash Europe in search of votes. *Spiegel Online*. http://www.spiegel.de/international/world/socialism-and-welfare-republicans-bash-europe-in-search-of-votes-a-808044.html.

Foroohar, R. "The end of Europe." *Time*. http://www.time.com/time/magazine/article/0,9171,2088040,00.html (August 22, 2011).

Freeman, R. "Epistemological bricolage: How practitioners make sense of learning." *Administration & Society* 39, no. 4 (2007): 476–96.

Geoghegan, T. *Were you born on the wrong continent? How the European model can help you get a life*. New York: New Press, 2011.

Gilardi, F. "Who learns what in policy diffusion processes." *American Journal of Political Science* 54, no. 3 (2010): 650–66.

Gilardi, F., K. Fuglister, and S. Luyet. "Learning from others: The diffusion of hospital financing reforms in OECD countries." *Comparative Political Studies* 42, no. 4 (2009): 549–73.

Gingrich, N. *A nation like no other: Why American exceptionalism matters*. Washington, DC: Regnery Publishing, 2011.

Haas, P. M. "Introduction: Epistemic communities and international policy coordination." *International Organization* 46, no. 1 (1992): 1–35.

Hacker, J. *The divided welfare state: The battle over public and private social benefits in the United States*. New York: Cambridge University Press, 2002.

Hall, P. "Policy paradigms, social learning, and the state: The case of economic policymaking in Britain." *Comparative Politics* 25, no. 3 (1993): 275–96.

Hartney, C. *US rates of incarceration: A global perspective*. Oakland, CA: National Council on Crime and Delinquency, 2006.

Hamilton, D. and J. Quinlan. *The transatlantic economy 2013: Annual survey of jobs, trade and investment between the United States and Europe*. Washington, DC: Center for Transatlantic Relations, 2013.

Hartz, L. *The liberal tradition in America*. New York: Harcourt Brace (1955).

Heclo, H. *Modern social politics in Britain and Sweden: From relief to income maintenance*. New Haven: Yale University Press, 1974.

Hill, S. *Europe's promise: Why the European way is the best hope in an insecure age*. Berkeley: University of California Press, 2010.

———. "President Obama wants America to be like Germany What does that really mean?" *The Atlantic*. http://www.theatlantic.com/business/archive/2013/02/president-obama-wants-america-to-be-like-germany-what-does-that-really-mean/273318 (February 21, 2013).

Ignatieff, M. *American exceptionalism and human rights*. Princeton, NJ: Princeton University Press, 2005.

Jackson, J. *The U.S. financial crisis: Lessons from Sweden*. CRS Report 22962. Washington, DC: Congressional Research Service. http://assets.opencrs.com/rpts/RS22962_20080929.pdf (September 29, 2008).

James, O., and M. Lodge. "The limitations of policy transfer and lesson drawing for public policy research." *Political Studies Review* 1, no. 2 (2003): 179–93.

Kagan, R. *Of paradise and power*. New York: Vintage, 2004.

Kingdon, J. *America the unusual*. New York: Worth, 1999.

Krugman, P. "The austerity delusion." *New York Times,* March 24, 2011. http://www.nytimes.com/2011/03/25/opinion/25krugman.html.

———."Learning from Europe." *New York Times,* January 11, 2010. http://www.nytimes.com/2010/01/11/opinion/11krugman.html?_r=0.

Lacqueur, W. *After the fall: The end of the European dream and the decline of a continent*. New York: Thomas Dunne Books, 2012.

Lepgold, J., and T. McKeown. "Is American foreign policy exceptional? An empirical analysis." *Political Science Quarterly* 110, no. 3 (1995): 369–84.

Lipset, S. M. *American exceptionalism: A double-edged sword*. New York: W. W. Norton, 1996.

Lipset, S. M., and G. Marks. *It didn't happen here: Why socialism failed in the United States*. New York: W. W. Norton, 2011.

MacCoun, R., and P. Reuter. "Evaluating alternative cannabis regimes." *British Journal of Psychiatry* 178, (2001): 123–28.

Madsen, D. *American exceptionalism*. Edinburgh: Edinburgh University Press, 1998.

Makse, T., and C. Volden. "The role of policy attributes in the diffusion of innovations." *Journal of Politics* 73, no. 1 (2011): 108–24.

Markovitz, A., and S. Hellerman. *Offside: Soccer and American exceptionalism*. Princeton, NJ: Princeton University Press, 2001.

Marquand, D. *The end of the west: The once and future Europe*. Princeton, NJ: Princeton University Press, 2011.

Mauer, M. *Comparative international rates of incarceration: An examination of causes and trends.* Washington, DC: Sentencing Project, 2003.

McPake, B., and A. Mills. "What can we learn from international comparisons of health systems and health system reform?" *Bulletin of the World Health Organization* 78, no. 6 (2000): 811–20.

Mehta, S. "Romney, Obama and God: Who sees America as more divine?" *Los Angeles Times,* April 13, 2012. http://articles.latimes.com/2012/apr/13/news/la-pn-obama-romney-america-exceptional-20120413.

Morgan, K., and A. L. Campbell. *The delegated welfare state: Medicare, markets, and the governance of social policy*. New York: Oxford University Press, 2011.

Panknin, Knut. *Germany's lessons for a strong economy*. Center for American Progress. http://www.americanprogress.org/issues/economy/news/2012/06/26/11796/germanys-lessons-for-a-strong-economy (June 26, 2012).

Pease, D. *The new American exceptionalism*. Minneapolis: University of Minnesota Press, 2009.

Rattner, S. "The secrets of Germany's success: What Europe's manufacturing powerhouse can teach America." *Foreign Affairs* (July/August, 2011). http://www.foreignaffairs.com/articles/67899/steven-rattner/the-secrets-of-germanys-success.

Reid, T. R. *The healing of America: A global quest for better, cheaper and fairer health care*. New York: Penguin Press, 2009.

Rifkin, J. *The European dream: How Europe's vision of the future is quietly eclipsing the American dream.* Cambridge: Polity Press, 2004.

Rose, R. "What is lesson-drawing?" *Public Policy* 11, no. 1 (1991): 3–30.

———. *Lesson-drawing in public policy*. London: Chatham House Publishers, 1993.

———. *Ten steps in learning lessons from abroad*. Working Paper: Report EUI RSC 2002/05. San Domenico di Fiesole: European University Institute, 2002.

———. *Learning from comparative public policy: A practical guide*. New York: Routledge, 2005.

Sahlberg, P. *Finnish lessons: What can the world learn from educational change in Finland*. New York: Teachers College Press, 2011.

Schafer, B., ed. *Is America different? A new look at American exceptionalism*. New York: Oxford University Press, 1991.

Schulz, T. "We need to learn from Germany: How the German economy became a model." *Spiegel Online*. http://www.spiegel.de/international/business/the-us-discovers-germany-as-an-economic-role-model-a-822167.html (March 21, 2012).

Stone, D. "Learning lessons and transferring policy across time, space and disciplines." *Politics* 19, no. 1 (1999): 51–9.

Tocqueville, Alexis de. *Democracy in America*. Vol. 2. New York: Vintage Books, 1990.

Tonry, M. "Explanations of American punishment policies." *Punishment & Society* 11, no. 3 (2009): 377–94.

Volden, C., M. M. Ting, and D. P. Carpenter. "A formal model of learning and policy diffusion." *American Political Science Review* 102, no. 3 (2008): 319–32.

Voss, K. *The making of American exceptionalism: The knights of labor and class formation in the nineteenth century*. Ithaca, NY: Cornell University Press, 1994.

Waldfogel, J. *Britain's war on poverty*. New York: Russell Sage Foundation, 2010.

Waltman, J. *Copying other nations' policies: Two American case studies*. Cambridge: Schenkman, 1980.

Weyland, K. *Bounded rationality and policy diffusion*. Princeton, NJ: Princeton University Press, 2006.

CHAPTER 2

Gender, Employment, and Parenthood: The Consequences of Work–Family Policies

Janet C. Gornick[1] and Ariane Hegewisch

Since the founding of the European Union (EU) in 1957, much has changed in relation to women, men, work, and family. Yet while women overall, particularly mothers, are much more likely to be in paid work, and men are somewhat more likely to perform unpaid family work, men are still the majority of paid workers and women still perform the lion's share of unpaid family work. In both the United States and Europe, having and raising children—and looking after relatives who are elderly or have disabilities—still takes time, and the majority of that work, whether it is paid or unpaid, is performed by women.

In the United States and throughout Europe, the Organisation for Economic Co-operation and Development (OECD 2012) reports that the great majority of part-time workers are women, as are the majority of workers who take time out of paid employment for caregiving purposes. In both settings, there is substantial evidence indicating that this unequal division of labor has negative effects on women's position in the labor market. In the United States and across Europe, relative to their male counterparts, women are less likely to be employed, spend fewer hours in paid work, earn less, are less likely to hold senior jobs, and are more likely to be in lower quality or contingent jobs, even if the extent of such inequality varies greatly between countries.

Yet while Europe, during the last fifty years, has seen the development of a substantial policy framework and infrastructure to support families' caregiving tasks, the same is not true in the United States. Europe, of course, continues to be diverse in many aspects of relevance to gender, work, and family—reflecting divergent conceptions of the role of the family, gender equality, and the state. This diversity provides a natural experiment that allows us to explore, within Europe and between Europe and the United States, the consequences associated with national work–family reconciliation policy provisions.

This chapter will address lessons from Europe with respect to institutions that help workers to reconcile the competing demands of parenthood and employment. More specifically, we will focus on three core components of work–family reconciliation policy: (1) family and parental leave policies, (2) working–time regulations and workplace flexibility, and (3) publicly supported child care. In each case, we provide a brief outline of European Union regulations, and summarize policy variation, as of 2008–2010, across twelve European Union countries—Austria, Belgium, Denmark, Finland, France, Germany, Italy, Luxembourg, Netherlands, Spain, Sweden, and the United Kingdom—as well as in the United States. In the latter part of the chapter, we present outcomes for fertility, labor force participation, and poverty across this same group of countries.

In each of these three policy areas, the institutional landscape in Europe—at the supranational level and, in many cases, at the national level—is markedly different from what is operating in the United States. While the availability and generosity of US social policy provisions in some areas (e.g., old-age pensions, disability benefits, unemployment insurance) are fair-to-middling compared with typical European policies, public provisions that support work-family reconciliation are extremely meager in the United States, in comparative terms. Indeed, in the United States, at both the federal and state level, public expenditures on work-family policies (e.g., paid leave, child care) are way below European levels, and employment rights (e.g., maximum weekly work hours, minimum periods of annual leave) are substantially more limited. Welfare state researchers disagree on the causes and consequences of this policy contrast, but they rarely contest the observation that, with respect to work-family reconciliation policies, US provisions are remarkably limited. In short, in no other social policy arena is American exceptionalism this stark.

It is also crucial to emphasize that these work-family reconciliation policies are not always, or even often, motivated by concerns about gender equality. Policy priorities related to gender, work, and family are diverse, and they continually shift and change. Work-family policies have been justified and adopted for a diversity of reasons in addition to enhancing gender equality—for example, alleviating labor shortages, encouraging work sharing and reducing unemployment, sustaining social insurance revenues, enhancing work–life balance, reducing family poverty and social inequality, improving children's educational outcomes, and raising birth rates. Nevertheless, these policies all affect both mothers' and fathers' engagement in paid work and their effects can linger throughout parents' life course and spill over to nonparents as well.

A large and growing research literature has established that public work-family policies can strengthen gender equality in employment, but they can also deter it.

Concerns about possible negative consequences for women's employment (or for gender equality) tend to focus on policies that encourage long periods of leave taking, part-time employment, or both, especially among women. Whether work-family policies are primarily advantageous or disadvantageous for gender equality is influenced by specific elements of policy design, including financing structures, coverage and eligibility rules, reimbursement levels, and benefit duration. As such, all of these public policies contribute to shaping gender equality in employment—and they do so in complex ways.

Policymaking in the European Union on Gender and Work–Family Reconciliation

Equality between men and women in employment was a founding principle of the 1957 Treaty of Rome that founded the European Economic Community (the forerunner of today's EU). Article 119 of the treaty prohibited unequal pay for equal work. Even though the motivation for addressing pay discrimination was the elimination of unfair competition for firms that were unable to benefit from women's lower-wage labor, rather than a concern with gender inequality itself, Article 119 subsequently served as the basis for policies and approaches more directly aimed at gender equality. Article 119 (now Article 157 of the Treaty on the Functioning of the European Union [TFEU]) was developed into a more explicit framework for nondiscrimination in employment, both through binding European Court of Justice case law and through a number of directives, starting from the 1975 Equal Pay Directive (which, unlike the US Equal Pay Act of 1967, explicitly addresses not only equal pay but also "equal value/comparable worth") and the 1976 Equal Treatment Directive (which, like Title VII of the 1964 Civil Rights Act, addresses discrimination in all other aspects of employment, from recruitment to promotion, training and dismissal) to the latest 2010 Parental Leave Directive (Council of Ministers 2010) which "lays down minimum requirements designed to facilitate the reconciliation of parental and professional responsibilities for working parents" (Clause II.1).

The European Court of Justice has variously confirmed the rights of women as primary caregivers to work reduced hours and has confirmed that employers must carry some of the costs of raising future generations and must provide some accommodation to women when they provide such tasks. The Part-Time Work Directive ensures that part-time workers are entitled to equal treatment (vis-à-vis their full-time counterparts), including pro rata pay and benefits. In all EU member states, as well as in the United States, women are at least twice as likely as men to work part time (see Table 2.2 below); thus, conditioning access to employment benefits, such as employer-supported pensions, health insurance, or paid time off, on full-time work disproportionately disadvantages women. The European Court of Justice has found in various judgments that unequal or adverse treatment of part-time workers constitutes disparate impact (or indirect sex discrimination) because the majority of part-time workers are women working reduced time because of their responsibilities as primary care givers (see Heron 2005 for a more detailed description of the evolution of case law in this area).

In the United States, the exclusion of part-time workers from employer-provided health care and occupational pensions is a defining feature of the labor market. As recently as August 2011, a US federal judge rejected a case charging unequal treatment of pregnant women and women returning from maternity leave by quoting Jack Welsh, the CEO of General Electric as saying, "There's no such thing as work–life balance. There are work–life choices, and you make them, and they have consequences," and by going on to say "The law does not mandate 'work–life balance.' It does not require companies to ignore employees' work-family tradeoffs—and they are tradeoffs—when deciding about employee pay and promotions."[2] While the US Equal Employment Opportunity Commission has officially issued guidance in "family caregiver discrimination" in recognition that mothers and other caregivers might face disadvantages in access to employment and advancement at work, this does not oblige employers to accommodate caregiving needs; it just clarifies that stereotyping or unequal treatment of workers with caregiving needs is illegal.

Even though not directly framed as a gender discrimination issue, the EU's basic regulatory framework for working hours, rest periods, and paid leave arguably provides another important building block in facilitating work–life balance, and, for those with family responsibilities, work-family reconciliation. The importance of providing paid annual leave was recognized in the 1957 Treaty of Rome (Article 120, now Article 158 of the TFEU), and the scope of the European Commission to address issues of working time and health and safety of workers was likewise recognized. More recently, the 2002 EU Working Time Directive 2003/88/EC (which updated earlier directives from 2000 and 1993) has established the daily right to at least eleven hours of rest in a twenty-four-hour period, one day off in seven days, and a minimum of eight hours for night shifts, as well as a minimum of twenty days paid leave per year (prorated for people working less than full time). The directive also sets a maximum working week of forty-eight hours—albeit with considerable scope for exceeding this maximum in the short term and with exemptions for managerial staff. There are no equivalent federal regulations in the United States. The Fair Labor Standards Act of 1938 set the forty-hour week as a basic standard after which hourly paid workers must be paid at 150 percent of their basic hourly wage; but, unlike in the EU, there are no absolute limits on hours worked, no mandate to provide rest periods either during or between working days, and no right to paid days off.

During the last two decades, the place of work-family reconciliation in European policy debates has changed considerably. As we report in Table 2.1, fertility rates have fallen to record lows in some countries and in all EU countries are now below the replacement level of 2.1. As a result, there is a growing imbalance between young people entering the workforce, people of working age, and people of retirement age, and this imbalance is threatening the viability of social insurance systems.

Policymakers are concerned with the impact of the shrinking workforce on the growth prospects of the European economy and are seeking measures to increase labor supply. The lagging labor force participation rates of mothers in many European countries have become a target for intervention and have led to a growing recognition of barriers to women's employment. At the 2000 Lisbon European Summit, the council set targets: to increase the average employment rate from 61 to 70 percent by 2010 and to increase women's labor force participation rate from 51 to 60 percent over the same period.

If the goal of increasing labor force participation is to be met, child care is recognized as an important building block. Early childhood education and care have been on the EU policy agenda since the early 1970s when the first European Social Action Program was launched in 1974, calling for "giving immediate priority to the problems of providing facilities to enable women to reconcile family responsibilities with job aspirations."[3] Incidentally, at broadly the same time, the US Congress passed a law guaranteeing universal child care from age one onward, a law that was subsequently vetoed by President Richard Nixon. The European Commission also established a network of experts, funded various studies, and issued recommendations for states to develop child care services but did not mandate change. The commission continues to exhort member states to increase support for quality child care services. At the 2002 Barcelona Summit, EU member states agreed to a target rate of child care services for 33 percent of children ages zero to three and coverage for 90 percent of three- to five-year-olds by the end of the decade. Yet while the EU can set basic standards regarding the conditions of employment, its role in relation to education and social policy, such as child care, is limited mainly to encouraging good practice and developing joint policy and action agendas.

Diverse Practices: Work–Family Reconciliation Supports in Europe and the United States

All EU member states are bound by the same minimum standards for maternity leave, job-protected parental leave, and paid annual leave—and they are bound by EU-wide rules on maximum weekly work hours. Yet, within this framework, provisions in Europe vary widely. In the field of social and employment policy, the EU operates only by setting minimum standards, establishing networks of experts that disseminate good practices and providing funding through the European Social Fund, thus allowing widely different standards in different member countries.

Maternity, Paternity, and Parental Leave

Maternity, paternity, and parental leave policies across the EU are far more generous than those in the United States, though these policies vary substantially among member states with regard to both their generosity and the degree to which they encourage both men and women (fathers and mothers) to take leave. The EU's role in leave policy is limited to setting some minimum standards that all member states must meet and well illustrates the principle of national social policy sovereignty within Europe. All EU member states are subject to Directive 92/85/EEC (Council of Ministers 1992) on the health and safety of pregnant workers, which guarantees fourteen weeks of job-protected maternity leave, payable at least at the rate of statutory sick pay in each country. Additionally, under the 2010 Parental Leave Directive 2010/19/EU (which amends an earlier 1996 directive), each parent (mothers and fathers, including adoptive parents) has an individual right to at least four months of job-protected leave while the child is young; the parental leave directive does not include a right to paid leave. On their return to work, workers may request a temporary change to their working hours, which must be considered in good faith by their employer.

In most European countries, parents are entitled to substantially longer leave than required by EU regulations. Leave provisions vary substantially both in terms of the overall duration of job-protected leave available and the level of wage replacement provided during leave, reflecting different traditions of social welfare and collective bargaining. All countries provide a basic period of paid leave that is reserved for the birth mother around the time of birth; paid paternity leave is less universal, although a number of countries provide rights to at least two weeks' leave (Moss 2011). Parental leave, that is, leave beyond the period around the time of birth, is available to both mothers and fathers. In some countries, leaves are granted to couples, who may share the entitlement however they wish, while in other countries rights are individualized and nontransferable; several countries combine these approaches, granting both a shared allocation and periods reserved for individual parents.

Recent scholarship on leave (most extensively, by Gornick and colleagues) has emphasized that leave policy designs vary across countries on two largely independent dimensions—their generosity and the extent to which the policy designs are gender egalitarian (see, e.g., Gornick and Meyers 2003; Ray, Gornick, and Schmitt 2010). The generosity of leave available to mothers across eleven of our twelve European countries (Luxembourg was not included), and the United States, is reported in Figure 2.1 (Ray, Gornick, and Schmitt 2010). This figure reports the maximum entitlements for mothers who are part of a couple, assuming that they take all of the leave to which they are specifically entitled, plus all of the fathers' leave that can be transferred to them. All countries provide mothers with at least some job-protected leave, with three countries—France, Germany, and Spain—granting more than three years of leave at one end of the spectrum and with Netherlands and Belgium with job-protected leaves of up to seven months. The least generous country is the United States, at twelve weeks.

Across these countries, the generosity of *paid* leave for mothers, expressed in "full time equivalent" (FTE) units, that is, the wage replacement rate multiplied by the duration, is substantially less than with total leave. Only two of these countries provide mothers six months or more of paid leave (expressed in FTEs): Germany with forty-two weeks and Sweden with forty weeks. Only the United States refuses mothers paid time off after childbirth or adoption.

Just as important as the generosity of leave, is the extent to which the architecture—the underlying rules—enables and encourages gender-egalitarian leave taking. The expanding literature on the gendered consequences of leave designs shows that where couples are free to share leave, and where there is low or no wage replacement during leave, fathers are unlikely to take leave (Hegewisch and Gornick 2011). Ray, Gornick, and Schmitt (2010) assigned each country's leave policies a

FIGURE 2.1   Leave for Mothers: Unpaid, Paid, and Total Leave, in Weeks, 2009

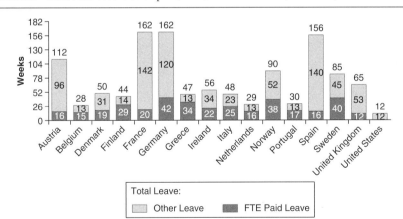

Source: Ray, Gornick, and Schmitt 2010.

Note: Results for Luxembourg are not available.

score on their 15-point three-component Gender Equality Index (see Figure 2.2): the portion of couples' leave that is available to fathers (worth 9 points), the wage replacement rate during the fathers' leave (worth 5 points), and additional incentives or disincentives for fathers to take parental leave (worth one point, positive or negative). The higher the index score, the more the leave policy enables and encourages mothers and fathers to allocate leave symmetrically between them (see Ray, Gornick, and Schmitt 2010 for details).

These results indicate that among our study countries, Sweden earns the highest score on this index, with 14 points. Finland earns 12 points, and Belgium follows with 11 points. France, Italy, and Spain each receive 10 points. Germany and the United States are tied at 9 points, with Denmark, the Netherlands, and the United Kingdom each scoring 8 points. Austria has the lowest score, at 7 points.

The United States is alone among high-income countries, and one of only four countries in the world without a statutory right to paid job-protected maternity leave.[4] Federal law in the United States provides twelve weeks of unpaid job-protected leave for self-care or care of seriously ill relatives for workers in larger

FIGURE 2.2   Gender Equality Index, 2009

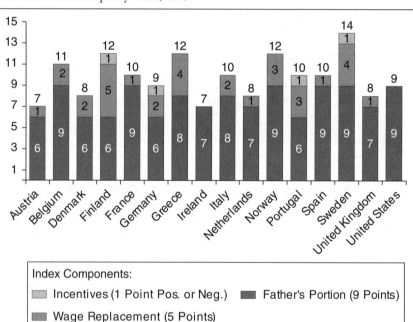

Source: Ray, Gornick, and Schmitt 2010.

Note: Results for Luxembourg are not available.

firms (with at least 50 employees), and this includes leave related to the care of infants. Men and women have identical entitlements to this unpaid leave; that explains the moderate score for the United States on the Gender Equality Index. On the other hand, the absence of wage replacement discourages male leave takers and depresses the US' score. In addition, in five US states, women on maternity leave are entitled to paid leave via temporary disability insurance (typically for six weeks); in two of these states, California and New Jersey, additional partial wage replacement is available to both new mothers and new fathers. However, the majority of US workers are left without any financial supports during leaves related to infant care; voluntarily provided employer provision has failed to bridge the gap left by the lack of public mandates (Hara and Hegewisch 2013), and that is especially true for lower-paid, less-skilled workers. Between 2006 and 2008, only slightly more than half of all women workers who worked during their pregnancy received any paid maternity leave (Laughlin 2011).

Working Time Regulation and Workplace Flexibility

While there is less diversity regarding working hours, the influence of different national frameworks is nevertheless apparent. In Figure 2.3, we report two key indicators of working time regulation. The first is the minimum number of paid days off as set by national law, which in effect defines the length of the standard work year. The second is the length of the standard work week; this indicator captures the lesser of either (1) the legal weekly work hour maximum, or (2), where there is no legal maximum, the standard work week as set by the average collective agreement (see Gornick and Meyers 2003 for a detailed explanation of this measure).

All of these European countries grant workers between twenty (the EU minimum) and twenty-five days of paid annual leave, and some collective agreements lengthen those entitlements. In addition, these twelve European countries all standardize the length of the work week at between thirty-five and thirty-nine hours, with Luxembourg an exception at forty hours.

Ensuring minimum paid annual leave and limiting weekly work hours are important tools for parents who are navigating the reconciliation of work and family. Increasingly, in Europe, another dimension of working time regulation is being added—flexibility in work hours. Parents are being given greater control over the scheduling of hours, the number of hours worked, and the location of work (Hegewisch and Gornick 2009). In Sweden since the late 1970s, parents have had the right to reduce their working hours to 75 percent (with prorated compensation) until their children reach school age. No other country has adopted a similarly comprehensive approach. The 1997 EU Part-Time Work Directive 97/81/EC, while not mandating such approaches, called on member states to provide greater workplace flexibility and to find mechanisms to ensure

FIGURE 2.3   Statutory Paid Annual Leave (Days) and the Length of the Standard Work
Week (Hours), 2010

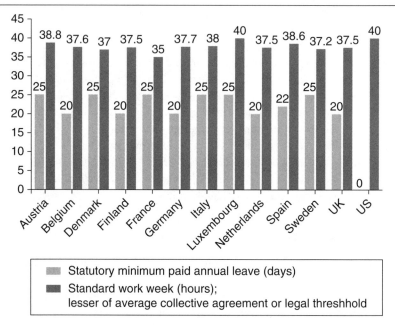

Legend:
- Statutory minimum paid annual leave (days)
- Standard work week (hours); lesser of average collective agreement or legal threshhold

Source: EIRO *Working time developments,* 2010. http://www.eurofound.europa.eu/eiro/studies/tn1106010s/tn1106010s.htm#hd2.

that such flexibility was to the mutual benefit of workers and employers. A number of countries, including the Netherlands, Germany, France, and the United Kingdom, adopted legislation in the early 2000s to give workers a right to request reduced hours, changed schedules, or home-based work. The 2010 Parental Leave Directive includes a right to request a temporary change in working hours for all parents returning from parental leave. In addition, nearly all European countries grant parents time off to care for their children (or themselves) during times of ill health—either routine sickness, serious illness, or both (Gornick and Meyers 2003).

The working time regulation landscape in the United States is quite different. With one exception, the recently passed New York State Domestic Workers Bill of Rights (A1470B/S2311E), which entitles domestic care workers to three days paid leave per year, no laws, either national or state level, grant private-sector workers a minimum number of paid days off each year. The nationally established standard work week (secured by the Fair Labor Standards Act) remains set at forty hours per week, a level that has been unchanged for over seven decades. While unions win some annual leave or shorter work weeks for their covered workers, the limited reach of unions in the United States means that the legal standards generally prevail. While many high-earning workers are granted annual vacation rights by their employers, low-paid workers often have no leave rights. Furthermore, in the United States, while the potential of workplace flexibility measures to provide win-win solutions for workers and employers has received much attention—including during a 2010 Summit on Workplace Flexibility convened at the White House[5]—no relevant federal legislation has been passed. In 2013, however, Vermont became the first state to give workers a right to request flexible working, with a legislative design directly drawing on the UK's flexible working statute of 2009 (2009 No. 595). The 1990 Americans with Disabilities Act (amended in 2008 and 2010) provides some right to accommodations in working hours for those who are disabled, but such rights to accommodation do not extend to an employee caring for persons with a disability (EEOC 2011.) Finally, in the United States, there is no national policy granting paid time off for sickness; however, the state of Connecticut and a few US cities (e.g., New York; Seattle; San Francisco; Washington, DC) have enacted laws granting workers some paid sick days.

Early Childhood Education and Care

Provision of publicly supported child care for preschool-age children varies significantly across European countries, but generally the level of support available, particularly for three- and four-year-olds, greatly exceeds that available in the United States. Figure 2.4 reports the share of children who are enrolled in formal child care (daycare centers or preschool) for two age groups: children under age three and children ages three to five. Such provisions may be full day or part day and may be primarily for educational reasons or for providing care for children during parents' working hours. In all countries apart from Italy, parents are entitled by statute to at least some early childhood education and care. Five countries— Belgium, Denmark, Finland, France, and Sweden—provide a statutory right to a subsidized child care place following the end of job-protected parental leave, and such places are available on a full-time basis (Moss 2011). Other countries provide less seamless support, leaving parents to their own financial and organizational devices for a period of time between the end of leave, when they directly provide care for their child, and the beginning of publicly supported child care. Austria is the only country in which formal public provision begins only at age five; in the Netherlands, provision begins at age four, whereas elsewhere the starting point is age three (though provision is part-time only in Austria, Germany, the Netherlands, and the United Kingdom). Luxembourg goes further; early childhood education is compulsory at age four.

FIGURE 2.4   Enrollment of Children in Formal Early Childhood Education and Care, 2009

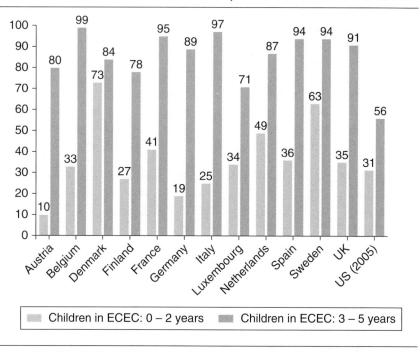

Source: OECD 2010: For children: the US, Early Childhood Program Participation Survey (2005); European countries, EU-SILC (2008) except Germany: administrative data; Nordic countries: NOSOSCO (2007-08); Moss 2011.

It is important to note that not all formal care is publicly supported, so formal care enrollment is not always a good proxy for countries' *public* support for child care. Data on the share of children enrolled in publicly supported care—generally, meaning that 75 percent or more of the cost is paid by the state—are difficult to obtain. The most recent available data, to our knowledge, pertain to the early 2000s. Based on these data, Gornick and Meyers (2003) report that, across Europe, especially in western and northern Europe, typically, at least two-thirds of three- to five-year-olds are in publicly supported settings, usually as part of preschool provisions. In most countries, substantially smaller percentages of "under threes" are in publicly supported care. In Denmark, as many as 74 percent of children ages one to three are in publicly supported care, but in most European countries, that share is 50 percent, and in some cases less than 20 percent.

In the United States, just more than half of children in this older age group (3–5 years old) are in publicly supported care, and the great majority of those children are five-year-olds in kindergarten programs. Although all US states offer some public kindergarten programs, many do not make kindergarten mandatory, and often the only available slots are part-time. In the United States, child care supports for three- and four-year-olds are narrowly targeted on children from low-income families (mainly through the Head Start program); in 2010, only 4 percent of three- and four-year-olds with employed mothers were cared for through Head Start programs (US Census Bureau 2011, Table 1). Public supports for child care for children younger than age three are especially meager in the United States, limited almost exclusively to child care vouchers for children in the poorest families. These programs are rarely structured as entitlements and waiting lists are often long, further limiting the reach of public child care supports for the "under threes."

Policy Impacts: Preliminary Lessons from Europe

Even though European countries are governed by common minimum standards, overall, work-family policies are characterized by substantial diversity in the supports that are provided for working parents. Just as work-family supports vary, so do basic features of women's family and employment outcomes. A substantial empirical literature suggests that these are causally linked. Broadly, countries with better work-family supports have higher rates of both fertility and maternal employment, and vice versa. As we described above, the aging of European populations has focused policymakers' attention on raising both fertility rates and women's employment to ensure that the growth of European economies is not held back by labor shortages and to enhance the sustainability of social insurance systems.

Birth Rates

While policies such as child care or paid parental leave are, of course, not the only factors influencing fertility, there is a clear correlation between these policies and fertility rates. Countries with the least extensive supports for working mothers tend to have the lowest fertility rates (see Table 2.1), and this relationship is confirmed by more thorough research on the relationship between work-family policies and fertility rates over time (McDonald 2000a, 2000b). Consider Austria, Germany, Italy, and Spain, where fertility rates have been below 1.5 children per woman for the last two or three decades, and they all fall below 1.5 as of 2009. All of these countries have meager supports for working mothers: Italy grants no statutory right to preschool child care; in Austria, such a right only begins at age five and, in Germany and Spain, there is no public provision prior to age three. With the exception of the United Kingdom, the European countries with the highest fertility rates all have extensive publicly supported child care and school hours that correspond fairly well to parents' employment hours. As we discuss below, the United States presents an anomaly in this regard, combining meager supports for working mothers with a relatively high fertility rate, exceeding 2 births per woman.

TABLE 2.1   Fertility Rates in Selected European Countries and the US, 1980–2009

	1980	1990	2000	2009
Austria	1.65	1.46	1.36	1.39
Belgium	1.68	1.62	1.67	1.83
Denmark	1.55	1.67	1.77	1.84
Finland	1.63	1.78	1.73	1.86
France	1.95	1.78	1.87	1.99
Germany*	1.43	1.45	1.38	1.36
Italy	1.64	1.33	1.26	1.41
Luxembourg	1.50	1.76	1.76	1.59
Netherlands	1.60	1.62	1.72	1.79
Spain	2.20	1.23	1.23	1.40
Sweden	1.68	2.13	1.54	1.94
UK*	1.90	1.83	1.64	1.94
US*	1.80	2.04	2.01	2.01

Sources: For 2009, all countries: OECD Family Database at http://www.oecd.org/document/ 4/0,3746,en_2649_37419_37836996_1_1_1_37419,00.html; other years Eurostat. 2010. Fertility Services. http://epp.eurostat.ec.europa.eu/statistics_explained/index.php/Fertil- ity_statistics; with the following exceptions: Germany 1980 and 1990 (West Germany only) and US 1980, 1990, 2000: Max Planck Institute. 2011. Human Fertility Database; online at http://www.humanfertility.org/cgi-bin/country.php?country=DEUTW&tab=si&t1= 1&t2=2.

Note: German fertility rates pre-2000 are for West Germany only.

Publicly supported child care is only one component of work-family supports, and we do not suggest it is the main factor in families' decisions about parenthood. But it is one indicator of attitudes to mothers and work. While child care in Denmark and Sweden is typically of high quality, including in its developmental components, it is designed with working parents in mind. Arguably, this is much less the case in Germany and Spain, where child development issues are more prominent (and, in any case, the statutory right covers only three hours per day). Maternity and paternity leave also seem to matter. Mothers in Germany, for exam- ple, are entitled to three years of job-protected leave per child, suggesting to employers and mothers alike that the place of a mother of young children is at home rather than in the workplace. In the four countries with the lowest fertility rates, traditional perceptions of the superiority of maternal over other forms of child care are strong; many women, particularly women with higher levels of education, when faced with a choice between motherhood and career, choose not to have children.

Many labor market scholars and demographers have puzzled over the paradox of the US result. Why, with such weak public work-family supports, do US women maintain comparatively high fertility? Two demographic factors contribute; high birth rates among both teenagers and immigrants (combined with a relatively high level of immigration) push up aggregate birth rates. Some structural factors matter as well. Most notably, the United States has an exceptionally large low-wage labor market, much of it unregulated, which enables working parents to buy inexpensive child care and to outsource other household services, thus "replacing" the meager public supports. Finally, cultural factors may contribute. It may be that US women are raised to expect that combining parenting and employment will be difficult—work–life stress is said to be a *way of life* in the US—so the realization that reconciliation will be difficult may have less of a deterrent effect on childbearing behavior. This question demands further interdisciplinary study.

Employment Outcomes

One basic indicator of women's economic achievement is their labor force participation rate, which captures the share of the population (in a given age group) that is either employed or actively seeking employment. Men's labor force participation rates are higher than women's in all of our study countries, but the magnitude of the gender gap varies from more than twenty percentage points in Italy to less than five percentage points in Finland (see Table 2.2).

Table 2.2 also reports employment rates for mothers with children below age 15.[6] Here, we see substantial variation across these European countries. Maternal employment rates vary from a low of 55 percent in Italy; to 60 to 69 percent in Luxembourg, Spain, and the United Kingdom, as well as in the United States; to 70 to 79 percent in Austria, Belgium, Finland, France, Germany, and the Netherlands; and up to 80 percent or higher in Denmark and Sweden.

As noted, mothers' employment rates are highest in Denmark and Sweden, and in both countries, differences between female and male labor force participation rates are comparatively low. At the other end of the spectrum are Italy and Spain. A substantial literature confirms the role of both leave policies and child care provisions in shoring up women's labor force participation rates. Studies confirm that leave policies affect women's individual employment decisions:

TABLE 2.2   Maternal Employment, Labor Force Participation, and Part-Time Work Rates, Selected European Countries and US, 2009–2010

	Maternal employment rate– child under 15[a]	Labor force participation (15–64) Women[b]	Labor force participation (15–64) Men[b]	Part-time work (<30 hours): Women[b]	Part-time work (<30 hours): Men[b]
	2009*	2010	2010	2010	2010
Austria	75.4	69.3	80.9	33.0	7.0
Belgium	70.9	61.8	73.4	31.7	6.7
Denmark	84.0	76.1	82.7	25.9	13.6
Finland	77.2	72.5	76.7	16.0	9.2
France	73.6	66.1	74.9	22.3	5.7
Germany	70.8	70.8	82.4	37.9	7.9
Italy	55.2	51.1	73.3	31.1	6.3
Luxembourg	68.4	60.3	76.0	30.4	4.6
Netherlands	78.5	72.6	83.8	60.6	17.2
Spain	60.0	66.8	81.9	21.7	4.9
Sweden	80.3	76.7	82.2	18.8	9.7
United Kingdom	67.1	70.2	82.5	39.4	11.6
United States	66.7	68.4	79.6	18.4	8.8

Sources: (a) OECD 2011: Chart LMF1.2.A: 2009 (*2010 for Denmark); (b) OECD 2012; Table A3.7.1.

Where mothers have job-protected leave, they are likely to make use of such leave, and will return to work at the end of such leave, whether leave is relatively short, as in Belgium, or long, as in Germany (see, for example, Hofferth and Curtin 2009). The introduction of 12 weeks of job-protected leave in the United States had an immediate impact on women's return to work after childbirth (Waldfogel 1998), with the strongest effect seen among women who have access to paid rather than unpaid leave.

Table 2.2 further illustrates the prevalence of part-time work (among the employed), using the thirty-hour cutoff adopted in the European Labor Force Surveys. (Note that that cutoff underestimates part-time work in countries such as the United States and Sweden, where a substantial number of women work between thirty and thirty-five hours per week). In any case, part-time employment has played an important role in enabling women to combine work with motherhood. Yet, while the majority of female part-time workers are "voluntary"—meaning that they have sought part-time employment—part-time work often requires women to take jobs below their professional experience and qualifications. As we discussed earlier, policymakers in the EU are concerned with ensuring the supply of skilled workers to the European economies. The loss of a trained woman worker, who, for example, may give up a job as a nurse because she cannot find a part-time nursing job and instead takes a part-time job as a cashier or receptionist—represents a loss to the economy as a whole. This reasoning is behind the widespread introduction of rights to request part-time and other forms of flexible working (see Hegewisch and Gornick 2011).

Social values vary across countries regarding the most appropriate way to care for children. Nevertheless, a substantial research literature has established that whatever the national setting, where child care is available, of reasonable quality and affordable, women are more likely to be in employment and to hold better jobs. Where child care is expensive or of poor quality, women are more likely to hold lower-quality jobs and to have more interrupted working lives (Gornick and Hegewisch forthcoming). Yet the impact of child care on labor force participation rates is somewhat less direct than the impact of leave policies because child care may be offered for only a few hours per day, not designed with working parents in mind, and may be used by parents primarily for educational reasons, whether they are in work or not (Jaumotte 2003).

Poverty

The link between the provision of work-family policies and family poverty rates is complex, as it is mediated by multiple features of the labor market as well as national tax and transfer policies. Nevertheless, we can at least draw this important conclusion: Generous and gender-egalitarian work-family policy is consistent with impressive poverty outcomes for families (see Table 2.3). Among our study countries, the lowest poverty rates are reported in Denmark, Finland, and Sweden, three Nordic countries with extensive work-family supports, and, with respect to leave, policy features that are structured to encourage men's engagement in child care at home.

At the other end of the spectrum is the United States, with the highest poverty rates among these countries: a remarkably high 47 percent among single-parent families and 15 percent in couple-headed families with children. The link between work-family supports and work attachment and advancement is well established in the United States, as are the negative consequences of not having such supports (Lee 2007). This is particularly so for single mothers. In addition, the lack of work-family supports has worrisome consequences for children's well-being. Quality, affordable child care provides long-term developmental benefits for children, as well as allowing their mothers to seek employment and, with this employment, increase their families' standard of living.

TABLE 2.3   Poverty Rates, Single-Parent Households, and Couple-Headed Households, 2008

	Single-parent households	Couple-headed households with children
Austria	30.8	5.6
Belgium	34.0	7.3
Denmark	9.9	2.5
Finland	14.2	3.8
France	22.6	4.9
Germany	26.5	4.5
Italy	31.5	13.2
Luxembourg	56.2	9.7
Netherlands	31.9	5.3
Spain	33.1	15.7
Sweden	17.9	3.8
United Kingdom	28.5	8.3
United States	46.9	15.0

Source: OECD Family Database *CO2.2: Child poverty* based on OECD Income distribution questionnaire, version October 2011.

Note: Poverty defined as income of 50 percent or less than national median; data for Denmark for 2007.

Unintended Consequences

One of the most active areas of scholarship on work-family reconciliation policy, especially in cross-national perspective, concerns the possibility that some features of these policies may unintentionally harm women's employment outcomes. In this section, we take a brief look at the question of unintended negative consequences, highlighting some recent studies that address this question. Concerns about negative consequences are focused almost exclusively on policies that enable workers to spend time out of the workplace, with or without compensation, through various leave, reduced-hour, or part-time work schemes. Concerns are also largely focused on higher-skilled, higher-earning workers. Public provision of nonparental child care is widely understood to have the opposite effect: It encourages time spent at the workplace and thus unambiguously strengthens women's ties to employment. Unless employers are mandated to provide and finance child care for their own employees (as is the case is some lower-income countries), government support for child care rarely prompts concerns about harmful consequences on women's employment.

The possibility that work-family policies could worsen some women's labor market outcomes is the subject of a contentious and growing empirical literature (see Pettit and Hook 2009). The core questions addressed in this literature are: Do public provisions that grant leaves and other measures, such as the right to part-time work, worsen the prospect that women will be employed in higher-skilled, higher-paid jobs or occupations? Do generous policies lower the glass ceiling or make it more impenetrable, in turn, worsening the gender wage gap, especially at the top?

Two distinct causal arguments have been suggested. The most commonly invoked argument focuses on the demand side; that is, employers' behavior is seen as the main culprit leading to negative consequences for gender equality at work. According to this view, where leaves and reduced-hour work options are widely available and generous, employers are more likely to discriminate against women in hiring and advancement—and pay (either directly or indirectly)—on the grounds that women more often than men take up the options to which they are entitled. Discriminatory employer behavior, it is argued, would be targeted mostly on higher-skilled workers, as their temporary or intermittent absences are perceived by employers to be the most difficult to manage and as incompatible with male norms of career commitment.

At the same time, some offer a supply-side argument, suggesting that the causal mechanism operates largely through workers' (not employers') decision making and behavior. From this vantage point, employed women who take up leave and part-time work options self-select into less-competitive, less-remunerative occupations and jobs, partly because they prefer to work side by side with others whose employment behavior resembles their own. Thus, the leave and part-time work options themselves may indirectly reduce women's focus on career advancement. The two arguments have in common the prediction that generous work-family policies will be associated with more job or occupational sex segregation and, in turn, a larger gender earnings gap, especially at the top of the earnings distribution.

The empirical literature on the question of harmful consequences of these policies is limited and has not clarified the extent to which the causal link (if there is one) originates on the demand side or on the supply side. In one often-cited study, Mandel and Semyonov (2005) argue that some forms of paid leave can have harmful consequences. They conclude that "although mother-friendly policies enable more women to become economically active, they exacerbate gender occupational inequality" (949). Specifically, they find that the generosity of publicly provided maternity leave worsens gender earnings inequality. Importantly, they find that two other measures of work-family policy generosity (publicly funded child care and public-sector employment) have no significant effect on the gender earnings gap. A few other studies indicate possible harmful effects of work-family supports on women's employment outcomes (e.g., Shalev 2008).

Other researchers, however, question these conclusions. Korpi, Ferrarini, and Englund (2009) argue that the existing research on the harmful consequences of public work-family provisions has, largely, reached erroneous conclusions. They claim that the existing literature has multiple weaknesses and conclude, "in para-phrasing Mark Twain . . . that rumors about the suicide of gender egalitarianism are greatly exaggerated" (26).

Although this literature continues to evolve—and more research is clearly needed—one conclusion seems clear: The length of leave periods matters. While several studies indicate that relatively short leaves increase women's labor force participation, raise the probability that women return to paid work after birth or adoption, reduce the likelihood of changing employers, and lower the "mommy tax" associated with leave taking (see Hegewisch and Gornick 2011), longer leaves seem to be much more problematic. One study comparing trends in women's labor force participation across OECD countries suggests that leave entitlements of more than nine months might have a comparatively negative impact (Jaumotte 2003). Labor force participation, of course, is not the only relevant outcome; other research suggests that lengthy leaves, as were long in place in Germany, also rein-force traditional gender roles in caregiving at home (Morgan and Zippel 2003).

Conclusion

The approaches to work-family reconciliation in place in many European coun-tries provide a wealth of potential lessons for policymakers. These lessons are far ranging; they relate, for example, to the design and financing of parental leave systems, the features of leave design that encourage men's participation in family care, the design of working time regulations that are compatible with both employer and employee needs, and the value of coordination between the educa-tional and care functions of child care services. At the same time, there are also potential lessons from the "soft" coordination of work-family policies in Europe and its emphasis on minimum standards, as well as gradual improvements through the sharing of best practices, knowledge networks, and financial supports for innovation. Lessons are as much about what not to do as they are about positive practices. Yet perhaps the largest lesson to be drawn is that the neglect of work-family reconciliation can lead to costly economic and social consequences, by reducing current and future workforces, exacerbating skill shortages, and increas-ing multiple facets of inequality.

Reflections: Prospects for Policy Development in the United States

There is no question that, among wealthy countries, the United States lags dramatically in the provision of public work–family reconciliation supports; that observation is uncontested. American work-family provisions, in comparative perspective, are vastly different from those in place in many European countries. Is this form of US exceptionalism inevitable and immutable? It is often argued that publicly provided work-family reconciliation policies, overall, are incompatible with the American context. Some analysts claim that the United States will never adopt European-style policies because they are incompatible with American political culture and preferences, especially the demand for small government and the sanctification of individual choice. Others stress that Americans would never be willing to pay for the costs of these services and supports, were they to be provided publicly. While a full assessment of these claims is outside the scope of this chapter, several points are worth making—and together, they suggest that the longer-term prospects for developing European-style work-family policy in the United States may be substantially greater than popular wisdom suggests (Gornick and Meyers 2003).

First, while Americans tend to be skeptical of large-scale public programs, a closer look at US history demonstrates that Americans generally react favorably to public programs that enable and encourage paid work. Many components of the work-family policy package have this feature. Public work supports are likely to become more politically attractive when the United States faces the labor shortages that ongoing demographic shifts will surely catalyze. In fact, employment rates among college-educated women in the United States are already lower than in several other major economies, suggesting that the lack of work-family supports may be pushing at least some workers out of the labor force, resulting in a loss of human capital to the American economy. Lost human capital will become less and less acceptable over time.

Second, a growing body of research demonstrates that European-style work-family programs provide ample room both for individual choices, and for variation across local communities and, conversely, that the absence of such programs actually constrains Americans' choices and, in some cases, forces them to choose from among unattractive options. The US' lack of paid maternity policy, for example, forces millions of American women to choose between returning to paid work before it is safe and feasible or taking a leave and absorbing an income loss at exactly the moment that their families have expanded. The scarcity of high-quality, reduced-hour jobs forces many parents (mostly women) to choose been high-quality employment with unwanted hours and lower-quality work with attractive hours. The absence of affordable child care makes choosing paid work infeasible for many mothers, effectively forcing them to opt for unpaid caregiving at home. Advocates of work-family policy expansion have made these arguments, with increasing vigor, in recent years.

Third, the costs of an expanded system of work-family policy would be substantial. But it is also true that the needed outlays might be less than expected. Even the highest-providing countries in our study devote a surprisingly small share of their gross domestic product (GDP) to these programs. Sweden, with arguably the most extensive benefits, spends about 2.5 percent of its GDP on family leave and child care; Denmark and Finland each spend just under 2 percent of GDP; France, with somewhat less extensive leave benefits, spends about 1.3 percent. And, indeed, the United States spends much less than these amounts: approximately 0.2 percent of its GDP on publicly financed child care and a negligible amount on public paid-leave provisions (Gornick and Meyers 2004).

Might Americans be willing to pay more—perhaps up to 1.5 or 2 percent of GDP—on supports for families with young children? It is notable that Americans have historically contributed to another form of support for children and families: public education. Although the United States is a laggard in many areas of social welfare spending, it was one of the early leaders in extending public education to all children. The United States continues to make substantial investments in the public education of its children, spending about 3.4 percent of GDP on primary and secondary public education. Were the United States to increase its public investments in supports for younger children (either directly or via their parents) to levels proportionate to current expenditures on school-age children (a population that is roughly twice as large), that level of funding would suffice to support a generous system of work-family policies, along the lines of programs operating in my countries in Europe (Gornick and Meyers 2004).

In short then, the needed costs for supports for our younger children are not out of line with current American investments made on behalf of older children, via public primary and secondary education. Furthermore, several economists from across the political spectrum—most notably, Nobel laureate James Heckman—have recently joined the call for more public investments in younger children, arguing that waiting until age six (or even five) to invest in children may cause irreversible losses in many children's development and, in the long term, in their economic potential.

What does the future hold in the United States? It is impossible to predict. What we do know is that American work-family policy advocates have been popularizing these claims for years, arguing that these programs support paid work, that they allow choice and flexibility, and that the investments in children are likely to be recovered. And, there is some evidence that US policymakers are increasingly open to enacting work-family policies. In the period just prior to the onset of the current global financial crisis (that is, in 2006–2007), there was a marked groundswell of work-family legislative activity in the United States, at the national level and in many states, activity that was halted with the sharp economic downturn. It is reasonable to imagine that, when the US economy recovers and when deficit reduction seems within reach, the next public policy area to undergo expansion will be work-family reconciliation policy.

Endnotes

1. Authorship is in alphabetical order; both authors contributed equally.
2. EEOC v. Bloomberg LLP, Opinion & Order: Case 1:07-cv-08383-LAP Document 202; p. 60-61 Filed 08/16/11.
3. Council Resolution of 21 January 1974 concerning a Social Action program, cited in Children in Scotland 2010:4.
4. The other three are Swaziland, Papua New Guinea, and Lesotho (http://www.ilo.org/wcmsp5/groups/public/@dgreports/@dcomm/@publ/documents/publication/wcms_124442.pdf).
5. The White House: Forum on Workplace Flexibility, March 31, 2010, (http://www.whitehouse.gov/the-press-office/president-and-first-lady-host-white-house-forum-workplace-flexibility).
6. We expect the maternal employment rates (reported in column 1) to be higher than the female labor force participation rate (in column 2) because mothers of dependent children are younger than women overall. At the same time, controlling for age, employment rates are systematically lower than labor force participation rates, because they exclude those seeking employment. Thus, we do not compare the two indicators to each other.

References

Children in Scotland. *Working for inclusion: An overview of European early years services and their workforce.* Edinburgh: Children in Scotland, 2010. http://www.childreninscotland.org.uk/docs/WFI_Researchoverviewreport_Jan10.pdf (September 20, 2011).

Council of Ministers. "Council Directive 75/117/EEC of 10 February 1975 on the approximation of the laws of the Member States relating to the application of the principle of equal pay for men and women" (Equal Pay Directive of 1975). *Official Journal L 04,* 19/02/1975 P. 0019–0020 (1975).

———. "Council Directive 76/207/EEC of 9 February 1976 on the implementation of the principle of equal treatment for men and women as regards access to employment, vocational training and promotion, and working conditions" (Equal Treatment Directive of 1976). *Official Journal L 039,* 14/02/1976 P. 0040–0042 (1976).

———. "Council Directive 92/85/EEC of 19 October 1992 on the introduction of measures to encourage improvements in the safety and health at work of pregnant workers and workers who have recently given birth or are breastfeeding (tenth individual Directive within the meaning of Article 16 (1) of Directive 89/391/EEC)." *Official Journal L 348,* 28/11/1992 P. 0001–0008 (1992).

———. "Council Directive 96/34/EC of 3 June 1996 on the framework agreement on parental leave concluded by UNICE, CEEP and the ETUC." *Official Journal L 145,* 19/06/1996 P. 0004–0009 (1996).

———. "Council Directive 2010/18/EU of 8 March 2010 implementing the revised Framework Agreement on parental leave concluded by BUSINESSEUROPE, UEAPME, CEEP and ETUC and repealing Directive 96/34/EC." *Official Journal L 68,18.3.2010* (2010): 13–20.

Gornick, J. C., and M. K. Meyers. *Families that work: Policies for reconciling parenthood and employment.* New York: Russell Sage Foundation Press, 2003.

———. "More alike than different: Revisiting the long-term prospects for developing 'European-style' work/family policies in the United States." *Journal of Comparative Policy Analysis: Research and Practice* 6, no. 3 (2004): 251–73. http://www.baruch.cuny.edu/wsas/academics/political_science/documents/JCPAarticle2004.pdf.

Gornick, J. C., and A. Hegewisch. *The impact of "family-friendly policies" on women's employment outcomes and on the costs and benefits of doing business.* (Research review, World Bank: Washington DC, forthcoming).

Hara, Y., and A. Hegewisch. *Maternity, paternity, and adoption leave in the United States.* Briefing Paper. Institute for Women's Policy Research, 2013. http://www.iwpr.org/publications/pubs/maternity-paternity-and-adoption-leave-in-the-united-states-1.

Hegewisch, A., and J. C. Gornick. "The impact of work-family policies on women's employment: A review of research from OECD countries." *Community, Work & Family* 14, no. 2 (2011): 119–38.

———. *Statutory routes to workplace flexibility in cross-national perspective.* Institute for Women's Policy Research Report No. B258. Washington DC: Institute for Women's Policy Research, 2009. http://www.lisdatacenter.org/wp-content/uploads/2011/02/flex-work-report.pdf.

Hofferth, S. L., and S. C. Curtin. "The impact of parental leave on maternal return to work after childbirth in the United States." *OECD Social, Employment and Migration Working Papers 7.* Paris: OECD. http://www.sourceoecd.org/10.1787/826588878522 (February 23, 2009).

Jaumotte, F. "Female labor force participation: Past trends and main determinants in OECD countries." *OECD Economics Department Working Papers No. 376,* 2003. http://www.oecd.org/eco/labour/31743836.pdf.

Korpi, W., T. Ferrarini, and S. Englund. *Egalitarian gender paradise lost? Re-examining gender inequalities in different types of welfare states.* Paper prepared for the EMPLOY-FAMNET Workshop, 2009. http://www.equalsoc.org/uploaded_files/publications/Korpi,Ferrarini,Englund,Berlin May11,2009.pdf.

Laughlin, L. *Maternity leave and employment patterns of first-time mothers: 1961–2008.* Current Population Reports P70-128. Washington DC: U.S. Census Bureau (October 2011). http://www.census.gov/prod/2011pubs/p70-128.pdf (June 14, 2013).

Lee, S. *Keeping moms on the job: The impacts of health insurance and childcare on job retention and mobility among low-income mothers.* Washington DC: Institute for Women's Policy Research, 2007. http://www.iwpr.org/pdf/C360KeepingMoms.pdf.

Mandel, H., and M. Semyonov. "Family policies, wage structures, and gender gaps: Sources of earnings inequality in 20 countries." *American Sociological Review* 70 (2005): 949–67.

McDonald, P. "Gender equity in theories of fertility transition." *Population Development Review* 26, no. 3 (2000b): 427–39.

———. "Gender equity, social institutions and the future of fertility. "*Journal of Population Research* 17, no.1 (2000a): 1–16.

Moss, P., ed. *International review of leave policies and related research 2011.* London: Institute of Education University of London, 2011. http://www.leavenetwork.org/fileadmin/Leavenetwork/Annual_reviews/Complete_review_2011.pdf.

Organisation for Economic Co-operation and Development. *OECD family database: Table PF3.1: Public spending on child care and early education.* Paris: OECD, 2010. http://www.oecd.org/redirect/social/family/PF3.1%20Public%20spending%20on%20childcare%20and%20early%20education%20-%20181012.pdf.

———. *PF3.1: Public spending on child care and early education.* Paris: OECD, 2011. http://www.oecd.org/els/family/PF3.1%20Public%20spending%20on%20childcare%20and%20early%20education%20-%20290713.pdf (September 30, 2011).

———. *LMF1.5: Gender pay gaps for full-time workers and earnings differentials by educational attainment.* Paris: OECD, last updated 04/11/2011. http://www.oecd.org/els/soc/LMF1.5%20Gender%20pay%20gaps%20for%20full%20time%20workers%20-%20updated%20290712.pdf.

———. *Gender equality in education, employment and entrepreneurship: Final report to the MCM 2012.* Paris: OECD, 2012. http://www.oecd.org/dataoecd/20/5/50423364.pdf (June 5, 2012).

Pettit, B., and J. L. Hook. *Gendered tradeoffs: Family, social policy, and economic inequality in twenty-one countries.* New York: Russell Sage Foundation, 2009.

Platenga, J., and C. Remery. *The provision of child care services: A comparative review of 30 European countrie*s. Brussels: European Commission's Expert Group on Gender and Employment Issues (EGGE), 2009.

Ray, R., J. C. Gornick, and J. Schmitt. "Who cares? Assessing generosity and gender equality in parental leave policy designs in 21 countries." *Journal of European Social Policy* 20 (2010): 196–216.

Shalev, M. "Class divisions among women." *Politics & Society* 36 (2008): 421–44.

US Census Bureau. *Who's minding the kids: Child Care Arrangements: Spring 2011—Detailed tables.* Washington DC: U.S. Census Bureau, 2011. http://www.census.gov/hhes/childcare/data/sipp/2010/tables.html (May 9, 2012).

US Equal Opportunities Commission. *Questions and answers about the association provision of the Americans with Disabilities Act.* Washington DC: U.S. Equal Opportunities Commission, 2011. http://www.eeoc.gov/facts/association_ada.html.

Waldfogel, J. The family gap for young women in the United States and Britain: Can maternity leave make a difference? *Journal of Labor Economics* 16 (1998): 505–45.

CHAPTER 3

The Role of Regulation in Health Care Policy

Lawrence D. Brown

In international comparisons of the performance of health care systems, the United States disappoints in at least three ways. First, the nation's spending on health care far surpasses that of its peers. The United States spends more than twice as much per capita on health as do other industrialized countries. Health care spending accounts for 17.6 percent of US gross domestic product (GDP), while the highest spending European countries—the Netherlands, France, and Germany—devote approximately 12 percent of GDP to health care (OECD, 2012). Second, the United States has left roughly 50 million of its residents—close to 20 percent of the non-aged population—without health care coverage.[1] Third, the US system is said to deliver poor value for money; that is, it fails to use the vast sums it spends in cost effective fashion.

Gauging the performance of any health care system is, to be sure, a tricky business. "The" health care system contains a range of subsystems—delivery of medical care, allocation of coverage, impact of social determinants of health, and cultural and behavioral factors, for instance—that contribute to health outcomes and costs. Warning against jumps to superficial cross-national conclusions from aggregate data, Peter Baldwin (2009, 41) concludes that the performance of the US health system is less remote from European norms than is often alleged. The system, he contends, "is neither equitable nor efficient. But nor is it entirely ineffective."

All the same, the ability of European nations to attain and maintain affordable universal coverage has long triggered curiosity and admiration among cross-national policy scholars in the United States (Rodgers 1998). This chapter tries to boil down this vast and complex topic by exploring differences and similarities between Europe and United States with respect to regulation of funding, coverage, benefits, allocation of funds, payments to providers, and governance of the supply side of the system. It concludes with ruminations on whether the Affordable Care Act (ACA) indicates a new-found willingness in the United States to learn from Europe or, rather, it derives from homegrown innovations that may partly correlate with European developments but were inspired by them little if at all.

Regulating Health Care

In the United States, health care providers, insurers, businesspeople, and conservatives from all walks of life depict health care "regulation" as meddlesome intervention by ignorant public officials that invariably produces unintended consequences. In the either/or frameworks that so often dominate health policy debate in the United States, regulation is viewed as a threat to such purported social benefits as professional autonomy, private provision, market competition, and correct financial incentives. Health care regulations therefore are adopted by policymakers not as a first choice but as a last resort. Regulations are introduced often by policymakers who have concluded that in exigent circumstances they have no other choice: They ruefully adopt regulatory measures they hedge about with constraints while continuing to search for workable alternatives that reject "the regulatory approach."

Since the 1970s, the United States has deployed a range of national and state regulatory interventions that seek to change the behavior of, or the payment received by, health care providers (Brown 1992). These include Professional Standards Review Organizations (PSROs) and their successors, the Peer Review Organizations and Quality Improvement Organizations; certificate of need legislation; health planning bodies (Health Systems Agencies); state setting of hospital rates, prospective payment for hospitals in Medicare, and rules on HMOs and health insurers more broadly. With the partial exceptions of rate setting and insurance regulation, these measures can be summed up as more than simply symbolic but less than substantively successful. They represent a distinctive set of tools, placed deliberately far back and nearly out of reach on the strategic shelf. Policymakers turn to them only as a last resort when they are under pressure not to sit there but instead to "do something."

The image of regulation that dominates American health care debates has very little resonance in European health care systems. Health policy systems in Europe are not based on a belief that one must choose between competition and regulation, between government-based approaches and markets, or other of the antinomies that misguide health policy debates in the United States. European societies regard regulations as rules of the game without which their health care systems would be unaffordable, nonuniversal, and incoherent. For them regulation is not only a discrete strategy or tool in the toolbox, but also rather the scaffolding that gives strength to systems of affordable universal coverage, the indispensable body of protections absent which market forces, competition, and the rest would surely run amok (as they do for instance in the United States). In Europe, then, regulation is less a discrete arena than a framework that pervades and rationalizes health care policy, giving it structure and substance.

The main regulatory strategies of intervention deployed in European systems are pretty much the same as those found in, or at least available to, policymakers in the United States. Differences lie less in the type of regulation than in the greater uniformity of application and tighter control over the actors to whom they apply in Europe than in the US health care system, which is wedded to what might be called regulatory particularism. For Europeans, the rules of the game are the coping mechanisms of systems under pressure—the best laid plans for managing the chronic stress in keeping affordable universal coverage both affordable and universal.

Funding

Funds for the US health care system flow from multiple, uncoordinated sources. The employer-based sector is an amalgam of millions of individual decisions taken by employers and workers about whether to buy coverage and on what terms. Medicare draws on social insurance contributions and general revenues at the national level, and many beneficiaries supplement their coverage with privately purchased Medigap plans. Medicaid is funded by general revenues appropriated by the federal and state governments. Separate, and separately financed systems, cover veterans, Native Americans, and federal employees. Care delivered to the uninsured is sustained by a mishmash of publicly appropriated funds, cross-subsidies financed by public and private payers, philanthropic programs, and more. In short, no rules of the funding game unite these subsystems, each of which deals with its fiscal strains in its own fashion.

Although the Right in the United States labors to persuade the public that European health care systems are one and all exemplars of socialized medicine (and thence the road to serfdom), these systems in fact display quite a range of options in organization and funding. Government may "own" large parts of the health care system as in England, but it need not do so. French doctors for nearly a century have proudly defended their independence from the state under the banner *le medicine liberale*, for example, and the French system contains both public and private hospitals. What matters to Europeans is not ownership or control of the system, but rather the power and capacity of government to set rules of the game that keep the system running without the myriad failures, market based and other, that bedevil a system as unruly as is the American.

In broad terms, health systems in Europe have been traditionally categorized as *Beveridge* or *Bismarck*, with Beveridge systems funded by general tax revenues and Bismarck systems funded by social insurance schemes to which employers and workers contribute. But Bismarckian systems, as found in France and Germany for example, have begun to supplement social insurance payments with general tax revenues, and both types of system increasingly seek extra revenues by means of modest out-of-pocket payments and taxes on, for instance, alcohol, tobacco, vehicle registrations, and the like. Since 2006, the Netherlands finances its system with a combination of flat payments by individuals (offset by subsidies for the less affluent) and earmarked employer contributions.

No European system finances health care entirely from a unique source of revenues, though the specific mix of funding sources varies from nation to nation. Unlike the United States, however, these systems derive these funds under national rules that apply to all entities that contribute funding to health care (e.g., corporations, households, workers, employers, and consumers) and channel the funds to nationally defined agents of coverage and payment (e.g., a national health service, provincial health ministries, sickness funds, or special offices that ensure coverage for the unemployed). These agents of coverage and payment in turn disburse the funds to health care providers or occasionally to consumers under systemwide, uniform rules. These systems, then, preside over something that can reasonably be termed a "national health care budget." The relative unity and uniformity of budgetary arrangements supply a concentrated focus and degree of leverage to contain costs that elude the multiple, fragmented, and weakly accountable systems in the United States that set their own funding rules for their particular health care games. European systems, for example, can modify coverage for the whole population in the light of new evidence of cost effectiveness, apply new payment methods across the universe of providers, adjust the flow of funds into their health care systems— or subnational systems—and set firm limits on the entrepreneurial energies of hospitals and other providers where these would drive up costs excessively. Although the budgeting process in European systems may be more transparent and facilitate greater accountability, these systems' struggles to control and contain costs are arguably harder than those that bedevil the higher-spending US system. Simply refusing to provide coverage for nearly 50 million people and declining to pay fees acceptable to many physicians in Medicaid, as the United States has done for years, is a relatively easy way to contain costs, compared to the highly contested decisions about the content of coverage that European health care policymakers have had to make to control costs.

Governance of Coverage

The institutions that manage health care coverage in the United States are as motley and disjointed as the sources of the funds that flow through them. On the private side, insured workers get coverage from insurance companies, such as Blue Cross, Aetna, and United, with which their employers contract, or directly from employers who elect to "self-insure" as do the great majority of large companies. The Centers for Medicare and Medicaid Services within the federal Department of Health and Human Services runs Medicare, while state-based Medicaid agencies manage Medicaid in each of the 50 states. Eligibility for Medicare commences at age 65, but eligibility for work-based coverage is entirely up to the employer, and eligibility for Medicaid is established by each state individually, except for some federal mandates for selected populations such as poor women and children. The ACA made the Medicaid system more uniform, establishing a national eligibility threshold of 133 percent of the federal poverty level, although a subsequent ruling of the US Supreme Court leaves each state free to choose whether or not to participate in this expansion of coverage.

Many European nations use no insurers at all for basic health care coverage. The British National Health Service (NHS) provides services directly to citizens and residents. Those who seek quicker access to health care services than the NHS can provide may purchase private health insurance, as does about 10 percent of the British population. The Scandinavian nations (and Canada) likewise supply coverage and care without resorting to insurers. Private insurers' role in the health field is confined to selling supplemental policies that cover services not included in the basic national health package. France, Germany, and most other countries on the European continent rely on *sickness funds*, which are private nonprofit institutions "with a public purpose" that is enshrined in firm regulations. For instance, these regulations control sickness funds' enrollment and rate-setting practices. Since 2006, the Netherlands allows for-profit entities to sell basic health insurance. Switzerland permits for-profit firms to sell health coverage; however, they are not allowed to earn on a profit on the basic package of nationally mandated health insurance. They can only make a profit selling their clients supplementary coverage (which might include dental care, private hospital rooms, extra preventive services, and more generous coverage of home health care, for instance) beyond what is required in the basic package. Enticed by the supposedly superior efficiency of market forces, the Dutch and the Swiss, and on a more constricted scale, the Germans, have adopted managed competition among sickness funds, but these arrangements stand worlds apart from laissez-faire. These nations not only regulate their sickness funds tightly in order to deter bias against poorer risks (i.e., people with poorer health) but also make extra risk-adjusted payments to sickness funds that may happen to end up with a relatively unfavorable mix of risks (i.e., clients with poorer health than the clients of other sickness funds). These systems understand that competition, like heath insurance and insurers themselves, is but a means to important egalitarian and solidaristic social ends. They seek to harness market forces to achieve their social objectives and work to refine their systems to ensure that these market-based means do not inadvertently subvert or corrode their underlying objective of providing universal access to healthcare.[2]

Consciously and conspicuously missing from the European picture is an "industry" of private firms like that found in the United States that has sought to maximize profits or revenues by practicing "preferred risk selection," that is, rejecting or penalizing bad risks (i.e., people who were likely to make expensive health insurance claims). The risk selection techniques practiced by for-profit firms, including for instance underwriting, setting premiums according to likely or actual use of services, rescission, and exclusions or waiting periods before the commencement of coverage for specific conditions, became well known in the context of the debate over health care reform in the United States. Controversy over these techniques helped trigger demands for redress to which the federal government responded with tighter regulations in the Health Insurance Portability and Accountability Act of 1996 and the ACA of 2010, which limit the discretion of insurers to deny coverage for people with preexisting conditions, to set annual and lifetime limits on coverage, to devote more than 80 to 85 percent (depending on the size of insurer) of their revenues to nonmedical expenses, and to set premiums as they please. Impressive as they are, however, these provisions still leave US coverage short of the European pattern, in which access to care is either supplied directly by the state or, if mediated by insurance institutions, governed by firm and uniform public rules that prohibit variations in coverage and prices according to health history.

These reforms also do not alter another prominent difference between the United States and European systems of coverage—namely, the high administrative costs US insurers incur to design, launch, and sustain marketing campaigns and then pass on to purchasers; to review, contest, and possibly deny payment of claims; to adjudicate appeals of delayed or denied claims; to secure preauthorization of referrals; and more. Estimates of administrative costs are notoriously complex and contentious, but the magnitude of the difference between the administrative costs of for-profit US insurers and nonprofit insurers in the United States and abroad is arresting indeed. Private insurance plans in the United States spend on the order of 16 to 20 percent of their revenues on administration, while Medicare and the Veterans Health Administration spend only about 3 percent (Wilensky 2009, 4–5). US spending on administrative costs also stands out in cross-national comparisons. The United States ran second only to Luxembourg among Organisation for Economic Co-operation and Development (OECD) nations in 2004, with spending on health administration and insurance costs that is twice as high as nation number three on the list (France) and more than four times greater than the OECD average (Congressional Research Service [CRS] 2007, 30).

Contents of Coverage

The two major US programs of public coverage—Medicare and Medicaid—have standard packages of benefits, although the former allows some regional variations in interpretations of coverage and the latter permits states to exceed and get federal matching funds for designated services above the basic package. The fifty states can elect to mandate that private insurers cover specific services, but employers that self-insure are exempt from such requirements, and those that do not self-insure have broad discretion as to what services they will buy for their workers and on what terms. The benefits and costs of employer-based coverage are therefore highly variable.

Most European societies authorize coverage for medically necessary and appropriate care (or words to that effect) and then specify the services in question in law, regulation, and payment formulas. In principle, then, all citizens and residents have access to the same set of services on equal and uniform terms. In practice, of course, access is not so straightforward: Providers exercise judgment as to who should get what care, when, and where; geographic variations in facilities, technologies, staff, and physicians shape the distribution of care; and social classes and cultural groups show different degrees of inclination to approach the system and distinct degrees of savvy in "working" it. The United States not only faces these complexities but also aggravates them severely by means of a multiplex structure of benefits that varies according to whether the citizen is covered by traditional Medicare, Medicare Advantage, Medicaid (in its fifty different iterations), or one of thousands of distinct employer-based plans.

Advances in medical technology coupled with rising expectations of consumers continue to drive health care costs upward. These trends oblige all Western health systems to ponder how to draw lines around medical care, coverage, and costs and how to make such decisions stick politically. Although the American Right invokes these efforts as evidence that a larger role for big government in health affairs entails an allegedly un-American "rationing" of care, in fact, the term is often used to depict any method of allocation of resources, whether public or private. In Europe, rationing mainly takes the form of waiting lists for specialist referrals and elective surgeries, and these tend to be longer in Beveridge-type systems than in Bismarckian ones (Or et al. 2010). These systems also examine drug formularies in hopes of delisting or restricting coverage for drugs that are not clinically effective or cost effective, and may, as in the case of the National Institute for Health and Clinical Excellence (NICE) in the United Kingdom, refuse to authorize coverage for innovative but very costly drugs or medical devices. But the US system that relies so heavily on private, for-profit insurers also rations care. For instance, leaving many millions of citizens without coverage or inadequately covered, permitting insurers to refuse to pay for allegedly insured medical treatments, shifting more of the costs of coverage and care to consumers, and encumbering care seeking with obstacles called "managed care," all constitute forms of rationing practiced by private insurers in the United States. The rationing strategies that predominate in the United States strike European policymakers as socially pernicious expedients which they prefer to avoid.

Some nations have labored to devise packages of basic benefits that explicitly identify care that falls outside a plausible definition of community responsibility and exclude those suspect services from basic coverage. To date, however, earnest marshalling of philosophical argument and energetic mining of clinical evidence on cost effectiveness—even by sophisticated analytical bodies such as NICE in the NHS—have identified few interventions that belong beyond the pale. In vitro fertilization, or perhaps more than the first try at it, seems to be the modal target, and new drugs that extend life briefly at high cost are perennially controversial. Some European systems have increased cost sharing—mainly copayments for physician visits, hospital stays, and prescription drugs—but seldom more than nominally. The NHS has from its beginning channeled access to specialists by means of gate-keeping general practitioners, but, notwithstanding low-key efforts in this direction in France and Germany, few systems push this strategy very hard. Many encourage the spread of supplementary or complementary insurance coverage for services beyond those provided by the basic national health system in hopes of easing strains on it.

In sum, regulatory efforts to fine-tune and rationalize the benefits that national health insurance promises proceed vigorously all across the West, but in Europe the bedrock premise that the public sector should assure universal access on terms that honor uniformity and equity remains culturally and politically undisturbed. Nor is the coverage formally embodied in the health insurance regimes of these nations the only type of benefit that influences the health of their populations. European welfare states also extend social protections by means of pensions, unemployment allowances, disability benefits, and family payments. These measures target the "social determinants" of health and may contribute more to explaining the higher rankings of those nations than the United States on myriad cross-national measures of health status than do features specific to health care systems per se.

(Re)distribution of Funds

The US health care system consists of diverse coverage "pools," each with redistribution patterns of its own. Medicare, the nation's closest approximation to universal coverage (for everyone above age 65) draws legitimacy from its being identified with social insurance rather than with welfare. Medicare beneficiaries bankroll through their working careers the care they will get once they retire and enter Medicare, so there is a perception that they have earned the benefits they receive. In fact, the value of the Medicare coverage that beneficiaries receive tends to exceed the value of their contributions, and therefore Medicare requires transfers from current workers to current retirees. Medicaid is funded by annual appropriations of general revenues by state governments and the federal government.

These funding sources give Medicaid a strongly redistributive cast—but solely for that subset of the disadvantaged population that meets its eligibility criteria. In their early years, voluntary health insurance plans in the employer-based system often set community-rated premiums through which more affluent and healthier subscribers subsidized less affluent and sicker ones. Beginning in the 1940s, the entry into the health insurance market of private commercial plans that offered so-called experience rates reflecting the use, or likely future use, of health services by subscribers, however, in time pushed community rating and its cross-subsidies to the sidelines of the system. No coherent social philosophy guides US arrangements, which confine entitlements to health care coverage to the aged and some of the poor while leaving the commercially insured population to the mercies of "actuarial fairness" (Stone 1993) and the market. Before ACA, the actuarial principle that good risks (i.e., those unlikely to make insurance claims) deserve good rates predominated and defeated federal efforts to pool risk among large groups. When large firms with market muscle shop for coverage for large pools of employees, this tendency can be overcome, but people in the small-group and individual markets have been at the mercy of insurers' assessments of their risk profiles. This is precisely the problem that ACA's health insurance exchanges and new regulations are intended to solve.

The root rationale for affordable universal coverage in Europe—that no one should fail to seek, or should be denied, health care for financial reasons—demands redistribution and cross-subsidies as a requisite of the equity and solidarity that give these systems their moral, cultural, and political foundation. Equity and solidarity require—indeed they mean—that the young, employed, better off, and healthier cross-subsidize the aged, the unemployed, the less well off, and the sick within the health insurance regime amid other components of the welfare state. Moreover, evidence that these redistributive allocations have not entirely eliminated inequalities ("disparities" in American parlance) in access, treatments, and health status has spurred proposals and programs to invest more heavily in regions and subpopulations that do not share fully the fruits of universal coverage. In recent years, European systems have sought to improve health services in underserved regions (so-called medical deserts), to address the social determinants of health, and to encourage physical exercise, healthy eating, cessation of smoking, and other public health interventions that disproportionately benefit disadvantaged residents.

Arrangements that explicitly equate equity with redistribution do not go entirely unchallenged in Europe. Health care takes a big bite from social resources, and its steadily increasing costs lead to grumbling, familiar to American ears and avidly rebroadcast by conservative US critics of the welfare state, about excessive tax burdens and whether the benefits the system assures for the well-off justify the financial burdens they bear for the sake of their less advantaged countrymen (Judt

2011, 147–51). Research findings, increasingly prominent in both academia and the popular media, that highlight the importance of lifestyle choices and behavioral variables in morbidity and mortality also trigger debates on both sides of the Atlantic about the wisdom—and equity—of making society pay for the health care of those who are deficient in personal responsibility and refuse to take proper care of their health. These and other corrosive forces may conceivably undercut the commitments to equity, solidarity, and (therefore) redistribution that animate contemporary European systems. To date, however, the most striking (and strikingly un-American) features of these systems are the strength of the consensus that lack of money should never preclude access to health care and the continuing commitment to redistributive rules that sustain affordable universal coverage.

Provider Compensation

Physicians and hospitals in the United States get paid for their services by a mix of payers, each of which uses various techniques to determine how much health care providers will be compensated for their services. First, there are dozens of private insurers, each of which sets its own fees for outpatient visits, inpatient procedures, and so on. Second, there is Medicare, which relies on various payment commissions and federal officials who use arcane methods, such as prospective payments based on diagnosis-related groups for hospital care and resource-based relative-value-scale, fee-based schedules to pay physicians. Third, fifty different state Medicaid agencies provide payment for services to patients covered by Medicaid, and each agency enjoys wide discretion over who gets paid how much for what services. Private payers differ in generosity, depending on their market leverage. Medicare payments usually fall below those of the private plans, and Medicaid in turn generally pays even less than Medicare, leading some physicians to refuse to see patients covered by these public plans (especially Medicaid). Notwithstanding these variations, on average US physicians (particularly specialists) get paid at rates far above those of their European counterparts (Anderson et al. 2003; Laugesen and Glied 2011; Reid 2009).

European systems craft fee schedules that list reimbursable acts, attach monetary coefficients to them, and apply them to all physicians and hospitals. These schedules are typically negotiated annually between representatives of providers (unions or associations of physicians or hospitals) and payers (associations of sickness funds, a national health ministry, subnational health ministries, or regional authorities). Most European societies have concluded that such structured "health insurance bargaining" (Glaser 1978; White 1995) is necessary but insufficient to keep their systems affordable; therefore, they have experimented with strategies that cap or constrain the negotiators by limiting increases in payments to providers and for drugs to the rates of increase in gross domestic product, consumer price index, average wages of workers, or some similar metric. The regulatory challenges in devising, enforcing, and fine-tuning such constructs are formidable, however, and in some systems have generated regulatory fatigue that spurs the search for market mechanisms that would finally give providers an incentive to practice more efficiently, or in other words, a direct interest in "managing" care and competition (Brown 1998).

All such systems, moreover, seek in some form or fashion to rationalize clinical practice by means of some combination of evidence-based medicine, practice guidelines, best practices, pay for performance, and other techniques that seek to harness knowledge drawn from health services and clinical research to the simultaneous improvement of quality and efficiency of care (Chalkidou et al. 2009). These systems tend to deploy these interventions as reinforcements at the margin of firm regulatory policies. None pretends, as does the United States (Oberlander 2011), that analytical techniques can successfully substitute for a well-articulated regulatory framework.

In no such system do the politics of payment unfold without stress. Despite familiar tales of the decline of the cultural authority, professional sovereignty, and dominance of providers, physicians and hospitals retain enormous legitimacy and sophisticated organizational representation—resources that often enable them to replenish political capital diminished by critiques of excessive use of services, medical errors, and other increasingly documented malfunctions that afflict systems of affordable universal coverage.

Supply-Side Governance

US health care policy tends to act as if more of the supply side—more biomedical research, more technology, more hospitals, more physicians, and so on—is almost always better. This stance follows more or less logically from the "medical cultural nexus" (Brown 2008), which equates such advances with high quality of care. US policymakers have tried various regulatory expedients to bring resources better into line with needs—PSROs to deter unnecessary hospital care in Medicare, state certificate of need programs to constrain excessive expansion of hospitals and untrammeled diffusion of technologies, health system agencies to instill planning into local health care systems, and more. The implementation of these programs was never smooth and seldom successful, and their staying power has been, on the whole, unimpressive.

European societies recognize that universal coverage cannot be kept affordable if (almost) anything goes on the supply side of the system. They therefore work to assure a number and distribution of physicians and hospitals sufficient to give their citizens timely access to primary and specialty care and avail themselves of pretty much the same medical devices, procedures, and drugs as does the United States. European citizens visit doctors, are admitted to hospitals, and consume drugs at rates close to or above those of Americans. Compared to the OECD average, the United States has fewer hospital admissions, doctor visits, hospital beds, and practicing physicians per population, and about average lengths of hospital stay. On the other hand, the United States surpasses the OECD average in percentage of specialists, costs of outpatient care, supply of advanced technologies (e.g., CT scanners and MRI machines), and heart procedures per population (CRS 2007, 58). European societies use regulation to hold the line on the number of specialists, the diffusion of technologies, the entrepreneurial energies of hospital leaders, and the drugs fully covered by their national plans. As a consequence, their systems are less service intensive than is that of the United States, a source of efficiency that combines with payments to providers that are markedly lower than those in the United States to explain why their spending on health care per capita and as a share of GDP falls well below that of the United States.

Health Care Reform and Lessons from Europe

European nations tend to view regulation as an enfolding set of uniform rules that are part and parcel of, indeed not easily distinguishable from, the health policy game, whereas the United States treats regulation as a package of disjointed and particularized interventions, reluctantly inflicted on private or voluntary forces run amok in the health care system. Often these regulatory interventions are branded in turn as a cause or aggravation of the private and voluntary misadventures the regulators hoped to correct. Because the title of the landmark legislation adopted in the United States in 2010 promises "patient protection" and "affordable care," one might reasonably expect the new law to move toward a European approach to regulation. The ACA adds substantially to the statutory stock of regulatory particulars, to be sure, but its designers, resolved to withhold ammunition from opponents who would scare the electorate by conjuring upon visions of "comprehensive" overhauling of the system, retained the basic features of the status quo. This meant retaining much of the US system's regulatory fragmentation.

When ACA is implemented, funds for health coverage will continue to flow from multiple sources. Medicare will, as now, cover the aged (among whom the affluent will pay more), Medicaid may cover 16 million or so more lower-income Americans, and the employer-based system of private coverage, very much intact, will be supplemented by income-related public subsidies to help individuals and workers in small businesses who lack employer coverage but are not eligible for public programs to buy private coverage in new health insurance exchanges. The federal Department of Health and Human Services, state Medicaid agencies, and state insurance regulators will continue to govern their distinct pieces of the action, though new rules limiting the discretion of private insurers to exclude or otherwise discriminate against the sick are one of the ACA's signal achievements.

The law mandates that insurers and Medicare cover various preventive services without cost sharing and the states will be required to define "essential health benefits" to be sold in the exchanges, but the breadth and contents of benefits will continue to differ markedly among sources of coverage. ACA's new taxes on the investment income of affluent taxpayers and on the insurance and medical device industries, its generous financial offer to the states to expand Medicaid eligibility to 133 percent of the federal poverty line, and the new income-related subsidies are, as Thomas Rice notes, "a progressive turn of events," in which for "the first time in a very long while the United States has passed a law that makes the tax system more progressive." (Rice 2011, 491). Whether a restive public will tolerate the taxes needed to sustain the new public coverage and the premium increases that may ensue from the law's assault on selection of preferred risks remains to be seen—especially if the health cost curve declines to bend.

The law takes several new regulatory steps toward cost containment. For example, public authorities are charged with reviewing "unreasonable" increases in insurance premiums, a review panel will propose cuts if Medicare spending targets are exceeded, a new institute will study the comparative effectiveness of medical technologies, and hospitals with excessive readmissions of their patients will face financial penalties. Whether these and kindred innovations set the United States on the road toward controlling costs at long last, as proponents contend, or are timid and toothless alternatives to methods the success of which is on display across the nations of Europe, as critics charge (Oberlander 2011) time will tell. Finally, although the ACA authorizes higher payments and other incentives for primary care physicians and much expands the number and budgets of community health centers, it does little to discipline the service-intensive practice style the nation has long equated with high-quality care.

In short, ACA impressively expands the health care regulatory agenda of the federal and state governments, but it does so by adding to the pile of regulatory particulars, not by assembling the multiplying strategic fragments into the uniform set of systemwide rules that European policymakers think crucial to attaining and maintaining equity and efficiency alike. No wonder then that Marc Rodwin's (2011) astute summary of the scope and limits of the law, written in 2011, was titled "Why We Need Health Reform Now." No less post- than pre-ACA, European systems arguably have much to teach Americans about the costs of the fragmentation and particularism of our own system and the benefits of uniformity in regulatory matters. But ACA is an exercise in incremental adjustment and gap filling that bears traces on each and every page of the intricate political accommodations and compromises required to keep the reform afloat and finally to get it passed. "Styles" of health care regulation, like other political products, emerge from exigent and nationally distinct cultural and institutional filters that would dependably constrain cross-national comprehension even if Americans unaccountably acquired a taste for it.

Conclusion

It would be pleasant to conclude this review by averring that the passage of the ACA in 2010 constitutes the fruit of learning from Europe—better late than never. Such a contention would, however, confound correlation with causation. The ACA does indeed bring the US system closer to European norms by moving nearer to universal coverage, by imposing tougher public rules on private health insurers, and by taking steps to slow the growth of costs. "Close," however, does not mean "similar," for the United States retains multiple and nonuniform systems of coverage, private insurers continue to enjoy substantial discretion, and the prospects for the ACA's cost containment are murky. Moreover, this partial rapprochement between the United States and Europe is best explained not by "learning from" Europe but rather by the need on both sides of the Atlantic to address broadly similar challenges (e.g., costs, equity, technology, and so on) with broadly similar strategic tools (e.g., coverage decisions, payment methods, health technology assessments, and the like). In deciding how to apply tools to tasks, the United States fashioned ACA around lessons mainly from within its federal system—from the individual mandate, insurance exchange, Medicaid expansion, and income-related subsidies successfully adopted by Massachusetts in 2006.

The superior record of European performance in health affairs stood as a constant reminder of the challenges the United States faced, and a persistent spur to facing up to them. However, the cultural aversion of sizable parts of the US population to anything resembling "European socialism" (including of course socialized medicine and a "government take-over of the system") and the institutional encumbrances of the US legislative and party systems (for example the need for sixty Senate votes to break filibusters, and a prominent cadre of conservatives within the Democratic party) would have made any overt display of learning from, not to mention emulation of, Europe a heavy political liability. The ACA may represent a kind of new frontier in health policy, however, and perhaps it will prove to be one along which getting from here—US arrangements—to there—European achievements—may proceed more smoothly than it has to date.

Endnotes

1. As discussed below, this will of course change with the enactment of the Affordable Care Act of 2010, which aims to bring coverage up to approximately 95 percent of the population.
2. On the evolution of the Dutch system, see the articles in HEPL 2011: 109–45.

References

Anderson, G. F., U. E. Reinhardt, P. S. Hussey, and V. Petrosyan. "It's the prices, stupid: Why the United States is so different from other countries." *Health Affairs* 22, no. 3 (2003): 89–105.

Baldwin, Peter. *The narcissism of minor differences: How America and Europe are alike.* New York: Oxford University Press, 2009.

Brown, L. D. "Political evolution of federal health care regulation." *Health Affairs* 11, no. 4 (1992): 17–37.

————. "Exceptionalism as the rule? US health policy innovation and cross-national learning." *Journal of Health Politics, Policy and Law* 23, no. 1 (1998): 35–51.

————. "The amazing noncollapsing US health care system—Is reform finally at hand?" *New England Journal of Medicine* 358, no. 4 (2008): 325–27.

Chalkidou, K., S. Tunis, R. Lopert, L. Rochaix, P. T. Sawicki, M. Nasser, and B. Xerri. "Comparative effectiveness research and evidence-based health policy: Experience from four countries." *Milbank Quarterly* 87, no. 3 (2009): 339–67.

Congressional Research Service. *U.S. health care spending: Comparisons with other OECD countries.* Washington, DC: CRS, 2007.

Glaser, W. A. *Health insurance bargaining: Foreign lessons for Americans.* New York: Gardner Press, 1978.

Judt, T. *Ill fares the land: A treatise on our present discontents.* Penguin UK, 2011.

Laugesen, M. J., and S. A. Glied. "Higher fees paid to US physicians drive higher spending for physician services compared to other countries." *Health Affairs* 30, no. 9 (2011): 1647–56.

Oberlander, J. "Throwing darts: Americans' elusive search for health care cost control." *Journal of Health Politics, Policy and Law* 36, no. 3 (2011): 477–84.

Or, Z., C. Cases, M. Lisac, K. Vrangbæk, U. Winblad, and G. Bevan. "Are health problems systemic? Politics of access and choice under Beveridge and Bismarck systems." *Health Economics, Policy and Law* 5, no. 3 (2010): 269.

Organisation for Economic Co-operation and Development. *OECD Health Data 2012.* Paris: OECD, 2012. http://www.oecd.org.

Reid, T. R. *The healing of America.* New York: Penguin, 2009.

Rice, T. "A progressive turn of events." *Journal of Health Politics, Policy and Law* 36, no. 3 (2011): 491–94.

Rodwin, M. "Why we need health care reform now." *Journal of Health Politics, Policy and Law* 36, no. 3 (2011): 597.

Rodgers, D. T. *Atlantic crossings: Social politics in a progressive age.* Cambridge: Harvard University Press, 1998.

Stone, D. A. "The struggle for the soul of health insurance." *Journal of Health Politics, Policy and Law* 18, no. 2 (1993): 287–317.

White, Joseph. *Competing solutions: American health care proposals and international experience.* Washington, DC: Brookings Institution, 1995.

Wilensky, H. L. "US health care and real health in comparative perspective: Lessons from abroad." *The Forum* 7, no. 2 (2009): 1–18.

CHAPTER 4

Pensions: Who Is Learning from Whom?

Mitchell A. Orenstein

As the United States (US) faces a massive fiscal crisis and reevaluates its spending on entitlement programs including Social Security, it seems relevant to ask whether the United States can learn from the experiences of other developed countries addressing similar issues (Orenstein 2009; Skocpol 1995; Weaver 2005). Are there lessons from Europe?

In a broad sense, European pension systems mainly provide negative lessons of what not to do. The generous European pension systems that were built up in many countries since the late nineteenth century have been in crisis for years and have been forced to cut back. Many of these systems offered very high income-replacement rates, aiming not only to prevent old-age poverty but also to help middle- and upper-income earners maintain retirement incomes similar to those they enjoyed as workers. However, as the aging of European populations has swelled the number of pensioners and as global economic competition has created pressure to reduce labor costs, this level of state pension provision has become impossible to sustain. The global financial crisis has only intensified this trend, once again showing many European states that they cannot afford as generous pension schemes as they did in the past (Casey 2012; Tinios 2012). The resulting cuts have been truly transformative. Greece and other countries in crisis have been forced to cut back suddenly and dramatically. The pension systems of Germany, Sweden, and other European countries that have experienced more orderly retrenchment have come to resemble that of the United States with its smaller, redistributive state Social Security system and workplace 401(k) system of voluntary individual accounts (Scherman 2012). Indeed, at the broadest, macrolevel of pension system design, it seems that recently Europe has learned more from the United States than vice versa. The overarching lesson from Europe is that, however comfortable and desirable they had become, the European pension systems proved

59

unsustainable. They also crowded out needed investments in young people and families, which became a growing focus of European welfare states (see Gornick and Hegewisch, chap. 2).

Yet, not all the lessons from Europe concerning pensions are negative ones. On the positive side, as European countries have shifted toward a more free market "liberal" model like that found in the United States in recent years, they have accumulated microlevel experiences in innovative pension system design that could be valuable to the United States. As I discuss below, the US workplace pension system suffers from high fees and low coverage, just as increasing numbers of Americans are being forced to rely on it. America's broken workplace pension system will need to be reformed, and recent European experiences transforming workplace pensions can provide useful lessons for successful reform in the United States. Drawing together these lessons—both negative and positive ones—highlights two overarching points: While Americans tend to believe that Social Security is in crisis, the European experience shows that, quite to the contrary, Social Security is relatively healthy; rather, it is the workplace pension system that is in crisis and could benefit the most from lessons from Europe.

A Reversal of Direction

The theme of transatlantic learning is not a new one in welfare state research. Historians have shown that the United States drew many lessons from Europe during the development of its welfare state (Rodgers 1998). Probably the most famous account of US lesson drawing from Europe is Daniel Rodgers's 1998 book, *Atlantic Crossings,* in which he details the many different ways in which US Progressives adopted European welfare state models. He argues that during the Progressive Era from approximately 1870 until the Second World War, the United States eschewed its typically parochial view of American exceptionalism and was uniquely open to European influence. With the rise of the United States after the Second World War, American exceptionalism returned with its tendency to look down on the corrupt old continent. But during the Progressive Era, he writes, "Tap into debates that swirled through the United States and industrialized Europe over the problems and miseries of 'great city' life, the insecurities of wage work, the social backwardness of the country-side, or the instabilities of the market itself, and one finds oneself pulled into an intense, transnational traffic in reform ideas" (1998, 3). While a rich and complex transatlantic discourse on policies and institutions existed then and exists today, during the Progressive Era, it was common practice in the United States for policymakers and citizens to look to and learn from European experience.

There is no doubt: European countries were pioneers in welfare state development and most of the lessons traveled west across the Atlantic. In the 1890s,

Chancellor Otto von Bismarck made Germany the first country to initiate comprehensive, national old-age and medical insurance systems. He did this to dampen workers' enthusiasm for socialism and tie their interests more closely to the state. Britain and other European countries followed suit within the next two decades, under the advice of contemporary policy entrepreneurs (Dawson 1912). However, progress was much slower in the United States. While the Civil War pension system that channeled cash payments to widows and children of veterans since the 1870s was a precursor to the development of a national welfare state in the United States (Skocpol 1995), it was not until after the Great Depression in 1935 that President Franklin Delano Roosevelt's New Deal established a comprehensive national welfare state including a Social Security pension system with old-age and disability insurance. The United States thus lagged Europe by three to four decades in welfare state development, similar to other new world countries such as Chile.

Rodgers (1998) devotes his book to analyzing many of the different pathways that reform ideas and lessons were transferred from Europe to the United States. First, US social policy academics trained at European universities, particularly in Germany, where they learned from social democratic scholars steeped in a growing critique of British laissez-faire economics. Study in Europe became de rigueur for top scholars at leading universities such as Columbia and University of Pennsylvania. Second, new government agencies such as the Bureau of Labor devoted many of their publications to spreading word of social policy innovations in Europe. Third, political leaders at the local level debated the merits of various European models when considering policies to address social ills of great US cities, seeing them as essentially analogous. Fourth, Rodgers focuses a great deal on particular social policy entrepreneurs and argues that they created the institution of a sociological "grand tour" of Europe, bringing back ideas and lessons.

Even today, lesson drawing from Europe remains commonplace in US universities, where many academics continue to draw inspiration from social policies in European social democracies. One of my professors in graduate school was voicing an everyday reality of the academic world when he once asked disdainfully whether a book I was perusing was "one of those books that argues that the US should be more like Sweden." Nevertheless, in a broader sense, the heyday of lesson drawing from Europe has clearly past. The rise of US dominance in the international system after the Second World War caused a return to a more typical and parochial sense of American exceptionalism that looked down on and eschewed European influence (Rodgers 1998). This rejection of Europe was reinforced by the turn to neoliberalism after 1980. Since that time, the free market liberal (in the US parlance, *conservative*) mainstream of US social policy thinking has criticized progressive thought for being too European and sought to follow a more indigenous business-like model. Indeed, this critique has become part of the Republican attack on President Barack Obama's health care plan. Meanwhile, modern US Progressives have been unable to gain traction for policies that mimic European social accomplishments. Though there is much evidence of the ways that the United States could learn from Europe in the social and environmental spheres (Hill 2010), many Americans believe that the European social model is threatened with collapse. This view has spread in the wake of the eurozone economic crisis and has further damaged the image of Europe's social and economic models in American eyes (Kelemen, chap. 1).

Another factor that explains the dominance of free market liberals in transatlantic welfare state discourse from 1980 to 2008 is that welfare states seemed to have reached their natural limits and entered an era of retrenchment (Pierson 1994). European and American countries that had expanded welfare guarantees in previous years found them increasingly difficult to finance and entered a period of permanent budgetary austerity—even before the recent economic crisis. The second oil crisis of the 1970s brought a period of cheap oil to a close and halted the dramatic postwar expansion of the Western economies. Globalization forced developed country labor markets to be more competitive versus their less-developed-country peers. Demographic aging caused by declining fertility rates had a strong impact on pension systems in developed countries. These systems had been created under very different demographic circumstances, with high ratios of workers to retirees. As the number of workers per retiree declined, this put the finances of state-managed, pay-as-you-go pension systems under permanent pressure and raised questions about how to manage the baby boom generation's retirement. Free market liberal discourse seemed to provide answers to these problems during a period of permanent austerity.

As a result of these trends, pension innovation that had flowed primarily from Europe to the Americas in the late nineteenth and early twentieth centuries began to flow mainly in the opposite direction since 1980. This reversal in the direction of transatlantic learning is clearly visible through a comparison of the diffusion of first pension systems worldwide and the diffusion of pension privatization—the most important trend in pension system design since 1980—starting in 1981. Whereas the establishment of national pension systems shows a clear regional diffusion pattern stretching from Continental Europe to the United Kingdom (UK), the Americas, and later to Asia and Africa, pension privatization started in Latin America and the United Kingdom and then spread quickly to Central and Eastern Europe (Orenstein 2008). More generally, in recent decades, lessons concerning pension system reform have been flowing with the jet stream eastward across the Atlantic.

Lessons from the United States for Europe

Since Europe and the United States ended a period of welfare state "development" and entered one of "retrenchment" (Pierson 1994), the US's laggard status came to be seen as a strength and a model for European liberals who sought to pare back overgenerous European pension guarantees. Some of the most dramatic pension reforms in Europe in the 1990s and 2000s resulted in systems that mirrored the US model of a relatively small public pension system combined with voluntary private savings through individual pension savings accounts such as 401(k)s. Perhaps the most dramatic example is Germany's Riester reforms of the 2000s, which transformed Germany's pension system from a Bismarckian one in which upper-middle-class pensioners could expect generous state pensions to a much more modest state pension coupled with voluntary individual savings (Ebbinghaus 2011; Palier 2010). The extent of the pension cuts that Germany has phased in over time is enormous. Replacement rates for pensions are predicted to decline from between 60 and 70 percent of prior earnings to 42 percent when the reforms are fully implemented (Borsch-Supan and Wilke 2003; Organisation for Economic Co-operation and Development [OECD] 2009), a cut of more than a third. This will give Germany the lowest public pension replacement rate for low-income workers in the developed western states of the OECD and nearly 20 percent lower than similar pensions in the United States (OECD 2009). Germans can make up the difference through voluntary savings in subsidized individual accounts, which are expected to produce an additional 17 percent of prior earnings, making up much of the difference between the old and new replacement rates. However, these returns are contingent on savings behavior, take-up, and investment returns. Not everyone will receive one and not everyone will reach that 17 percent level. The old German pension system is gone, at least for future generations of retirees.

Germany is not the only European welfare state to drastically reduce the generosity of its pension system in the 1990s and 2000s, inspired by the free market liberal policies of the United States and United Kingdom. Karl-Gustav Scherman, a former president of the International Social Security Administration, estimates that the 1990s reforms in Sweden will cut average replacement rates in Sweden from around 55 to 65 percent of prior earnings under different scenarios to around 30 to 40 percent by 2050 (Scherman 2009, 2012). Sweden's reforms also created a system of individual pension savings accounts, funded by a 2.5 percent payroll tax contribution. Sweden enacted a so-called *notional defined contribution* system for its income-related pension system that ties benefits closely to contributions. Under this system, replacement rates have dropped further than expected.

European leaders made these and other changes because they came to believe that they could not afford to sustain their generous pension systems at a time of slow economic growth, demographic aging, and need for human capital investment in younger people. While the results of these reforms will take two to four decades to fully realize, the reality is that the generous European pension systems previous and current generations knew have been gutted. The new systems put in place converge to a great extent with the previously much-maligned US model. In some cases, they are less generous than the United States (Scherman 2009). The lesson from Europe: The US system has had the right combination all along of a smaller, redistributive state Social Security system supplemented by savings in voluntary individual savings accounts.

Another major way in which the US pension system seems to be leading the way for Europeans is in increasing the retirement age. The European Union's *White Paper* on pension reforms recommended that European countries increase the retirement age as the primary means of reaching fiscal balance. Yet, the United States had already voted in 1983 to raise its retirement age to 67 years. Germany and Spain followed suit, initiating an increase in their retirement ages to 67 in 2007 and 2011 respectively. In 2010, France started to raise its minimum retirement age from 60 to 62.

Perhaps the most important example of Europe learning from the Americas comes from pension privatization, which traveled from Latin America to Eastern Europe in the 1990s and 2000s via the Washington-based international financial institutions (IFIs) and particularly the World Bank. Now, historian Matthias Leimgruber (2008) has pointed to the Swiss roots of the three-pillar World Bank model of pension privatization, and indeed, some of the key ideas behind pension privatization arose from a 1970s reform in Switzerland that created a system of individual pension savings accounts and was transmitted via European insurance and financial circles. However, few European countries followed the Swiss model and it was ultimately refined and popularized in the Americas before being re-exported to Europe—primarily to Central and Eastern Europe— from 1997 to 2004.

Pension privatization was popularized in the Americas because of the close association of the University of Chicago and the dictatorship of Augusto Pinochet in Chile. Free market, liberal welfare state reform ideas pioneered at the University of Chicago in the 1970s were transmitted to Latin America through a United States Agency for International Development (USAID) program to train Chilean economists at leading US universities. This produced a cadre of "Chicago boys" who later held top positions in the Pinochet government in Chile. These economists led the privatization of the Chilean social security system, replacing it with a system of individual pension savings accounts. Pension privatization came to be seen as one of the policies responsible for the dramatic turnaround of the Chilean economy and, as a result, spread throughout Latin America starting in the 1990s. Peru was one of the first countries to adopt the Chilean model in 1992. Argentina followed in 1994. At the same time, pension privatization captured the imagination of the World Bank, which issued a major report in 1994 entitled, "Averting the Old Age Crisis" (World Bank 1994). While not part of the original Washington consensus on development, pension privatization became one of a set of second-stage reforms advocated by the Washington-based IFIs.

The lessons of pension privatization in the Americas were learned quickly in Central and Eastern Europe. More than a dozen Central and East European countries adopted pension privatization in the years between 1997 and 2004, making this region the greatest locus of pension privatization outside of Latin America. Central and East European countries adopted pension privatization in part because the collapse of communism had kicked the political supports out from under the existing systems of social insurance. Trust in trade unions and the state declined precipitously. At the same time, budget deficits grew. The World Bank hired Latin American pension experts to advise on reform in Central and Eastern Europe. The head of the World Bank Institute's pension programs, for instance, was a prominent Argentine reformer. As part of its technical assistance, the World Bank often brought Central and East European opinion leaders on study tours of Chile and Argentina to learn about their reforms, trips that had a significant impact on their opinions. The Bank also often sponsored talks by Jose Piñera, famous Chilean minister of labor who has conducted a worldwide crusade for pension privatization in cooperation with the US-based, libertarian CATO Institute.

Hungary privatized its pension system in 1997 and Poland did so in 1998. A dozen other countries followed suit between 1998 and 2004, in an example of rapid intraregional diffusion. Most of these reforms followed the model set out in the 1994 World Bank report, which advocated a reduced state pay-as-you-go system complemented by a newly designed system of private pension savings accounts. Although these countries also had access to European advisers and European pension system models, these countries did not follow the existent West European models to anywhere near the same extent, attesting to the way in which pension advice emanating from the Americas had become dominant in social policy reform (Appel and Orenstein 2013). It is particularly remarkable that countries of Central and Eastern Europe were adopting Latin American–inspired pension privatization during a period when many of them were otherwise focused on adopting the laws and regulatory regimes (the so-called *acquis communautaire*) required for them to gain membership in the European Union. In other words, despite the fact that Central and East European countries were focused on adopting West European regulatory frameworks in many other fields, they clearly did not find West European pension systems to be attractive models. Part of the reason for the lack of reliance on Europe was that, at the time, European models were themselves under siege. Conversely, many West European leaders looked favorably on the pension privatization experiments in Eastern Europe and sought to use them as a lever to produce reforms at home.

Convergence of the Welfare Worlds

While Central and Eastern Europe experimented with pension privatization, the famously stable welfare state worlds of Western Europe began to hybridize and converge toward the liberal model of the United States and United Kingdom. In 1990, Gosta Esping-Andersen described three worlds of welfare capitalism: a liberal world of minimal safety nets, a Scandinavian world of high universal benefits, and a Continental or Bismarckian world of status-reproducing social insurance. For several decades, scholars verified these findings, showing that despite forces of globalization, European countries remained within their original worlds. Political pacts supporting these models and other institutional sources of *path dependency* won the day and held the models in place. Yet in the 2000s, this consensus began to break down. Scholars increasingly perceived that European welfare states had never been quite as differentiated as the typology suggested. And furthermore, forces of Europeanization seemed to be creating a trend toward hybridization of European welfare worlds (Heidenreich and Zeitlin 2009) with all the major states adopting aspects of the liberal model (Bridgen and Meyer 2011; Palier 2010).

This hybridization or convergence had many sources, but the main one was the adoption of liberal welfare policies in the Scandinavian and Bismarckian countries. Denmark famously adopted *flexicurity* policies that aimed to combine flexibility with security—creating a more liberal labor market supported by job training programs and other social supports. Sweden, as described above, liberalized its pension system through individual accounts. The Netherlands also embraced flexicurity and increased the coverage of and reliance on its preexisting private occupational pension system.

While Scandinavian countries remained distinct in some ways, they clearly adopted many aspects of a liberal economic program starting in the 1990s. Germany and other conservative welfare states were slower to change, but the Schröder reforms of the 2000s marked a watershed. German liberals had been trying to liberalize labor markets and social policies for years, but they finally succeeded under a pro-business Social Democratic government enacting the landmark Hartz reforms. France under Sarkozy got rid of the thirty-six-hour work week and made pension benefit eligibility more restrictive.

For pensions, this liberal trend meant an increased reliance on private savings and reduced state pay-as-you-go pension systems. The examples of Sweden and Germany were mentioned above. Sweden transformed its pension system by adopting a notional defined contribution, or NDC, system to replace its previous income-related benefit and also carved out room for a 2.5 percent payroll contribution to individual pension savings accounts. Germany drastically reduced its state pension system and created a new voluntary private savings scheme beside it. Netherlands and Denmark increased reliance on their preexisting occupational private pension systems. These are not isolated examples, but rather part of a widespread trend in Western Europe (Ebbinghaus 2011).

Much of the impetus for this convergence came from the European Union, which in the 1990s initiated a process for addressing continent-wide issues of pension system balance. This discussion centered around the Economic and Financial Affairs (ECOFIN) Council's attempt to create a dialogue on pension liberalization and the Social Policy (EPSCO) Council's attempt to articulate a defense of the European social model. The ultimate result of these debates was a European Commission 2012 *White Paper: An Agenda for Adequate, Sustainable, and Safe European Pension Systems* (European Commission 2012). The *White Paper* is a useful document because it both sums up the state of pension reform in Europe after thirty years of incremental liberalization and because it establishes common priorities for the future. The main one is to increase the retirement age. As the commission explained in its preparatory *Green Paper* (European Commission 2010, 2) on pension reform, "The recent financial and economic crisis has aggravated and amplified the impact of the severe trend in demographic ageing. Setbacks in economic growth, public budgets, financial stability and employment have made it more urgent to adjust retirement practices and the way people build up entitlements to pensions." Noting a distinct trend over the last decade to "lower the share of public pay-as-you-go pensions in total provision while giving an enhanced role to supplementary, prefunded private schemes, which are often of a Defined Contribution (DC) nature" (5), the commission advocates increases in the retirement age as the most promising option for restoring pension finances. The global financial crisis opened a window for such changes.

Impact of the Global Financial Crisis

The global financial crisis proved to be a watershed for European pension systems (Casey 2012). It remains unclear whether it will ultimately push Europe further in the direction of learning from the free market, liberal policies of the Americas or reverse this trend. So far, the results are mixed. On the one hand, the global financial crisis halted the impetus toward pension privatization worldwide (Orenstein 2011) and forced countries in Central and Eastern Europe to reevaluate their commitment to private pension systems (Drahokoupil and Domonkos 2012). On the other hand, it created pressure for countries to cut back on public pension spending as a way to address fiscal deficits in particular by raising retirement ages. Table 4.1 provides a summary of recent retirement age increases in selected countries in Western Europe.

Again, looking at these retirement age increases, it is hard to avoid the conclusion that Europe is learning from the United States, rather than vice versa. The United States, for instance, increased its retirement age from 65 to 67 in a

TABLE 4.1   Recent Retirement Age Increases in Europe (selected countries)

Country	Retirement Age Increase
France	From 60 to 62
Great Britain	From 60 to 65 for women by 2012
	Increasing to 68 starting in 2024
Germany	From 65 to 67 by 2029
Netherlands	From 65 to 66
Spain	From 65 to 67
Switzerland	From 64/65 to 67 by 2030

landmark 1983 reform. Germany legislated a similar increase in 2007, twenty-four years later. What lesson should the United States learn from this? The main lesson, it seems, is that the US Social Security system is in better shape that the US debate would suggest. The US approach of combining a modest state pension system with a large private and voluntary system of individual accounts subsidized through the tax system has been validated by recent European reforms.

Meanwhile, in Europe, the crisis has ruined the finances of state-managed, pay-as-you-go pension systems. No country was affected more than Greece. Greece had a famously profligate pension system, with replacement rates that far outpaced most European countries. It replaced, on average, nearly 100 percent of prior income. During the crisis, it was pared back by some 15 percent or more due to a variety of measures (Tinios 2012). Greece eliminated thirteenth- and fourteenth-month pensions for civil servants and reduced pensions in payment, a very unusual reform due to its high political costs. Greece was certainly late to reform its pension system in a liberal direction, but it was ultimately forced to do so, proving the necessity of at least some convergence toward the liberal model. Other European countries also cut back their public pay-as-you-go pension systems in the wake of the crisis. Romania enacted a 15 percent cut to pensions in payment only to have these reinstated by the constitutional court. The Baltic States also cut pensions in payment as part of an internal devaluation intended to keep them on a path to Euro membership. The depth of pension cuts depended on whether countries had scaled back pensions in an orderly fashion during good times and on the extent of the crisis.

The financial crisis also upset the momentum toward pension privatization. Central and East European countries that had privatized their pension systems were forced to reduce the percentage of payroll tax contributions channeled to individual accounts. Budgetary pressures and European Union fiscal deficit rules made it difficult to finance so-called transition costs of switching to the new system (Drahokoupil and Domonkos 2012). Postcrisis debt will inhibit pension privatization even in developed countries for years to come. Also, the World Bank stopped advocating pension privatization due to internal recognition of problems with the new private systems (Orenstein 2011). Hungary renationalized its privatized pension system altogether, seizing the assets held in private pension savings accounts and using them to pay down debt (Simonovits 2012). Poland is now considering such a measure. However, in most countries of Central and Eastern Europe, privatized pension systems are expected to survive, but at a lower level of funding than initially recommended by the World Bank. In 2011, the Czech Republic became the first European country since 2004 to privatize its pension system, but it did so with a much smaller, voluntary contribution to private accounts than its Central and Eastern European precursors. Again, the basic model continues to be the liberal welfare states of the United States and United Kingdom.

One general lesson the United States can draw from Europe is that the US Social Security system is in relatively good health. The US Congressional Budget Office (CBO) estimated in 2012 that the finances of the system would be secure through 2086 with a modest increase in the social security tax rate of 1.95 percent. Without that, its long term expenditures will exceed revenues by 10 percent (CBO 2012). Whereas domestically, the US Social Security system has endured decades of attacks from critics alleging that the system is on the brink of collapse, the health of Social Security is relatively good. In large part, this is due to the prescient 1983 reform engineered by Alan Greenspan (representing President Ronald Reagan) and New York Senator Daniel Patrick Moynihan. This bipartisan reform increased the retirement age, increased social security taxes, and made it possible to finance the retirement of the baby boom generation by creating a *social security trust fund* to save money for that purpose. While a new bipartisan reform is required to keep the system healthy in future decades, the United States had the prescience to enact these reforms early, while most European countries did not. The US Social Security system has also proved more durable than many of its European counterparts largely because of its basic design. Social Security provides a lower average replacement rate than many high-end European systems once did, around 40 percent (though much higher for low-income workers). It is also highly redistributive, geared toward poverty prevention. This type of modest system has stood the test of time, whereas the larger European pension systems that sought not only to prevent poverty but also to guarantee much higher retirement incomes for middle-class and upper-income workers have proven more vulnerable.

Lessons from Europe for the United States

While at the macrolevel, Europe has learned from the United States and other free market, liberal welfare states, at the microlevel, the new systems that the Europeans have designed to achieve goals of private savings contain important lessons for the United States.

The United States, like Europe, has gone through wrenching changes in its workplace pension system recently as employers have shifted from guaranteed *defined-benefit* pensions to uncertain 401(k) accounts, placing enormous risk on the shoulders of individual employees. With the retirement of the baby boom generation and the increased stress on Social Security, benefits are likely to be cut. The implication: Individuals will rely on workplace pensions even more. The problem is that the workplace pension system in the United States is not up to the challenge. Only a minority of workers are covered by a workplace pension. The vast majority of Americas rely solely on Social Security. While the workplace pension system benefits from enormous tax breaks, these tax breaks go primarily to those who need them least—the wealthy. The maximum tax breaks go to those who deposit the legal maximum of $17,500 per year into an individual pension account. Moreover, much of the money that goes into the workplace pension system never comes out in the form of pensions. First, between one-quarter to one-half of all funds are paid out in fees. Despite the large size of many US funds, the fees charged are up to five times higher than necessary, providing huge profits for financial firms but robbing pensioners of income. Second, there are many ways that people can tap their savings in 401(k) accounts; for instance, when buying a new home, changing jobs, or dealing with life emergencies. In some circumstances, people pay a penalty, but they still have access to these funds. Third, individuals are notoriously poor at making investment decisions. They often buy high and sell low. The result: Only about a third of Americans report significant retirement income coming from workplace pensions. Yet an increasing proportion of people will require additional income if social security benefits are cut. The US workplace pension system is in desperate need of reform.

It is exactly here that recent European experience provides some important lessons for the United States. As Weaver (2005) points out, a number of European countries have recently offered increased employer or voluntary or mandatory private pensions and many of the new program designs offer lessons for the United States. Sweden, for instance, has achieved low fees and a unique mix of individual choice and government regulation in its individual account system by using a single national clearinghouse for pension fund investments. Swedish accounts are unique. Rather than being marketed directly to individuals (as in the UK or US), individuals inform the government clearing house which funds they would like to select and that agency directs their contributions to the fund and issues statements. Fund companies do not know who their clients are, thus they cannot mis-sell their products using high-pressure sales tactics or tack on excessive fees. Sweden also created a default fund for people who do not wish to choose their own fund from some 700-plus options. This fund has low fees, creating competitive pressures on other fund fees, a sort of *public option* in pension choice. Sweden provides a unique counterpart to the US system of unregulated free choice marred by high fees and poor investment decisions.

The United Kingdom has recently adopted a system of automatic enrollment, where employees are automatically enrolled in a pension savings plan when they take a new job. Since employees seldom change their pension choice once it is made, this automatic enrollment is expected to create a much higher coverage rate for private pensions than in the United States. Automatic enrollment in pension savings plans was one of the recommendations made by Cass Sunstein, former head of the Office of Information and Regulatory Affairs in the Obama administration, in the book, *Nudge* (Thaler and Sunstein 2009), which seeks to apply principles of behavioral economics to public policy. The Netherlands and Denmark also have valuable experiences in extending an existing workplace pension system to the entire population, thus covering nearly everyone. Once the United States acknowledges the crisis of its workplace pension system, the next step will be to review options for reform emanating from Europe.

A growing number of European countries similarly have supplemented Social Security programs by making preexisting systems of workplace individual pension savings accounts mandatory. This approach was taken by the Netherlands starting in 1947, Switzerland in the 1960s, and Demark in the 1990s. Australia and New Zealand, English-speaking settler states like the United States, have also adopted this model. Australia introduced a major reform of its pension system in the 1990s, and New Zealand introduced its KiwiSaver program in 2007, which inspired the United Kingdom to legislate a similar National Employment Savings Trust (NEST) pension savings program in 2008 (OECD 2007). The experiences of English-speaking countries, such as Australia, New Zealand, and the United Kingdom, are the most relevant examples for the United States to follow, since these countries share a similar cultural heritage, reflected in their smaller Social Security systems, lesser reliance on the state, and greater trust in market provision.

The Netherlands has mandated workplace pensions since they were introduced in 1947, and many of them have been fully funded. Switzerland mandated workplace pensions after a 1972 referendum. In Switzerland, making workplace pensions mandatory began as a move by insurers and conservative politicians to prevent the formerly communist Labor Party from expanding the Social Security–type system (Leimgruber 2008; Rein and Turner 2001). Denmark moved toward mandatory workplace pensions in 1991 in an effort to provide adequate pensions for blue-collar workers. Eighty-two percent of Danes now are covered by a workplace pension (Green-Pedersen and Lindbom 2006). Until recently, the Dutch, Danish, and Swiss models were seen as outliers to the European norms, since these countries had smaller Social Security–type pension systems. However, a growing number of European and other countries have adopted this approach to pension reform.

In addition to the European models of mandatory workplace pensions, Australia's 1992 pension reform has provided an influential global model. The timing of Australia's new pension system coincided with the global trend toward pension privatization. Its design had a distinctly pro-market flavor that took inspiration from the Chilean model. The idea to mandate workplace pensions in Australia came out of negotiations between employers and trade unions. Trade unions wanted better pensions for workers and in 1986 agreed to accept lower wage increases in exchange for setting up a workplace pension system of so-called *superannuation* funds, funded by a 3 percent employer contribution. In 1992, the Australian government made this system mandatory and increased the contribution amount from 3 percent in 1992 to 7 percent in 2001 and 9 percent starting in 2002. Eighty-nine percent of all Australian workers are enrolled in one of the many workplace pension systems. Between 1990 and 2002, workplace pension funds experienced high returns of approximately 8 percent per annum, insuring the popularity of the program. However, it remains to be seen how lower returns may affect the system. Workplace pensions in Australia are very lightly regulated, with no guaranteed returns. A wide variety of funds offer a range of products with little government control and administrative fees are high, meaning that the funds may not necessarily provide the returns needed to support a secure retirement.

New Zealand passed its KiwiSaver pension system in 2006 and implemented it starting in 2007. Like Australia, New Zealand has a small state retirement pension paid for entirely by general tax revenues (rather than a special payroll tax contribution, as in the US and most other countries). Everyone is eligible to receive the state pension if residency requirements are met. Given the relatively small size of the benefits, however, many New Zealanders need to save to have an adequate pension; yet only 15 percent of employees were previously enrolled in a workplace pension system. This provided the impetus for the KiwiSaver program. Since 2007, all new employees are automatically enrolled in a KiwiSaver account to which they contribute 4 percent of earnings. Their investments are channeled to a default pension investment fund, unless they select another option, and they have eight weeks to opt out of the system if they choose to do so. Employers may also contribute to the accounts and receive a tax break on contributions. The New Zealand reform is unique in not requiring employer contributions as well as in making enrollment automatic, but optional (Toder and Khitatrakun 2006).

KiwiSaver proved inspirational in the United Kingdom, where successive Labor governments sought to re-reform the pension system after Thatcher's 1986 reforms that privatized part of the system in a misbegotten effort that produced substantial government liability when private companies oversold the benefits of switching to private pensions. The United Kingdom, like the United States, provides a relatively low level of Social Security pensions, which became increasingly insufficient as the population aged. A 2007 law increased protection for poorer pensioners while creating new opportunities for pension savings in the future. In 2008, the United Kingdom government proposed a new pension savings system that drew upon the KiwiSaver model of mandatory enrollment with an option for employees to opt out.

It proposed a mandatory contribution of 8 percent of earnings between 5,035 and 33,540 pounds (up to a maximum of 3,600 pounds per year) to an individual pension savings account. At least 3 percent of this contribution would be paid for by employers, with the rest paid by employees (and the government through tax breaks). The United Kingdom decided to phase in the contribution levels starting in 2013 with the 8 percent level to be reached in 2018. Pension savings accounts would be easily portable and a great deal of emphasis is placed on fair regulation of these funds, given the previous experience of the mis-selling of Thatcher-era funds. Employers with existing workplace pensions could maintain their current scheme if it was found to be more generous in a straightforward test. The government would work with the pension industry to design pension savings funds, place strict limits on fees, and insure low costs. Fees are meant to be limited to 0.3 percent of funds under management, but an initial 1.8 percent fee was enacted to fund the setup costs of the system. Lessons from these experiences concerning the design of workplace pensions may prove invaluable as the United States confronts how to reform its workplace system Social Security faces possible cuts.

In sum, the current 401(k)-based workplace pension system in the United States has serious problems. While employers have moved away from defined-benefit pension systems that guaranteed income based on previous salary and provided generous pensions to employees with long tenures at large firms, 401(k)-type workplace pension systems have had poor results in terms of creating an adequate retirement income for most Americans (Munnell and Sunden 2004). People do not contribute enough to their individual pension savings accounts, called *401(k)s* after a clause in the US tax code; they often cash out the balances when they leave their employers; they make poor investment decisions, for instance keeping too much in company stock; and they will most likely make poor decisions at retirement, taking lump sum payments instead of annuities. As a result, balances in most 401(k) accounts are too low to provide adequate benefits in retirement. The system needs to change now that more Americans are dependent on these accounts.

European and other international experience shows that the most promising way forward for US pension reform is to make enrollment in a workplace pension mandatory and create a new *public-option* pension savings fund that will prove attractive to both employees and employers. Generous, preexisting workplace pension schemes could opt out if they prove that their benefits will be equal or higher than the new savings system. This approach achieves the promise of benefit adequacy by limiting cuts to Social Security and mandating workplace pensions for all. Such a reform can be funded by replacing the tax breaks provided to the existing workplace pension system, which have increased dramatically in recent years. In doing so, the European pension systems could provide important lessons in how to achieve this, with an eye to low costs, flexibility, and targeting underserved populations.

Conclusion

In conclusion, the transatlantic flow of ideas has reversed since the Progressive Era, when social policy ideas flowed from the Old World to the New. Since 1980, in pensions at least, Europe has mainly learned from the Americas. This is because of broader political economic trends that resulted in the dominance of neoliberal policy worldwide. European social welfare systems have been pressured to converge to a more liberal model. The pace of this change accelerated during the global financial crisis, as European welfare states were forced to slash future social expenditures in part by increasing the retirement age to US or nearly US levels (67 years of age). Nevertheless, the United States can still clearly draw lessons today from European countries' experiences with pension reform. The lessons the United States can draw from Europe are mostly at the programmatic level in terms of finding the right balance between public and private pensions and learning from innovative new designs for voluntary, mandatory, and workplace private pensions that have been created in Europe. The transatlantic flow of ideas on pensions will always be with us, and the United States will be forced to consider its own reforms soon given the inadequacy of our 401(k)-based workplace pensions. When that time comes, Europe's recent experience with emulating and improving upon the US model should be kept in mind.

References

Appel, H., and M. A. Orenstein. "Ideas versus resources: Explaining the flat tax and pension privatization revolutions in Eastern Europe and the former Soviet Union." *Comparative Political Studies* 46, no. 2 (2013): 123–52.

Bridgen, P., and T. Meyer. "The impact of the new public and private pension settlements in Britain and Germany on citizens' income in old age." In *Converging worlds of welfare? British and German social policy in the 21ˢᵗ century*, edited by J. Clausen, 180–217. Oxford, UK: Oxford University Press, 2011.

Börsch-Supan, A., and C. B. Wilke. *The German public pension system: How it was, how it will be.* Working Paper No. 2003-041. Ann Arbor: Michigan Retirement Research Center, 2003. http://www.mrrc.isr.umich.edu/publications/papers/pdf/wp041.pdf.

Casey, B. H. "The implications of the economic crisis for pensions and pension policy in Europe." *Global Social Policy* 12, no. 3 (2012): 246–65.

Congressional Budget Office. *The 2012 long-term projections for Social Security: Additional information.* Publication Number 4520. Washington, DC: Congress of the United States, Congressional Budget Office, 2012.

Dawson, W. H. *Social insurance in Germany 1883–1911.* London: T. Fisher Unwin, 1912.

Department for Work and Pensions. *Pensions and ageing society.* London: GOV.UK. https://www.gov.uk/government/topics/pensions-and-ageing-society.

Drahokoupil, J., and S. Domonkos. "Averting the funding-gap crisis: East European pension reforms since 2008." *Global Social Policy* 12, no. 3 (2012): 283–99.

Ebbinghaus, B., ed. *The varieties of pension governance: Pension privatization in Europe.* Oxford, UK: Oxford University Press, 2011.

Esping-Andersen, G. *The three worlds of welfare capitalism.* Princeton, NJ: Princeton University Press, 1990.

European Commission. *Green paper towards adequate, sustainable and safe European pension systems.* COM (2010) 365 final. Brussels: European Commission, 2010.

————.*White paper: An agenda for adequate, safe and sustainable pensions.* COM (2012) 55 final. Brussels: European Commission, 2012.

Green-Pedersen, C., and A. Lindbom. "Politics within paths: Trajectories of Danish and Swedish earnings-related pensions." *Journal of European Social Policy* 16, no. 3 (2006): 245–58.

Heidenreich, M., and J. Zeitlin, eds. *Changing European employment and welfare regimes: The influence of the open method of coordination on national reforms.* New York: Routledge, 2009.

Hill, S. *Europe's promise: Why the European way is the best hope in an insecure age.* Berkeley: University of California Press, 2010.

Leimgruber, M. *Solidarity without the state: Business and the shaping of the Swiss welfare state, 1890–2000.* Cambridge: Cambridge University Press, 2008.

Munnell, A., and A. Sunden. *Coming up short: The challenge of 401(k) plans.* Washington, DC: Brookings Institution Press, 2004.

Organisation for Economic Co-operation and Development. "Public pensions and retirement savings." *OECD Economic Surveys*, no. 8 (2007): 51–78.

————. *Germany: Highlights from OECD pensions at a glance 2009.* Paris: OECD, 2009.

Orenstein, M. A. *Privatizing pensions: The transnational campaign for social security reform.* Princeton, NJ: Princeton University Press, 2008.

————. "Learning from international experience." In *Pensions, social security, and the privatization of risk,* edited by M. A. Orenstein, 108–27. New York: Columbia University Press, 2009.

————."Pension privatization in crisis: Death or rebirth of a global policy trend?" *International Social Security Review* 64, no. 3 (2011): 65–80.

Palier, B. *A long goodbye to Bismarck: The politics of welfare reform in continental Europe.* Amsterdam: Amsterdam University Press, 2010.

Pierson, P. *Dismantling the welfare state? Reagan, Thatcher, and the politics of retrenchment.* Cambridge: Cambridge University Press, 1994.

Rein, M., and J. Turner. "Public-private interactions: Mandatory pensions in Australia, the Netherlands and Switzerland." *Review of Population and Social Policy* 10 (2001): 107–53.

Rodgers, D. *Atlantic crossings: Social politics in a progressive age.* Cambridge: Harvard University Press, 1998.

Scherman, K. G. *The Swedish NDC system: A critical assessment.* Paper presented to the 2nd Colloquium of the Pension, Benefits, and Social Security Section of the International Actuarial Association. Helsinki, Finland, May 2009.

————. "The Swedish public pension under stress." *Global Social Policy* 12, no. 3 (2012): 336–39.

Simonovits, A. "Re-nationalizing the mandatory private pension pillar in Hungary." *Global Social Policy* 12, no. 3 (2012): 334–36.

Skocpol, T. *Protecting soldiers and mothers: The political origins of social policy in the United States.* Cambridge: Harvard University Press, 1995.

Thaler, R. H., and C. R. Sunstein. *Nudge: Improving decisions about health, wealth, and happiness.* New York: Penguin Books, 2009.

Tinios, P. "Greece: Extreme crisis in a monolithic unreformed pension system." *Global Social Policy* 12, no. 3 (2012): 332–34.

Toder, E., and S. Khitatrakun. *Final report to Inland Revenue: KiwiSaver evaluation literature review.* http://www.urban.org/publications/411400.html (December 2006).

Weaver, R. K. *Social security smörgåsbord? Lessons from Sweden's individual pension accounts.* Brookings Policy Brief Series 140. http://www.brookings.edu/research/papers/2005/06/saving-weaver (2005).

World Bank. *Averting the old age crisis: Policies to protect the old and promote growth.* Washington, DC: World Bank Publications, 1994.

CHAPTER 5

Labor Market Policy: Toward a "Flexicurity" Model in the United States?

Tobias Schulze-Cleven

As a result of the global financial crisis, the US unemployment rate had climbed to double digits by 2009. With Americans experiencing the highest level of unemployment in a generation and the highest rate of long-term unemployment in more than half a century, US unemployment briefly matched that of the European Union (EU). Four years into the recovery, US unemployment has dropped below 8 percent. But as the jobless struggle to reenter the workforce, underemployment remains widespread, and American families are suffering from financial hardship. Even though policymakers allocated increased funding for labor market policy during the recession, the United States remains uniquely weak among advanced industrialized democracies in its lack of policy programs to support the populace in engaging with the labor market.

US policymakers have long had little interest in learning from the experiences of other countries, considering American institutions to be both innately superior to foreign ones and better suited to American culture. Policymakers have been especially disdainful of the supposedly rigid and stifling labor market institutions of continental Europe. This attitude has been reinforced by recent developments in the eurozone, where unemployment has reached the record level of 12 percent, while the US labor market has shown signs of improvement. The record unemployment in Europe has been driven by a surge in unemployment and crippling austerity policies in countries wracked by the Eurozone crisis—Greece, Spain, Portugal, and Ireland—and by persistently high unemployment in Italy and France. Without question, some of these countries, such as Spain and Greece, offer powerful lessons about the negative consequences of distorting labor market policies—particularly for youth unemployment.

However, the high average unemployment across Europe obscures the fact that throughout the crisis, some EU countries, including Austria, Belgium, Denmark, Finland, Germany, and the Netherlands, have maintained unemployment rates lower than the Unites States'. The assumption that all European labor market policies are anticompetitive and underperforming is misguided. European countries have very different labor market policies, and some provide great flexibility, showing more compatibility with the US's emphasis on individual autonomy and freedom than skeptics would lead us to believe. Moreover, with Europe's leading performers exhibiting similar per capita rates of economic growth to those of the United States over the past decades, the empirical evidence provides no reason to believe that these countries' labor markets are inferior to that of the United States under normal economic conditions. During the crisis, their labor market institutions have arguably proven themselves to be better suited than their US equivalents to help families deal with economic dislocation, to cushion a recession's impact on individuals' livelihoods, and to support workers in their adaptation to new economic conditions.

The recent crisis has demonstrated that deregulated, hands-off economic policies not only undermine markets over the long term, they impose enormous costs on society. This has become as evident in worldwide financial markets as it has in the domestic market for labor. The number of programs and overall spending levels on American labor market policy have withered under laissez-faire approaches, suffering both from deliberate rollbacks (Weir 1992) and from policymakers' failure to respond to new social and economic needs (Hacker 2004). This has left the United States without the internal collective resources to address today's large-scale challenges, such as structural economic change, globalization, and demographic shifts. Unless the United States takes active steps to shore up its labor market policy, it is likely to drift as it has in the past, leading to the further deterioration of the nation's skill base and creating major long-term problems with unemployment and poverty. If increasing parts of the workforce are unable to meet labor market needs, this could have serious repercussions for the stability of the American economy and society.

This chapter moves beyond the typically narrow US-centric nature of domestic policy debates in Washington to expand the horizon of policy possibilities for the United States. By examining other countries' experiences with labor market policy and reform, the chapter provides a new way of looking at the challenges and options for US labor market policymaking. With respect to both labor market *policy* and the *policy process*, US policymakers could draw inspiration from other democracies' experiences and implement (albeit with great difficulty) new institutions that build on lessons from Europe. If the United States is ever to learn from other countries, the time may be now, when the US labor market is faced with such grave challenges.

In particular, this chapter argues for an approach to labor market policy that borrows extensively from the Danish model of coordinated and active labor market policies. Combining generous temporary support and intensive worker training with a strong emphasis on getting workers back into the labor force as quickly as possible, the country's labor market policies have helped produce desirable market outcomes. The country's policy mix has underwritten high levels of labor market flexibility and provided social security for unemployed workers. This so-called *flexicurity approach*, which was pioneered in Denmark and the Netherlands, has attracted the attention of policymakers across Europe, and the EU has promoted flexicurity as a model of reform for other EU member states. While there are substantial differences between Denmark and the United States, including the two countries' sizes, the United States could build on the ideas underlying successful policy programs in Denmark. Today, all industrialized nations face many of the same basic policy constraints and share many common goals: As international competition and technical change have taken their toll, countries have struggled with reducing unemployment and encouraging the provision of good jobs that pay decent wages. Moreover, they have sought to increase labor market flexibility, both in particular employment relationships and more broadly by encouraging national workforce adaptability in the face of increased labor market uncertainty.

Beyond providing inspiration for the substance of new policies, developments in Europe could also provide advocates of reform in the United States with a valuable comparative perspective on the processes through which labor policy reforms can be enacted. Here the German experience is particularly relevant because the country has a complex political system like that of the United States, in which complicated relationships between the federal states and the national government often impede reform and support the status quo. Yet Germany has shown real signs of changing its labor market policy over the last decade. By understanding Germany's successes and failures, Washington policymakers could find inspiration for how to plot a plausible pathway to major reforms in the United States. The German example illustrates how a reform strategy based on *layering*—grafting *new* elements onto *old* policies and institutions rather than immediately replacing them—can help circumvent blockages in the legislative processes and lead slowly to transformational changes (Streeck and Thelen 2005). Thus, if American policymakers were to find direct attempts to emulate Denmark blocked, they might consider pursuing a layering approach in order to deliver the more active and generous labor market institutions that many Americans have long desired. This paper explores one potential opportunity for layering-oriented reform of US labor market policies, which may open up as Washington seeks to boost US export performance and improve the United States' position in the global economy. Expanding the small, federal Trade Adjustment Assistance (TAA) program into a much more prominent part of US labor market policy could plausibly address domestic worries about globalization and improve the nation's export capacity. This could build on a broad pro-reform coalition with the potential to move beyond entrenched interest group conflict and bitter political partisanship.

The remainder of the chapter is divided into six sections. Section one discusses potential ways of addressing contemporary challenges in labor market policy. Section two reviews American labor market institutions, chronicling how they have been neglected throughout most of the twentieth century. A third section illustrates how Denmark has sustained impressive labor market outcomes through coordinated activation policies. The fourth section turns to Germany, Europe's largest economy and a country with political institutions that were partially modeled on American ones after World War II. The fifth section examines how US policymakers could build on European experiences. The final section concludes.

Labor Market Policies for the Global Era

Labor is often treated by economists as a simple production input, no different from land and capital. It is anything but this. Creating well-functioning labor markets is a *political* process, in which governments try to resolve the needs of the market with the social and physical needs of the workforce. Labor market policy seeks to reconcile the diverging goals of capitalism and democracy, the former of which allocates worth according to market demand and the latter of which seeks to protect the rights and freedoms of the entire population. Labor markets policies achieve this with *passive* measures such as unemployment insurance that help soften the blows to individuals caused by market dislocations, *active* measures such as worker training and job placement that intervene in the labor market to help the unemployed gain employment, and labor laws that regulate many aspects of the employment relationship, from pay to working hours to safety conditions.

Labor market policies can make employment more attractive and increase job satisfaction, and they can actually increase economic performance, for example by facilitating labor mobility from less productive to more productive sectors (Schulze-Cleven, Watson, and Zysman 2007). Job search assistance, placement services, and retraining opportunities can be crucial to enabling workers to pursue new professional opportunities and can drive economic growth in the process. Policies may also encourage workers to invest in firm- or sector-specific skills (Estevez-Abe, Iversen, and Soskice 2001) or to become entrepreneurs, secure in the knowledge that they have a safety net if they fail. The logic here is essentially the same as for limited-liability companies: Limiting downside risk encourages beneficial risk taking. Finally, the absence of this sort of social safety net may result in *job lock*, where employees feel unable to leave a current job to pursue new employment because doing so would entail a loss of their current benefits, especially health care.

Importantly, the changing terms of international competition and domestic socioeconomic transformations present new challenges for labor market policies. The doubling of the global labor market in the wake of the economic opening of the former Soviet Bloc, China, and India (Freeman 2005) and the arrival of knowledge-based competition leave skills as countries' scarcest resources (Mayer and Solga 2008). In all advanced democracies, the number of well-paying, manufacturing-based jobs has shrunk, and employment opportunities have become increasingly concentrated in services. While this new economy provides more opportunities and freedom for highly skilled professionals, it also increases the levels of vulnerability and risk for broad sections of the workforce. This change is expressed in cross-national trends toward unemployment of increasing duration, slower wage growth, rising income inequality, and higher earnings volatility.

Most commentators agree that labor markets need to be flexible in this environment, both to allow companies to stay competitive internationally and to allow countries to reach sustainable macroeconomic conditions. But how can flexibility best be achieved? For conservatives and neoliberals, achieving flexibility turns on removing labor market *rigidities* (Siebert 1997). In practice, this has often involved weakening unions and removing social protections—from job security regulations to unemployment benefits. However, this simplistic approach fails to appreciate how the rigidities of social protections are necessary parts of a well-functioning labor market. A more realistic and sustainable approach should seek to provide *flexible rigidities*, with durable institutions that deliver social protection in a manner that supports, rather than discourages, adaptation across the economy as a whole (Streeck 2005).

By understanding the importance of flexible rigidities, we can see how best to update social protection to suit today's global era. Contemporary policies should be dependable and inclusive, allowing people to access them when in need and providing help to all, particularly those individuals without other sources of support. Moreover, policies should help workers adapt to changes in a manner that is sustainable over the long term. Given existing funding constraints, it is important that social protection policies do not simply finance consumption with long-term payments to the unemployed but focus on investments that help the unemployed reengage in new work.

Instead of protecting particular jobs, social protection policies should protect workers with temporary income support when they become unemployed and provide lifelong learning opportunities and training to help them transition to new jobs when the old ones disappear. Dependable financial support during periods of unemployment is the most basic element of a social safety net, and inclusive continuing training effectively harnesses workers' productive potential over their entire life course. As the next section discusses, the United States entered the recent economic downturn with labor market policies that performed remarkably poorly by these criteria.

The Pathologies of American Labor Policy

Many of the United States' contemporary labor policy programs, including those for income support and training, are inadequate to the goal of achieving real flexibility. For instance, restrictive eligibility criteria typically leave more than half of the unemployed without assistance from the country's unemployment insurance scheme. Of course, the system is not designed to protect those who voluntarily leave their jobs, but it tends to leave the most vulnerable part of the workforce—contingent workers in temporary and part-time jobs—without any access to unemployment compensation and therefore completely exposed to the risks of job loss. Moreover, the funding for federal employment and training programs is at its lowest level in almost forty-five years, having fallen from a peak of 0.46 percent of American gross domestic product (GDP) in 1978 to 0.05 percent a few years ago (Rosen 2008a, 9). Thus, while American workers are increasingly exposed to labor market risks, they are not reliably protected from these risks by unemployment insurance or by continuing education and training policies.

Unemployment Insurance

The patchwork system of US unemployment insurance (UI) offers a low standard of income protection, paying lower benefits for less time than similar systems in other advanced countries. The UI system is administered by states according to federal and state guidelines, and it is financed through a complex mix of federal and state payroll taxes. With the exception of Hawaii, no state meets the insurance system's initial goal of replacing half of the previous wage level. The average national replacement rate is only a little more than a third of former wages, with almost all states limiting benefits to a maximum of between $200 and $500 a week (Kletzer and Rosen 2006).

Benefits are only regularly disbursed for up to twenty-six weeks in most states (Montana and Massachusetts are slightly more generous). As a result, because the average duration of unemployment has increased, about a third of UI recipients exhaust their benefits before they are able to find new employment. While there is a system of automatic triggers in place to extend benefits during cyclical downturns, rapid changes in the economy have rendered it ineffective. Congress has also passed emergency extensions during recessions, sometimes with great difficulty. However, not only have these temporary stopgap measures politicized unemployment assistance, they have also introduced strong elements of randomness and inequality into the level of protection, since extensions are usually only applied to those workers who have not yet exhausted their benefits.

The federal government's failure to continually adapt the UI program to new needs is best illustrated by the insufficient adjustment of the annual wage base on which federal unemployment insurance taxes—used to finance federal UI—are levied. Originally set at $3,000 in 1939, the taxable wage remained completely fixed for the first thirty-two years and has stayed at $7,000 since 1983. Simply indexing the taxable wage to inflation would have led to a taxable wage of $45,000 today, which would have collected far greater funds for the system. As a result, the federal UI tax system is highly regressive at what is basically a flat $42 per person annually and collects so little revenue that the states are left to finance 83 percent of the UI program's regular expenditures (Kletzer and Rosen 2006).

Training and Education Policy

Various publicly funded worker-training initiatives at the federal and state levels are not well integrated with unemployment insurance or with each other. Efforts to create more cohesive policy, such as the Workforce Investment Act (WIA) of 1998, which established 1,800 one-stop career centers across the country, have been undermined by meager funding, restrictive program rules, and lack of employer engagement. Thus, even though Congress has made new investments into the WIA during the recent recession, there remain many hindrances to the goal of better matching of worker skills to employer needs. During the current recovery, millions of available jobs remain unfilled as employers complain that they cannot find workers with the requisite skills to fill the positions they have advertised (Woellert 2012).

The higher education system, which is supposed to provide postsecondary education and training, is also falling short of expectations. While the system's historical achievements—the postwar baby boomers were the best-educated generation in the country's history—have continued to have extremely positive effects on the country's economy, tuition is rising sharply, and public support is not keeping up. For instance, in 1976, Pell Grants for low-income students covered 72 percent of the average cost of education at a four-year state institution; by 2003, they covered only 38 percent (Delbanco 2009). This is particularly a problem for the children of immigrants and for first-generation college attendees, as the increasing cost of higher education squeezes many of them out of the market.

The United States has long excelled at offering opportunities for workers to obtain qualifications later in life, but the country is struggling to adjust to changing student demographics, learners' time constraints, and students' greater interest in vocational courses. These days, only about one out of every six college students fits the profile of the traditional 18- to 22-year-old full-time residential undergraduate student (Delbanco 2005). For instance, 40 percent of college students are 25 and older (University Council for Educational Administration [UCEA] 2009). Community colleges—traditionally the most accessible providers of higher education—have been systematically neglected at a time when an increasing number of jobs require the skills and knowledge typically obtained in some form of postsecondary education (Padron and Marx 2013). Thus, as a result of demographic change and weakening commitments to accessible higher education, the new generation of workers replacing the retiring baby boomers in the labor market will, on average, have lower educational credentials (Callan 2009). This reality reveals the wide gap between American policymakers' inclination to preach the importance of education and learning and the sobering messages of experts about the contemporary state of the nation's education system.

More broadly, not only does the United States help workers less than other countries, but American workers face higher levels of social risks and barriers to security. Income inequality has sharply increased, with high-income earners—particularly the top 1 percent—having experienced disproportionate wage growth. Cross-nationally, higher income inequality is associated with lower intergenerational mobility, leaving the United States a worse performer than many European countries in supporting the American dream of upward income mobility (Krueger 2012; Sawhill and Morton 2008).

The mismatch between higher risk and inadequate protections has led to calls for greater protectionism. Workers fear that they will be made worse off by competition from abroad, as well as by the introduction of new production techniques at home. These are reasonable concerns, since the international reorganization of economic activity over the last few decades has been associated with American companies offshoring and outsourcing many activities that were previously sourced domestically. In the United States, offshoring now hits well-educated middle-class workers (e.g., software programmers), as well as blue-collar manufacturing workers. As the gains from globalization have been very unequally distributed, international economic integration has negatively affected many people, and it has strongly increased the level of uncertainty that American workers face in their daily lives. As argued by pro-free trade economists like Jagdish Bhagwati (2009), the provision of more dependable and effective mechanisms of social protection to help workers deal with higher uncertainty would go a long way toward increasing public support for global trade.

Denmark and Germany provide important lessons about how the United States might move in this direction. Denmark shows that social protection mechanisms, such as well-managed income replacement programs and continued training programs, are not only compatible with flexible markets but can enhance them. At the same time, Germany points to a reform strategy that might be feasible in the US context. Taken together, the two countries' experiences demonstrate how more dependable and effective social protection mechanisms in labor market policy are both practical and achievable.

Toward Labor Market Utopia? The Danish Case

Over the last few years, Denmark's institutional arrangement has received increasing journalistic and scholarly attention in the United States (Stinson 2006; Stokes 2006; Ilsøe 2007). Selectively displacing old institutions and converting others to new uses, the Danes have built labor market arrangements that provide flexicurity, combining the promotion of labor market flexibility with the guarantee of social security. While the flexicurity concept originated in the Dutch context, it has become most closely associated with the Danish system. Arguably, it is the Danish example that has provided the inspiration for the European Union's promotion of the concept to other member states.

The country's institutions support a unique system of *protected mobility*, where job mobility levels match those of the United States, and the social safety net is one of Europe's most effective. Social security is provided through generous income replacement schemes rather than regulations designed to prevent layoffs (Madsen 2004). Income replacement is provided by two programs: a union-run but state-sponsored voluntary unemployment insurance system and a means-tested social assistance scheme for everybody. The unemployment insurance system offers up to 90 percent replacement of the previous wage for low-income earners and about 60 percent of previous wages for a skilled manufacturing worker for up to two years. Importantly, these unemployment insurance benefits are only granted unconditionally for a delimited time, with continued payment linked to the recipient's compliance with an activation plan, which includes either an offer of further training or an employment position. Compared to the stigmatizing nature of the parallel American welfare-to-work program, Danish arrangements are far less punitive and more enabling by emphasizing positive over negative incentives for individuals to take up work. Moreover, the institutions have been adaptable, thus when the economy was experiencing labor shortages prior to the recession, training offers were scaled back and the system was oriented toward a work-first focus. Overall, the system has sustained higher rates of labor market participation than in the United States. In addition, while unemployment has increased during the recent recession, it has stayed below that of the United States. As a wealthy country with high average incomes, Denmark shows that economies with high costs per worker can remain competitive in global markets if its workers are highly skilled.

Denmark sees itself as a *learning society* and is the leading provider of continuing worker training among the countries in the Organisation for Economic Co-operation and Development (OECD). Denmark features participation rates in continuing training activities that are about twice the average of the European Union, and in a relatively recent survey, 56.2 percent of Danish respondents reported that they had participated in some form of education or training during the last year (European Centre for the Development of Vocational Training [Cedefop] 2003, 18). While Danish workers at all skill levels participate in lifelong learning programs, the degree of participation by people with low levels of formal education, who are most at risk from economic change, is especially striking by international standards. According to data from the mid-1990s, 42.3 percent of all blue-collar low-skilled workers in Denmark participated in adult education and training during the preceding year, but only 22.4 percent of Americans workers in the same category did so (Desjardins, Rubenson, and Milana 2006, 59–62). Even though, as in other countries, participation rates in lifelong learning activities increase in line with the level of prior education, the differences in participation rates between highly educated workers, skilled workers, and formally unskilled workers are far lower in Denmark than in other countries (Kailis and Pilos 2005). Thus Denmark's continuing education and training system helps sustain a more equal distribution of skills in the population than exists in other OECD countries, which helps to keep wages high.

The international market success of Danish companies indicates how much they have benefited from the labor market arrangements in their country. Both as independent operators in niche markets and as valuable subsidiaries of multinational corporations, Danish companies have proven very adept at playing global games by using domestic institutions to their competitive advantage (Kristensen and Zeitlin 2004). Danish health care companies such as Novo Nordisk, Novozymes, and Lundbeck are world leaders. The toy company Lego sells products that allow children to learn across the world. In their internal operations, Danish firms can grant their workers more autonomy than is common in foreign companies with less-skilled workforces. This has in turn left Danish workers with more discretion for decision making unconstrained by hierarchical supervision systems and provides the basis for effective organizational flexibility within firms (Dobbin and Boychuk 1999; Lorenz and Valeyre 2005). By facilitating close collaborations between companies' customers, production workers, and engineers, the internal organization of many Danish companies facilitates product and process innovations that keep Danish companies highly competitive.

Of course, Danish-style labor market policies do not come cheaply. Denmark has long been a leader among OECD countries in public investment in education and in spending on labor market programs. However, these resource commitments appear to have directly positive effects. Arguably, they have helped create a population that is not only highly skilled, but highly open to change and new economic opportunities, with 77 percent of the population seeing globalization as an opportunity and only 16 percent perceiving it as a threat (Eurobarometer 2006). These figures make Denmark the most trade-friendly country in Europe, as workers feel prepared to embrace international competition.

What general lessons could US policymakers take from the Danish experience? First, policymakers should recognize that it is possible to set up comprehensive social security and continuing training systems that work and play an active role in sustaining upward social mobility. Money invested in pooling labor market risks and underwriting skill acquisition tends to be well spent. It makes the labor market work better, both for employees and employers. Second, Danish arrangements offer evidence of the importance of public–private cooperation in job training. Danish companies have enjoyed considerable leeway in shaping training programs to meet their local needs (Kristensen and Zeitlin 2004), and they participate in active labor-market and social programs with the explicit goal of gaining access to a more highly skilled labor supply (Martin 2004, 41). Effective workforce development policy needs both state sponsored infrastructure and continuous input from companies about their changing requirements.

While the Danish case is instructive about what kinds of policies might be possible, the United States is not a blank slate. Any institutional changes in the United States would have to build on current institutions. Here, the experience of Germany—which introduced labor market reforms in a politically inflexible system—can be instructive. Developments in Germany illustrate that policymakers can change the character of an institutional system by introducing new elements rather than directly attempting broad institutional reform.

Policy Change Through Layering—The German Case

German labor market policies—from specific policies such as short-time work (*Kurzarbeit*) to general institutions such as codetermination—have helped Germany maintain low levels of unemployment during the Eurozone crisis and succeed as an export powerhouse (Panknin 2012; Rattner, 2012).[1] However, for the purposes of this chapter, the primary lessons drawn from Germany do not concern the substance of German policies but instead the process through which German labor market policies were reformed over the past decade. Given Germany's current excellent economic performance, it is easy to forget that a decade ago Germany was viewed as the "sick man of Europe" and as a "fallen superstar" (Steingart 2004). At that time, Germany had long been seen as needing to overhaul its labor market policy to introduce more flexible mechanisms of social protection. It was widely accepted then that the rules governing the standard employment relationship (*Normalarbeitsverhältnis*), and the social welfare programs supporting it, had left the country stuck in the "continental dilemma" (Scharpf 2000) of providing "welfare without work" (Esping-Andersen 1996). While expenditures for social protection were high, they went largely into income replacement, with much less focus on education and retraining (Allmendinger and Leibfried 2003). According to one assessment, the country needed nothing less than a transformation of its competitive infrastructure (Silvia 2003, 2). In spite of these near-uniform assessments of the need for reform in Germany's system, the policy process was stuck.

The country eventually overcame its long-running reform gridlock through a strategy of institutional layering. Rather than delivering fundamental changes by displacing old institutions, the government under Social Democratic Chancellor Schröder pursued selective deregulation that effectively layered new institutions on top of those that already existed. Following what amounted to a path of least resistance, the government embarked in 2003 on expanding a second-tier system of labor contracts by changing the country's rules for nonstandard types of employment. Almost no changes were made to the rules governing the first-tier standard employment relationship, which grants full-time workers an array of employment protections that make it difficult and costly for employers to lay off workers but which also potentially hinder the adaptability of the German labor market. Instead, the government focused on such measures as liberalizing temporary agency work by removing the limit that had restricted the employment of temporary workers by any one employer to a maximum of one year. The government also reformed the regulation of part-time jobs, which service-sector companies have been particularly keen to use.

These reforms are in many respects highly problematic when compared to the Danish model. They give employers greater flexibility in hiring decisions but come with lower levels of social protections (and often wages) for the least securely employed workers. They have increased employment, but their impact on individual welfare is more ambivalent. While a strategy of more broadly reforming existing institutions would have been more in line with the progressive ideology of the governing coalition, such fundamental reform was blocked by the institutional constraints of the German economic and political order.

Following these changes in the law, nonstandard forms of employment were widely embraced by employers. Indeed, the rapidity of the increase in atypical employment in Germany is without parallel in Europe. Between March 2002 and May 2006, while German businesses shed well over one million first-tier jobs, they simultaneously created almost exactly the same number of second-tier jobs. Already in 2004, one-third of dependent (as opposed to self-employed) workers and over 54 percent of female workers were employed in atypical employment relationships (Keller and Seifert 2006, 236). By 2011, the overall share of active workers in standard employment relationships had fallen to 60 percent (Möller 2011). Forms of nonstandard work include fractional employment in mini-jobs, as well as more extended part-time and fixed-term contracts. In particular, temporary agency work has boomed, with the number of workers in this category having tripled over the last decade (Federal Employment Agency 2013). So, while Germans continue to refer to jobs with standard labor contracts as *typical* jobs, these jobs have become both significantly less standard and typical. In turn, the "economic miracle" that Germany has experienced in recent years has in part been built on insecure and often low-paid jobs (Dempsey 2011).

More recently, the proliferation of second-tier employment prompted further reforms of labor market rules. In the spring of 2009, the government expanded its ability to set work conditions in specific sectors of the economy to protect the growing number of nonstandard workers. In the past, expanding the scope of government regulation to include work conditions such as minimum wages, rules about holiday provisions, and health and safety regulations would have been politically infeasible, as they were viewed as matters to be negotiated between employers and workers. Crucially, however, the initial reforms opened up the political room for this break with long-standing principles.

The main lesson from these reforms for American policymakers is one of *process* rather than *content*. German policymakers succeeded in overcoming stalemate by circumventing domestic opposition to reform from entrenched interest groups and political veto players. They did not attack the existing system head-on but instead sought to layer a new system, with a quite different employment relationship, on top of existing institutions and regulations. This suggests that one path to institutional change in a system involving many veto points can be through the creation of new programs, rather than through wholesale efforts at institutional reengineering. While layering approaches are likely to have only moderate success in the short term, they may, if carefully designed, unleash longer-term processes of institutional change. Over time, new programs can—if they prove successful—be expanded, or they may trigger further adaptation as happened in Germany.

Toward Institutional Innovation in the United States? A Strategy for Reform

In 2009, many hoped that the new Obama administration could seize on the economic crisis to overcome the complexity of the US federal system and push New Deal–style comprehensive reforms of US labor market policy through Congress. After all, President Franklin D. Roosevelt's legislative initiatives seemed to provide evidence that a crisis provided an incoming administration with opportunities for institution building that might not exist during more steady times.

These hopes were never very realistic. The New Deal itself was the result of unsatisfying political compromises. Moreover, it is much easier to build new institutions where there are no old ones to displace than it is to build such institutions in an environment where there are existing institutions, each with its own entrenched interest groups. While the Roosevelt administration was able to build new institutions on a relatively clean slate, today's administrations are constrained by a plethora of feedback effects from past institution building and policymaking. Add to that the high level of partisanship in contemporary American politics, which increasingly produces "legislative gridlock" (Binder 2003), and efforts at broader institutional reform look far less promising.

Nevertheless, some important changes in labor market and education programs have been made. For instance, the American Recovery and Reinvestment Act of 2009 (ARRA), commonly known as the Stimulus, included temporary extensions of, as well as small increases in, UI benefits, expanded tax credits for college attendance for students from low-income families, job training funds for green jobs, increases in the sizes of Pell Grants, and fiscal transfers to states that were geared toward preventing cuts in education. The Obama administration also succeeded in ending the bank-based system of originating student loans by starting a program of direct government lending, and then invested the projected savings into increased Pell Grant amounts. At that point, however, the political winds turned. First, Congress only appropriated two of the twelve billion dollars the President's American Graduation Initiative had proposed for long-term investment in the capacity of community colleges (Basken 2010). Since then, many programs, including funding for the Workforce Investment Act and Pell Grants, have become the focus of budgetary politics.

Ultimately, political opposition can hinder legislative initiatives at many points in the policy process. Given that a significant share of Washington policymakers tends to view labor market adjustment policies as "welfare" (Destler 2005), and given that the Republican Party seems bent on noncooperation, there are many barriers to emulating Danish employment policies. Given all of the impediments to promoting a Danish flexicurity-type policy approach in the United States, US policymakers could consider using the trade debate to reframe the issues of labor market policy in the context of economic globalization and to promote reform by layering trade-related labor policies onto the existing system of labor market support. By making the expansion of the federal government's Trade Adjustment Assistance (TAA) program a constitutive part of discussions on trade matters, reform advocates could assemble a broad social coalition in support of a legislative agenda that both sustains international cooperation on trade and converts a small backwater program, TAA, into an important element of US labor market policy.

In recent years, the United States has sought to strengthen bilateral trade relations with many nations. Congress has passed the trade agreements the Bush administration had negotiated with South Korea, Panama, and Colombia, and the United States recently announced the launch of talks with the European Union over a Transatlantic Trade and Investment Partnership. Of all the strategic options open to policymakers for shrinking the gap between what the United States produces and what it consumes (just before the recession, the US trade deficit was more than 5 percent of GDP), export promotion is one of the best and least painful for the population. However, to maintain an open global trading system and succeed in export promotion, protectionist pressures must be contained at home.

Congressional support for deepening trade relations, particularly within the Democratic Caucus in the House, has fallen as the share of trade in the economy has increased over the years. While Republican lawmakers are more supportive of free trade than Democrats, they too have noticed that their constituents are often unenthusiastic about expanding levels of international trade. The strongest objections to free trade come from communities that are hit when new international competition leads to job losses in particular sectors. To address the negative consequences for these communities, most of the major federal trade bills have been accompanied by reforms of TAA. Originally introduced in 1962 and building on an idea proposed by the president of the United Steelworkers, TAA seeks to help workers who have lost their jobs as a result of foreign trade. Today, TAA provides job training, income support, job search and relocation allowances, a tax credit to help pay the costs of health insurance, and—for certain reemployed trade-affected workers aged fifty years and above—a wage insurance supplement.

At present, the positive effects of the TAA are severely hampered by problems typical to targeted programs. Few potential beneficiaries know about the program, so it has very low take-up rates, with only about 10 percent of the estimated group of potentially eligible workers having received assistance between 1974 and 2002 (Kletzer and Rosen 2005, 317). More recently, not only did many eligible workers fail to get income support, even fewer received training (Rosen 2006, 89; 2008b, 3). The program's administration is also contentious, with regular union complaints about "improper denials" of assistance (AFL-CIO 2004) and a US court's criticism of the program's poor implementation. Finally, even after recent reforms of TAA as part of ARRA, the program solely focuses on import-competing industries and workers affected by companies moving overseas, leaving workers who lose jobs in export-oriented industries ineligible, let alone those who are displaced because of non–trade-related reasons.

Given the shortcomings of US labor market policies in helping workers cope with the dislocations that accompany trade liberalization, observers of US trade policy have long noted the need for a new social compact to maximize the country's overall gains from globalization while supporting the communities that experience economic losses as a result of globalization. One suggestion comes from trade policy expert I. M. Destler (2005) who stressed that such a compact should (1) broaden TAA eligibility for stipends and retraining to all Americans displaced from their jobs by economic change, (2) make wage insurance broadly available without current restrictions, and (3) provide employers with incentives to invest in human capital by offering on-the-job training to displaced workers.

If designed well, a revised TAA could become a cornerstone in a broader national strategy for responding to economic dislocations (Rosen 2008a). Alongside unemployment insurance, it could provide a second stream of income support, and it could strengthen support for training offered under the Workforce Investment Act. The program's administration should be simplified and local administrators should be empowered to make use of its benefits. Moreover, the program could be structured in such a way as to bolster the private–public partnership that is all too often missing in the local administration of WIA benefits. Recent reforms of TAA under ARRA go in the right direction, but they remain an inadequate foundation for a new social compact on trade. They have not changed the character of the program, including such long-standing issues as the burdensome petition process to establish eligibility and challenges to Department of Labor outreach. Policymakers would need to go further than in recent reforms to move toward the agenda suggested in this chapter.

This broad approach could be a winning idea for a majority of Americans. With the US population far less polarized than Washington politicians (Fiorina, Abrams, and Pope 2005; Hacker and Pierson 2005), one should not solely focus on the partisan rancor between Republicans and Democrats or the stark opposition on trade between such groups as the US Chamber of Commerce and the labor move-ment. Pre-crisis opinion polls have repeatedly shown that Americans tend to believe that globalization is beneficial for the United States, worry about globalization's negative effects on domestic job security, and would like to see the government do more to help workers who suffer from globalization-related job loss. Deeply com-mitted to Ronald Reagan's vision of the United States as an "opportunity society" (Haskins and Sawhill 2009), Americans are increasingly dissatisfied with rising economic inequalities that undermine the relative equality of opportunity (McCall and Kenworthy 2009). With the right framing, the existing majorities in society might be large enough to force Washington insiders' hands. Moreover, among organized interests, many larger pro-globalization businesses would likely come on board, since in contrast to smaller companies, they have long supported human capital investment policies and broader social policy interventions (Martin 2000).

Conclusion

To be clear, the proposed strategy of institutional layering does not provide an immediate solution to many of the challenges that the United States faces in its labor market policy. Indeed, the immediate impact on the social security of the average American might be quite small, since it would not initially move the coun-try very far toward a more broadly shared prosperity. Substantial progress in that direction will require far more reform, including paying serious attention to enforcing and updating labor and employment laws. Moreover, coordinated political initiatives to pursue market-shaping policies seem necessary to improve the number of quality jobs in the US labor market (Kochan 2010) and to promote innovation in work organization at the company level (Schulze-Cleven 2006). Finally, there is a strong need to find new ways for members of the middle class to make their voices heard, both at the workplace and in politics so that they can provide a counterweight to labor market policymaking based on more narrow economic interests. However, immediate progress on broad reforms does not look likely in the current US political climate, and any progress will likely require significant and sustained political leadership.

Layering a significantly converted TAA program onto US labor market policy would not preempt the need for these broader reforms. Instead, it could be the start of a process of institutional change that could lead to more substantial structural policy changes over time. As such, it could contribute to putting the country on a more sustainable—and more equitable—path of economic growth and job creation. It would also be in line with Americans' expressed preferences for indirect (e.g., education based) rather than direct (i.e., redistributive) mechanisms of addressing rising income inequality (McCall and Kenworthy 2009).

The extension of TAA-type assistance to all displaced workers would necessitate further reforms in the UI system. This need for policy coordination between TAA and other labor market programs could be one potential mechanism for future broader institutional change. Another one could be domestic policy learning. Research has shown that some displaced-worker adjustment programs have been quite effective in promoting suitable reemployment (Kletzer and Koch 2004). While Washington policymakers have continued to ignore these findings, if they are forced to address them, programs in this area could be expanded or new ones created.

At present, the combination of a political system that requires interparty cooperation and increasingly polarized political parties has undermined the country's ability to reform labor market policies in ways that would strengthen the US labor force. As it stands, any larger-scale policy shifts will require changes in US politics, US institutions, or both. In the interim, a strategy that draws on lessons from the content of Danish labor market policies and the process of German labor market reforms seems worth serious consideration for overcoming entrenched opposition.

Endnote

1. Short-time work is a work-sharing scheme in which the government temporarily complements the incomes of workers who had to be put on reduced hours by their employers. Codetermination rights give workers a say in the management of company

processes, such as work organization and hiring. Codetermination facilitates a high degree of internal flexibility that many German companies used during the recent recession to reduce the workforce's working time in order to hold on to—rather than lay off—valuable skilled labor.

References

AFL-CIO. *Breaking faith with workers: The Bush labor department's improper denials of trade adjustment assistance.* Issue Brief. Washington, DC: AFL-CIO, 2004.

Allmendinger, J., and S. Leibfried. "Education and the welfare state: The four worlds of competence production." *Journal of European Social Policy* 13, no. 1 (2003): 63–81.

Basken, P. "Historic victory for student aid is tinged by lost possibilities." *The Chronicle of Higher Education.* http://chronicle.com/article/Historic-Victory-for-Studen/64844 (March 25, 2010).

Bhagwati, J. "Check it." *The New Republic.* http://www.newrepublic.com/article/check-it (April 1, 2009).

Binder, S. A. *Stalemate: Causes and consequences of legislative gridlock.* Washington, DC: The Brookings Institution Press, 2003.

Callan, P. *California higher education, the Master Plan, and the erosion of college opportunity.* National Center Report 09-1. San Jose: The National Center for Public Policy and Higher Education, 2009.

Delbanco, A. "Colleges: An endangered species?" *New York Review of Books* 52, no. 4 (March 10, 2005).

———. "The universities in trouble." *New York Review of Books* 56, no. 8 (May 14, 2009).

Dempsey, J. "Economic miracle eludes Germany's lowest-paid." *New York Times.* http://www.nytimes.com/2011/08/19/business/global/many-germans-scrambling-as-economic-miracle-rolls-past.html?pagewanted=all&_r=1& (August 8, 2011).

Desjardins, R., K. Rubenson, and M. Milana. *Unequal chances to participate in adult learning: International perspectives.* Paris: UNESCO, 2006.

Destler, I. M. *American trade politics.* 4th ed. Washington, DC: Institute for International Economics, 2005.

Dobbin, F., and T. Boychuk. "National employment systems and job autonomy: Why job autonomy is high in the Nordic counties and low in the United States, Canada and Australia." *Organization Studies* 20, no. 2 (1999): 257–92.

Esping-Andersen, G. "The welfare states without work: The impasse of labour shedding and familialism in continental European social policy." In *Welfare states in transition: National adaptations in global economies,* edited by G. Esping-Andersen, 66–87. London: Sage, 1996.

Estevez-Abe, M., T. Iversen, and D. Soskice. "Social protection and the formation of skills: A reinterpretation of the welfare state." In *Varieties of capitalism: The institutional foundations of comparative advantage,* edited by P. Hall and D. Soskice, 145–83. Oxford: Oxford University Press, 2001.

Eurobarometer. *The future of Europe.* Brussels: European Commission, 2006.

European Centre for the Development of Vocational Training. *Lifelong learning: Citizens' views.* Luxembourg: Office for Official Publications of the European Communities, 2003.

Federal Employment Agency. *Arbeitsmarktberichterstattung: Der Arbeitsmarkt in Deutschland, Zeitarbeit in Deutschland—Aktuelle Entwicklungen.* Nuremberg: Federal Employment Agency, 2013.

Fiorina, M., with S. Abrams, and J. Pope. *Culture war? The myth of a polarized America.* New York: Pearson Longman, 2005.

Freeman, R. B. "What really ails Europe (and America): The doubling of the global workforce." *The Globalist.* http://www.theglobalist.com/storyid.aspx?StoryId=4542 (June 3, 2005).

Hacker, J. S. "Privatizing risk without privatizing the welfare state: The hidden politics of social policy retrenchment in the United States." *American Political Science Review* 98, no. 2 (May 2004): 243–60.

Hacker, J. S., and P. Pierson. *Off center: The Republican revolution and the erosion of American democracy.* New Haven, CT: Yale University Press, 2005.

Haskins, R., and I. Sawhill. *Creating an opportunity society*. Washington, DC: Brookings Institution Press, 2009.

Ilsøe, Anna. *The Danish flexicurity model—A lesson for the US?* Working Paper. Washington, DC: Center for Transatlantic Relations, John Hopkins University, 2007.

Kailis, E., and S. Pilos. *Lifelong learning in Europe. Statistics in Focus: Population and Social Conditions 8/2005*. Luxembourg: Eurostat, 2005.

Keller, B., and H. Seifert. "Atypische Beschäftigungsverhältnisse: Flexibilität, soziale Sicherheit und Prekarität." *WSI Mitteilungen* 5 (2006), 235–40.

Kletzer, L., and H. Rosen. "Easing the adjustment burden on US workers." In *The United States and the world economy*, edited by C. Fred Bergsten and The Institute for International Economics, 313–41. Washington, DC: Institute for International Economics, 2005.

———. *Reforming unemployment insurance for a twenty-first century workforce*. Discussion Paper 2006-06. Washington, DC: Hamilton Project, Brookings Institution, 2006.

Kletzer, L., and W. Koch. "International experience with job training: Lessons for the U.S." In *Job training policy in the United States*, edited by C. J. O'Leary, R. A. Straits, and S. Wandner, 247–87. Kalamazoo, MI: W. E. Upjohn Institute for Employment Research, 2004.

Kochan, T. *Waking up to the jobs' crisis: Welcome to the real America!* http://mitsloan.mit.edu/iwer (March 2010).

Kristensen, P., and J. Zeitlin. *Local players in global games: The strategic constitution of a multinational corporation*. Oxford: Oxford University Press, 2004.

Krueger, A. B. *The rise and consequences of inequality*. Presentation, Chairman of the Council of Economic Advisers, January 12, 2012. http://piketty.pse.ens.fr/files/Krueger2012.pdf.

Lorenz, E., and A. Valeyre. "Organisational innovation, human resource management and labour market structure: A comparison of the EU-15." *Journal of Industrial Relations* 47, no. 4 (2005): 424–42.

Madsen, P. K. "The Danish model of 'flexicurity': experiences and lessons." *Transfer: European Review of Labour and Research* 10, no. 2 (2013): 187–207.

Martin, C. J. "Reinventing welfare regimes: Employers and the implementation of active social policy." *World Politics* 57, no. 1 (2004): 39–69.

———. *Stuck in neutral: Business and the politics of human capital investment policy*. Princeton, NJ: Princeton University Press, 2000.

Mayer, K. U., and H. Solga, eds. *Skill formation—Interdisciplinary and cross-national perspectives*. Cambridge: Cambridge University Press, 2008.

McCall, L., and L. Kenworthy. "American's social policy preferences in the era of rising inequality." *Perspectives on Politics* 7, no. 3 (2009): 459–84.

Möller, Joachim. "Das Normalarbeitsverhältnis verschwindet—stimmt's?" *Spiegel Online*. http://www.spiegel.de/karriere/berufsleben/mythen-der-arbeit-das-normalarbeitsverhaeltnis-verschwindet-stimmt-s-a-767232.html (June 8, 2011).

Padron, E., and A. Marx. "Community colleges: Separate and unequal." *US News*. http://www.usnews.com/opinion/articles/2013/05/23/community-colleges-need-more-funding-for-services-they-provide (May 23, 2013).

Panknin, K. *Germany's lessons for a strong economy*. Center for American Progress. http://www.americanprogress.org/issues/economy/news/2012/06/26/11796/germanys-lessons-for-a-strong-economy (June 26, 2012).

Rattner, S. "The secrets of Germany's success: What Europe's manufacturing powerhouse can teach America." *Foreign Affairs*. http://www.foreignaffairs.com/articles/67899/steven-rattner/the-secrets-of-germanys-success (June 16, 2011).

Rosen, H. F. "Trade adjustment assistance: The more we change the more it stays the same." In *C. Fred Bergsten and the world economy*, edited by M. Mussa, 79–113. Washington, DC: Peterson Institute for International Economics, 2006.

———. *Designing a national strategy for responding to economic dislocation*. Testimony before the Subcommittee on Investigation and Oversight House Science and Technology Committee, June 24, 2008a.

———. *Strengthening trade adjustment assistance*. Policy Brief No. 2/08. Washington, DC: Peterson Institute for International Economics, 2008b.

————. *The export imperative.* Testimony prepared for the Senate Finance Committee Subcommittee on International Trade, December 9, 2009.

Sawhill, I., and J. Morton. *Economic mobility: Is the American dream alive and well?* Washington, DC: Economic Mobility Project, Pew Charitable Trust, 2008.

Scharpf, F. "Employment and the welfare state: A continental dilemma." In *Comparing welfare capitalism: Social policy and political economy in Europe, Japan and the USA,* edited by B. Ebbinghaus and P. Manow, 240–86. London: Routledge, 2000.

Schulze-Cleven, T. "The learning organization." In *How revolutionary was the revolution? National responses, market transitions, and global technology in the digital era,* edited by J. Zysman and A. Newman, 234–41. Stanford, CA: Stanford University Press, 2006.

Schulze-Cleven, T., B. Watson, and J. Zysman. "How wealthy nations can stay wealthy: Innovation and adaptability in a digital era." *New Political Economy* 12, no. 4 (2007): 451–75.

Siebert, H. "Labor market rigidities: At the root of unemployment in Europe." *Journal of Economic Perspectives* 11, no. 3 (1997): 37–54.

Silvia, S. *Reinventing the German economy.* AICGS Policy Report No. 8. Washington, DC: American Institute for Contemporary German Studies, 2003.

Steingart, G. *Deutschland: Abstieg eines Superstars.* Munich: Piper, 2004.

Stinson, J. "Denmark: A unique mix of welfare and economic growth." *USA Today.* http://usatoday30.usatoday.com/money/world/2007-03-06-denmark-usat_N.htm (March 5, 2006).

Stokes, B. "Jobless, the Danish way." *National Journal* (March 4, 2006), 28–34.

Streeck, W. "The sociology of labor markets and trade unions." In *The handbook of economic sociology,* edited by N. J. Smelser and R. Swedberg, 254–83. Princeton, NJ: Princeton University Press, 2005.

Streeck, W., and K. Thelen. "Introduction: Institutional change in advanced political economies." In Beyond continuity: Institutional change in advanced political economies, edited by W. Streeck and K. Thelen, 1–39. Oxford: Oxford University Press, 2005.

Weir, M. Politics and jobs: *The boundaries of employment policy in the United States.* Princeton, NJ: Princeton University Press, 1992.

Woellert, L. "Companies say 3 million unfilled positions in skill crisis: Jobs." *Bloomberg.* http://www.bloomberg.com/news/2012-07-25/companies-say-3-million-unfilled-positions-in-skill-crisis-jobs.html (July 24, 2012).

CHAPTER 6

Immigration Policy: A Transatlantic Comparison

Martin A. Schain

Any reasonable comparison of the development and management of immigration policy in Europe would have to conclude that immigration policy has been generally poor, badly managed, and with unanticipated results that have been increasingly negative. With few exceptions, policy has been poorly defined and often contradictory. The gap between policy outputs and outcomes has been considerable and appears to have nurtured the breakthrough and growth of radical-right political parties. Therefore, the lessons to be learned from Europe are generally negative: what not to do, and how not to do it. Indeed, the failures of European policy tend to highlight the considerable success of those aspects of American immigration policy that have worked well and that are generally accepted as beneficial. This chapter will examine three aspects of immigration policy in Europe and the United States: entry policy, integration policy, and border enforcement. It will also examine several proposals for policy change in the United States in light of the European experience.

Entry Policy

In many ways, entry policy is the most difficult area of immigration policy to analyze. Entry of immigrants for settlement into most European countries has been strictly limited for the last forty years. For most of Europe, the postwar surge in immigration, related to recovery and economic growth, ended with the economic crisis of the early 1970s. The relatively open immigration policies of the previous twenty-five years rapidly drew to a close, either through government decisions that ended the bilateral treaties of the German guest-worker program, administrative decisions that more or less ended open immigration to France, or legislation that redefined citizenship in the United Kingdom. At the same time that countries in Europe were developing more exclusionary policies, the United States began to implement more open policies, ending forty years of exclusionary policy.

Although the political framing of these policy decisions generally suggested that immigration for settlement would be limited at best (*zero immigration* was the phrase often used in France), in practice, immigrants continued to arrive each year. This happened for several reasons: first, because court decisions limited restriction on entry, particularly for family members of resident immigrants; second, because European countries still needed workers in some service sectors, construction, and some industries; and finally, because of the spurt of asylum seekers that were admitted during the 1990s (see Table 6.1). Thus, although the explicit rhetoric of immigration was and remains extremely restrictive, policies themselves remain, sometimes implicitly and sometimes explicitly, more nuanced. Since 2000, all major European countries have developed programs to attract highly skilled immigrants, although only the United Kingdom has been successful. In 2009, in an effort to attract highly skilled workers, the European Union (EU) introduced a European *Blue Card*—a residency and work permit designed to facilitate the entry of highly skilled immigrants into EU member states (Council Directive 2009/50/EC). All twenty-seven EU member states (EU-27) except for the United Kingdom, Ireland, and Denmark participate in the scheme. Nevertheless, the real growth in immigration of third-country nationals has been among the less skilled and among those who enter for family unification.[1]

The number of citizens of EU member states migrating to member states other than their own has also increased, by 10 percent a year since 2002, while immigration of non-EU nationals has remained stable since 2003. In 2006, EU nationals represented 40 percent of immigrants entering the (other) EU-27 countries. During the same period, EU nationals returning to their countries of origin declined by 20 percent (Herm 2008). This percentage has continued to grow (44 percent in 2008), contributing to the growing proportion of the resident foreign population in EU countries who come from other EU countries. More than a third of the foreign nationals in the EU-27 in 2009 were from other EU countries (Eurostat 2010). The general trend in Europe since 2002 has been for an increasing number of EU citizens to move to other EU countries for an extended period of time, indicating a relative success for free-movement policy. In recent years, the economic crisis has accelerated this trend as unemployed workers and young people from southern Europe have flocked to Germany seeking jobs (Adam 2013). Although most of the movement continued to come from Poland, Romania, and Bulgaria, since 2010, there has been more than a 40 percent increase from Spain, Portugal, Italy, and Greece.

Thus, there are decisions and some legislation throughout Europe that permit, and, in the case of highly skilled immigrants, sometimes encourage continued immigration. Although most countries have some sort of residency laws that define legal residency of noncitizens, however, no country in Europe has passed, or has

TABLE 6.1   Immigration and Immigrant Populations in France, Britain, and the United States, 1992–2009

A. Immigration Inflows for Permanent Settlement

	1992 total (thousands)	*Per 1000 population*	*2009 total (thousands)*	*Per 1000 population*
United Kingdom	175	3.0	471.3	7.1
France	116.6	2.0	126.2	2.0
United States	974	3.8	1130.8	3.7
EU 15/25	1727.6	4.7	2500	5.0

B. Immigrant Population

	Year	*Foreign-born (thousands)*	*Percentage of total population*
United Kingdom	2009	6899	11.3
France	2009	7235	11.6
United States[a]	2009	38948	12.7
EU 27	2010	47348	9.4

C. Inflows by Entry Country (2009)

	Total	*Family (percentage)*	*Work (percentage)*
France	178,700	49	12.6
United Kingdom	347,000	33.6	35.6
United States	1,130,200	88.8	5.8

Sources: Data from Organisation for Economic Co-operation and Development (OECD), *International Migration Outlook, Annual report 2011.* (Paris: OECD Publications, 2011), 281–83, 331, 341; *Trends in International Migration, Annual Report 2003* (Paris: OECD Publications, 2003), 117–94, 286, 291, 305–10; Katya Vasileva, "Population and Social Conditions," *Eurostat, Statistics in Focus* 34/2011, 2.

[a] Does not include those born of US citizens.

attempted to pass, a comprehensive law on immigration comparable to the US Immigration and Nationality Act, which defines in law both categories for entry and limits. Therefore, criteria for legal entry in Europe remain somewhat opaque, and often poorly defined, contributing to what radical right parties in Europe often call the gap between commitments to halt immigration and the realities of continuing immigration each year.

Moreover, the differences in entry requirements between Europe and the United States have been growing deeper over time. During the past decade, major

European countries have been moving toward linking entry with narrow concepts of integration that would tend to ensure cultural stability and minimize challenges to the cultural status quo from immigration (Caldwell 2009). Thus, requirements for entry in the Netherlands, France, Germany, and (to a lesser extent) the United Kingdom have increasingly demanded conformity with national social norms.

The most demanding (and controversial) program for entry was initiated in the Netherlands in 2006. Immigrants seeking residency visas were required to pass a *civic-integration examination* before entering the Netherlands. The examination consisted of a Dutch language test, as well as an examination that tested their understanding of Dutch liberal values. The most publicized part of the exam was a film that featured pictures of a nude beach and gay couples kissing. The point was that these scenes are part of normal life in the Netherlands. Since most of those taking the examination would be people entering under family unification, the intention was to target spouses and potential spouses and to discourage resident Muslim immigrants from importing wives from their home countries. Although the government has denied this interpretation, it is reinforced by the exemptions of immigrants from countries such as the United States, Canada, Japan, South Korea, Estonia, Latvia, Lithuania, Australia, and New Zealand (as well as the parliamentary debate on the legislation). Although 90 percent of those who took the examination passed during the first year, the number of applicants for family unification per year was cut in half after the examination was imposed in 2007 (Nana 2007; Scheffer 2011).

The Dutch initiative has been followed throughout Europe in various ways. In 2011, UK Prime Minister David Cameron, supported by France's President Sarkozy and Germany's Chancellor Merkel, called for "muscular liberalism" to bar state aid to groups that do not share Britain's liberal values. France has tightened admission requirements even for those seemingly eligible for family unification (Hollinger 2011).[2] After 2007, those applying for family unification were required to take two-month courses that constituted "an evaluation of language ability and the values of the Republic" in their home countries (Schain 2012, 57).

American policy on entry, by contrast, has moved decidedly in another direction. Since 1965, US entry law has been strongly biased toward a broad-based concept of family unification that effectively gives priority to families of those residents born abroad. At the most basic level, immigration law now favors and promotes diversity in other ways as well.

The Immigration Act of 1990 included a program of *diversity visas* that would eventually provide for the admission, on an annual basis, of fifty-five thousand immigrants from "underrepresented" countries. Entrants from these countries are required to have high school diplomas (or equivalent) or work experience but are then chosen by lottery. Thus, what began as an effort to relieve the backlog of applications from Ireland—the initiative had been taken by Senator Edward Kennedy on behalf of his Irish constituents—ended as a mechanism for increasing the diversity of the population of the United States.

Indeed, when the House and Senate conferees emerged with a final agreement on the 1990 legislation, they called their compromise agreement a victory for cultural diversity, "for family unity, and for job creation" (Tichenor 2002, 274). What makes this statement particularly striking is that, even as an afterthought, American political leaders were seeking to promote what European leaders either feared or sought to carefully manage—cultural diversity. The pattern of diversity could be accelerated by reform legislation that is now being considered by the US Congress (as this volume goes to press). It focuses on the fate of the roughly eleven million undocumented immigrants now in the United States, most (but not all) of whom are from Mexico and Central America, but is also likely to make it easier for high-tech companies to hire highly skilled foreign workers from other parts of the world (Sengupta 2013).

Integration Policy and Integration Success and Failure

The gap in immigrant integration policy is also widening between Europe and the United States. Immigrant integration policies are policies designed to encourage the integration of immigrants into the social, economic, and political life of the country to which they have immigrated. Such policies may address issues including education, language training, employment, and cultural integration. Integration policies can vary widely in their aims and means, some taking a less interventionist approach and encouraging multiculturalism and others taking pressuring more explicitly for cultural integration. Many European countries are beginning to develop explicit integration policies for immigrants that are consistent with their more muscular entry requirements. In March 2006, the interior ministers of the six largest EU countries (the so-called *G6*) agreed to pursue the idea of a harmonized *integration contract* at the EU level, using the French (and Dutch) model as a starting point. By the time of this initiative, the French and Dutch had already made evaluation of various cultural criteria of integration a condition for entry (see above).

The initial step was to create a committee of experts to investigate the procedures used in all member states. They then planned to propose such a policy to the other nineteen countries of the EU (Williamson 2006). Then, one of the first initiatives of the French presidency in 2008 was to propose a comprehensive, compulsory, EU integration program. The compulsory aspect was finally dropped in June of that year, but a European Pact on Immigration and Asylum was passed by the European Council in October 2008 that emphasized three criteria for acceptance and integration in Europe: language mastery of the receiving country, knowledge and commitment to the values of the receiving country, and access to employment (Council of the European Union 2008). By 2010, a council report noted that "significant efforts" had been made by member states to implement the pact (Council of the European Union 2010).

Much of this activity was generated by broad-based political perception that traditional—less interventionist—modes of integration had failed to produce desired results (Scheffer 2011). Although perceptions of policy failure on integration have been widespread and politically salient for the French, Germans, Dutch, and British, this issue has not been particularly salient for the Americans.

For the French, the political rhetoric of failure began in the early 1980s, with the beginning of cycles of urban violence that culminated with the nationwide riots in November, 2005. The policy debate has tended to focus on the failure of the school system to effectively integrate new waves of immigrants as effectively as it had previous waves, on spatial concentrations of immigrants, and on urban unrest (Fassin 2011). For the British, the perception of failure began in 2001 and grew in intensity after the suicide attacks in the London Underground and buses in July 2005. For the Germans, the rhetoric of failure has become the core of the presentation of Chancellor Merkel, who, in a speech before the youth group of her conservative Christian Democratic Union (CDU) in October 2010, famously declared that multiculturalism in Germany had "utterly failed" and that it was an illusion to think that Germans and foreign workers could "live happily side by side" (Spiegel Online 2010). Soon after, Prime Minister Cameron (supported by President Sarkozy and Chancellor Merkel) spoke more substantively and called for a movement toward muscular liberalism to bar state aid to groups that do not share Britain's liberal values. [3]

In the American case, the perception of failure, merged with analyses of race relations in the United States, was widespread among intellectuals during the decade of the 1990s but has faded since (Huntington 2005; Salins 1997; Schlessinger 1991). Indeed, there is a considerable gap in public opinion between the general optimism of Americans about immigrant integration and the relative pessimism in key European countries[4] (see Table 6.2). By the 1990s, proposals to cut back on legal immigration could gain no congressional support, and there was durable support for the multicultural model of America as a "nation of nations" (Schain 2012). If we compare recent developments in immigrant integration policy in the United States with those in France and the United Kingdom, we can understand some of the important differences in the approaches taken in Europe and their impact. In fact, despite the absence of explicit integration policies in the United States, integration *has* been generally more successful by most measures in the United States compared with Europe, although in Europe integration policies have sometimes been more successful than the political rhetoric would indicate. France's recent experience with immigrant integration policies illustrates both the efforts undertaken to better integrate immigrants and the shortcomings of these efforts to date.

In France, although cycles of urban unrest indicate both tension and anger among ethnic and minority populations (largely from Muslim countries in Africa and North Africa), civic-value orientations have generally been similar to the general population. France has been at least as accepting of immigrant populations as Britain, and by some measures, even more accepting. More than most countries in Europe, French respondents tend to have confidence in the willingness of immigrants from Muslim countries to adapt to French customs and even of devout Muslims to adapt to "modern" society (see Tables 6.2 and 6.3).

TABLE 6.2   Attitudes About Integration of Immigrant Populations (Percentages)

	US	France	UK	Germany	Netherlands	Italy
"Immigrants in general are integrating well."	59	44	43	41	36	37
"Muslim immigrants are integrating well."	45	45	37	25	36	37
"Hispanic immigrants are integrating well."	78					

Source: Data from German Marshall Fund of the United States (2011), 29.

TABLE 6.3   Attitudes Toward Immigrants and Muslims (Percentages)

	A good thing people from the Middle East and North Africa coming to your country: Agree	*Immigration having good influence on your country: Agree*	*Muslims in your country mostly want to adapt to national customs: Agree*	*No conflict between being a devout Muslim and living in modern society: Agree*	*Growing Islamic ID: Good*
French	58	46	45	74	11
British	57	43	22	35	27
Spanish	62	45	21	36	13
German	34	47	17	26	11
American		52	33	42	37

Sources: Data from Pew Research Center, *The Great Divide: How Westerners and Muslims View Each Other,* (Washington, DC: Pew Global Attitude Project, June 2006), 3, 6, 8, 10; Pew Global Attitudes Project, *Muslims in Europe: Economic Worries Top Concerns About Religious and Cultural Identity,* (Washington, DC: Pew Research, July 22, 2006); IPSOS Public Affairs, *Associated Press International Affairs Poll,* (Washington, DC: IPSOS Public Affairs, May 2006).

These societal attitudes are reflected in attitudinal patterns among the immigrant population, in particular those who identify as Muslim. French Muslims are far more integrative in their orientation and less conflicted between their Muslim and national identities (see Table 6.4) than other Muslim communities in Europe (Klausen 2005). Compared with native French respondents, there are certainly differences in civic and religious orientations, but some of these differences have diminished in succeeding generations (Brouard and Tiberj 2005; Tribalat 1995). These differences are also narrower than in Britain, for example.

On the other hand, there appears to be little tolerance in France for Muslim religious expression. The most recent report of the National Consultative Commission on the Rights of Man (CNCDH) indicates a sharp drop in toleration and a rise of anti-Muslim attitudes, which coincides with the deepening economic crisis since 2009 (Mayer, Michelet, and Tiberg 2013).[5] Moreover, reassertions of French secularism during the past decade—a culture that France shares with the Netherlands and other parts of Catholic Europe—have resulted in legislation that has banned young girls from wearing headscarves in public schools and all women from wearing full body covering (burqas) in public space. However, it is important to note that the opposition to these bans among the population from Muslim countries was not strong, and there was significant support for such bans among women of Muslim heritage.

French policy has not been particularly strong in developing tools for combating discrimination, and France has failed to create either employment or

TABLE 6.4   Muslims in Europe: Attitudes Toward Identity, Fellow Citizens, and Modernity (Percentages)

	Removing headscarf necessary for integration: Yes		Religion important part of your life: No	People with different religious practice threat to our way of life: Agree	Difference in ID with "country" and "religion": (Country-Religion)	Muslims in your country want to adopt national customs: Agree
	Men	Women				
Paris Muslims	9	20	23	6	+1	78
London Muslims	5	7	9	22	−12	41

Sources: Data from Zsolt Nyiri, "Muslims in Europe: Berlin, London, Paris: Bridges and Gaps in Public Opinion," (Princeton, NJ: Gallup World Poll, 2007); Pew Research Center, *The Great Divide: How Westerners and Muslims View Each Other* (Washington, DC: Pew Global Attitude Project, June 2006), 3, 11–12; Pew Global Attitudes Project, *Muslims in Europe: Economic Worries Top Concerns About Religious and Cultural Identity,* (Washington, DC: Pew Research, July 6, 2006; These results are for France and the UK).

educational opportunities for it minority populations. In 2004, France established an Equal Opportunities and Anti-Discrimination Commission (*Haute Autorité de Lutte contre les Discriminations et pour l'Egalité* [HALDE]) in response to two directives of the European Council in 2000 that obliged all EU countries to constitute commissions that would both monitor and act against patterns of racial discrimination (Council of the European Union 2000). The HALDE has been the principal instrument for combating discrimination in France, but compared to similar commissions in Britain and the United States, the HALDE lacks both the legal and financial resources to investigate patterns of discrimination. The HALDE investigates individual claims, and it has worked hard to facilitate the submission of these claims. However, few of the thousands of individual claims brought to the HALDE result in positive outcomes for complainants. For instance, of the more than six thousand cases that were closed in 2008, two-thirds were rejected because they were "inadmissible" or because they were deemed to be outside of the scope of powers of the HALDE, only approximately 8 percent resulted in some kind of positive outcome for complainants, and only 1.3 percent ended up in the courts (HALDE 2008).

The HALDE's effectiveness is limited by its dependence on individual claims and by legal restrictions on its ability to investigate patterns of discrimination in fields such as employment discrimination. In 2006, a French Sénate committee adopted an amendment that would have established "a typology of groups of people susceptible to discrimination because of their racial or ethnic origins."[6] The measure, which would have been used to measure diversity of origins in the civil service and some private companies, was rejected by the Constitutional Council (Van Eeckhout 2007). The failure to adequately address discrimination has been noted in the annual reports of the HALDE, as well as by scholars (Fassin 2002). Most recently, a Franco-American study of employment discrimination once again emphasized that it is clear that anti-Muslim discrimination is holding back Muslim economic success in France (Adida, Laitin, and Valfort 2010).

In addition, children from immigrant families in France have done comparatively poorly in the education system, although educational attainment is more complicated. On one hand, educational attainment among immigrant populations at the university level is as great as or greater than that of the native population in France, as it is in the United States and United Kingdom as well. On the other hand, the proportion of immigrants who never got to upper secondary education in 2010 was disastrously high in France but far lower in Britain and the United States (see Table 6.5). Moreover, compared with Britain and the United States, there has been little improvement in France during the past decade. These differences are confirmed by a cross-national analysis comparing achievement scores of immigrant children in reading, math, and science with those of native children. Low achievement scores were almost 40 percent higher in France compared to Britain (Schnepf 2004). In Britain, first generation immigrant children do as well (or as poorly) as others of the same age and socioeconomic class. In France, by contrast, even if we control for socioeconomic status, immigrant children have lower educational attainment than their native born counterparts (Schnepf 2004). This is important because educational attainment has a strong impact on unemployment rates for immigrants (for natives as well—see below).

France has not completely ignored this problem. The lead, however, has been taken at the level of higher education through a program initiated in 2001 by the Institut d'Etudes Politiques in Paris (Sciences Po). In a bold initiative, Sciences Po decided to establish a parallel admission program for lycée students from the Paris suburbs whose schools were located in Zones of Educational Priority (ZEP), a category of schools created in 1982 for special attention by the Ministry of Education. Although this was not a program explicitly aimed at immigrant populations (this would not conform to the standards of law), the definition of a ZEP included the percentage of immigrants. Sciences Po worked directly with the lycées in these zones, and between 2001 and 2008, recruited about 400 students (about 10 percent of its first-year students). In part because these students were pretrained and cherry-picked, the program has been quite successful and has spread to other elite institutions. The problem is that, while admirable, this program is directed at exactly that level where immigrant students have been most successful (see Table 6.5) (Langan 2008).

British integration policy has focused on school policy and curriculum, as well as antidiscrimination policy, since about 1966. The articulation of a positive approach toward multiculturalism began with and effort to improve race relations but very quickly evolved into a broader understanding of multiculturalism. Thus, Roy Jenkins, home secretary at the time, noted in 1966:

> I do not think that we need in this country a melting pot. . . . I define integration therefore, not as a flattening process of assimilation but as equal opportunity, accompanied by cultural diversity, in an atmosphere of mutual tolerance.[7]

Jenkins perspective was reinforced by a series of reports on education beginning with the Swann Report in 1985. The Swann Report (*Education for All*) strongly advocated a multicultural education system for all schools, regardless of institutions, location, age range, or ethnicity of staff or pupils. The report made a link between education and multiculturalism by noting that racism had an adverse effect on the educational experiences of black children in the United Kingdom. These conclusions have been reaffirmed by numerous reports since then. (Swann 1985)

Nevertheless, as in many countries, there has been growing pressure to assert the limits of multiculturalism and support a stronger sense of collective identity. By 2001, in the aftermath of urban riots in the summer and the attacks in the

TABLE 6.5   Educational Attainment of Immigrant Populations, 2004–2010 (Percentages)

	Less than upper-secondary education*				University degree or higher			
	Native born		Foreign born		Native born		Foreign born	
	2004	2008–2010	2004	2008–2010	2004	2008–2010	2004	2008–2010
France	35	29.9	56**	51.1	13	14.2	12	15.5
UK	49	24.0	45**	29.7	20	29.8	28	32.6
US	12.5	9.6	32.8	29.8	27	30.1	27	28.9

Sources: France and Britain data from OECD, *OECD in Figures 2005* (Paris: OECD, 2005), 65; Insee, *Enquête emploi* and *Enseignement-éducation,* (Paris: Insee, 2005, 2010; ages 15–65 working population); Christian Dustmann and Nikolous Theordoropoulos, *Ethnic Minority Immigrants and Their Children in Britain,* CDP No.10/06 (London: CReAM), 20; Christian Dustmann, Tommaso Frattini, and Gianandrea Lanzara, *Educational Achievement of Second Generation Immigrants: An International Comparison,* CDP No. 16/11 (London: CReAM), 27; United States data from US Census Bureau: David Brauser, *A Description of the Immigrant Population, November, 2004* (Washington, DC: Congressional Budget Office, 2004); US Census Bureau, *Current Population Survey: 2011* (Washington, DC: US Census Bureau, 2011), Table 40, Ages 25+, whole population with no high school degree and BA+.

Notes: *UK=ISCED 2 level or below; France=BEPC (first-cycle high school) or below, and US no high school degree.

**no qualification: UK=10% 2004; France=50% 2004

United States in September, government reports indicated the beginning of a reassertion of policies of civic integration into a society based on shared values.

The most important symbolic change in this direction has been the initiation of a citizenship test and a citizenship ceremony under legislation passed in 2002. Beginning November 1, 2005, all applicants for naturalization were required to pass a "Life in the UK" examination, together with certification in the English language. Although the Home Office denied that this was a "Britishness test," it was widely referred to in those terms by both the prime minister and in the press. Together with new citizenship ceremonies that include a pledge of allegiance, the civics and language tests are meant to create a meaningful gateway for integration, the kind that has never existed before in Britain. These ideas were then integrated into the Borders, Citizenship and Immigration Act of 2009 with a more demanding pathway to citizenship. This approach, now dubbed *muscular liberalism,* was given greater emphasis by the Tory-Liberal-Democratic government of David Cameron after 2010, who called on the government to bar state aid to groups that do not share Britain's liberal values (Schain 2012, 160–66).

Still, despite the tougher rhetoric and additional measures that have placed limits on the acceptance of multiculturalism, British policy remains far more multicultural than French policy, closer to the kind of multiculturalism that is accepted in the United States. The two pillars of this policy are in school curriculum, which has endured as an instrument of multiculturalism, and in antidiscrimination policy as applied to religious and ethnic groups. The British policy became a model for Europe, and influenced European Union directives that have established similar antidiscrimination programs throughout the European Union (Council of European Union 2000).

Multicultural education programs appear to have been relatively effective in both educational attainment and in relating educational attainment to employment (see Table 6.6). The British record of educational integration appears to have been relatively successful (even if we control for socioeconomic status), and the record of the United States somewhat less so; the French record, however, is the worst of the three. As Table 6.6 illustrates, unemployment in France, the United Kingdom, and the United States is higher among those with lower levels of education, regardless of whether they are natives or foreign born. Of course, this is not surprising. What is surprising is that higher education brings levels of unemployment down far less for foreign-born populations (for natives as well) in France than in either the United Kingdom or the United States.

The United States has had little by the way of explicit integration policies since the 1920s, with the exception of the evolving requirements of the citizenship examination. By 2008, the formal examination had become more demanding in requiring knowledge of history, civics, and English. Nevertheless, the study questions were available in English, Spanish, Chinese, Tagalog, Vietnamese, and Azerbaijani (Schneider 2010). Implicit American integration policy has become increasingly focused on antidiscrimination policy, which in turn has reinforced minority identity and legitimacy. This approach may change, since the

TABLE 6.6   Unemployment Rates of Foreign-Born Populations, by Level of Education Attainment, 2003–2004 (Percentages)

Country	Type	Low Education	Medium	High Education	Difference low/high
France	Foreign-born	18.4	14.4	11.8	−36
	Native	12.2	7.9	5.8	−52
UK	Foreign-born	12.2	7.9	4.2	−66
	Native	8.8	4.7	2.3	−74
US	Foreign-born	9.1	5.7	4.3	−53
	Native	15.5	6.7	3.2	−79

Source: Data from OECD, *International Migration Outlook* (Washington DC: OECD, 2007), 154.

immigration reform legislation proposed in 2013 may establish a federal office for immigrant integration that would coordinate programs of language training and integration. An unintended consequence of antidiscrimination policies has been to open and reinforce political opportunities. Opportunities for both political expression and access to the political system have been far greater in the United States than in any country in Europe, including Britain and France (DeSipio and de la Garza, 2009; Stepnick and Stepnick 2009).

The first national recognition of the growing importance of the Hispanic vote came during the first term of George W. Bush, when he decided to court the Latino and prospective Latino vote. Existing studies showed that Latinos (with the exception of Cubans) were strongly Democratic in orientation and became more so with increasing education and tenure in the United States. Nevertheless, as Republican governor of Texas, Bush had some success in attracting Latino voters, and the president seemed to feel that not making this effort would be to surrender the electoral future to the Democrats. Indeed, this gamble had some payoff in the 2004 presidential election. More than a third of the states (35 percent) and more than a third of the congressional districts (35 percent) in 2000 had immigrant populations of 10 percent or more, with a heavy proportion of Hispanics. This distribution of districts with a high proportion of immigrants is far greater than in France or Britain (about twice as great), and provides a reasonable measure of the potential electoral gains and the dangers of ignoring this population.

Therefore, the electoral stakes in the United States of such questions as illegal immigration and border control can be high. When such issues become politically salient, the electoral consequences can be both the mobilization of an anti-immigration electorate, as well as an immigrant electorate favorable to more open immigration policies. In the run-up to the 2012 election, Republican candidates outdid each other in attacking illegal immigration, and Republican strategists warned of the consequences, particularly in a tight presidential race. Hispanic Republicans did well in the 2010 congressional elections; they elected three governors and eight members of the House and the Senate for the first time. A presidential candidate with a strong anti-immigrant record is not likely to do well in those states with a large Hispanic electorate. Although Hispanic voters vote in smaller numbers (about 33 percent of those registered) than other groups, they also tend to be issue voters, who are likely to be mobilized by a presidential candidate perceived as militantly anti-immigrant. In the 2012 elections, the Democrats gained record percentages (well over 70 percent) among Hispanics as well as among Asian voters (Schain 2012, 279–82).

Border Enforcement

Although there appear to be similar political concerns in Europe and the United States about illegal immigration and about the permeability of borders, in fact, the

US border has been far more permeable than its European counterpart (the EU's common external *Schengen* border). The US border remains far more permeable despite the fact that the United States has devoted far more resources to border control than have European countries. This raises the question of whether Europe has developed a border control system that is more effective than that of the United States and whether we might draw lessons from it.

There are two dimensions to the status of legality or illegality in terms of border enforcement. The first is the legality of the border crossing itself. The second is how long the migrant has stayed. As one scholar has emphasized, "An immigrant in a legal situation can fall into illegality from one day to the next. For numerous immigrants, the situation of illegality can represent a temporary phase of the migration cycle, before obtaining a residency permit."[8] This was the case in France in the 1960s, when migrants who had entered the country could legalize their status with a work contract and has been the case in numerous countries (including France) that have permitted periodic amnesties (Tapinos 1999).

Estimating the number of undocumented migrants in any country is a formidable task, which always comes with political overtones. The task is complicated by a lack of any good way to know how many illegal immigrants have left the country. The difficulty is fully elaborated in the comparative report for the European Commission *Clandestino Project* (Triandafyllidou 2009). These estimates varied between 1.9 and 3.8 million for the EU-27 in 2008, relatively close to the more political figures released by governments during the past decade (see Table 6.7).

Government estimates vary with the political climate and whether it is more politically advantageous to maximize the estimate (e.g., to attract new budget allocations), or minimize the estimate (e.g., to demonstrate the effectiveness of border controls). What is striking about both the scholarly and the political estimates for illegal immigration in Europe is that they are relatively low compared with the United States, even if we consider variations by country. The estimate that illegal immigrants make up at most 0.68 percent of the population for France is considerably lower than in Britain (approximately 1.4 percent), and far lower than that of the United States where the 11 to 12 million undocumented make up roughly 3.8 percent of the population.[9]

The relatively low proportion of illegal immigrants in France has been attributed in part to the fact that until 2007 (and periodically since then), illegal immigrants were able to claim legal residency after ten years in the country. The low rate has also been attributed to the relatively small role that the informal labor market plays in France. In general, where labor markets are more deregulated, there is more labor mobility, more informal employment, and frequent hiring for the sorts of low-skilled entry-level jobs that attract many irregular migrants.

TABLE 6.7   Estimates of Undocumented Immigrant Populations, 2002–2008

Year	Immigrant Population (millions)		Immigrants (percentage of total population)	
	Minimum	*Maximum*	*Minimum*	*Maximum*
European Union				
2002 (EU-15)	3.1	5.3	0.8	1.4
2005	2.2	4.8	0.58	1.23
2008 (EU-27)	1.9	3.8	0.39	0.77
United States				
2002	9.0	9.9	2.9	3.2
2005	10.6	11.6	3.5	3.8
2008	11.1	12.1	3.6	3.9
2010	10.7	11.7	3.5	3.8

Sources: Data from Clandestino Research Project, *Size and Development of Irregular Migration to the EU* (Athens, Greece: Clandestino, 2009), 23; Jeffrey Passel and D'Vera Cohn, *Unauthorized Immigrant Population: National and State Trends, 2010* (Washington, DC: Pew Hispanic Center, 2011).

More generally, during the past decade, the number of undocumented immigrants in Europe seems to have been declining (by at least 40 percent), both at the European level and among most of the EU member states. The most notable exception is the United Kingdom, where the clearing of backlogs of asylum seekers has resulted in a sharp increase as a result of a change in status of the same people. In the United States, the undocumented immigrant population peaked about 2007 and has steadily diminished since, particularly in the wake of the economic crisis, which led many undocumented workers to leave the country due to a lack of job opportunities.

On balance, if we view the EU as a federal system, the governance of the border is principally in the hands of the member states, much as it was in the United States for most of the nineteenth century. The European model employed by these member state governments focuses, as Susan Martin has argued, on internal enforcement through required identity papers and controls on immigration status imposed in the labor market. Martin contrasts this process to the Anglo-Saxon "island model" of enforcement, with its emphasis on strong frontier controls and weaker internal enforcement mechanisms (Martin 2007). As a result, it has historically been easier for an undocumented immigrant to live and work in the United States than in European countries.

However in recent years in the United States, there has been a trend toward greater internal enforcement. The emphasis on the *Secure Communities* program since 2009 indicates a willingness by the federal government to employ the services of local police to roundup undocumented immigrants on a continuing basis (Preston 2012; Schain 2012). This is quite different from the emphasis on periodic operations during the last two years of the G. W. Bush Administration.

While the United States has been moving toward a more European-style model emphasizing internal controls on immigration, the trend of EU policy has been toward the US-style model of tough external border control. This tendency is being driven by the unevenness of frontier controls among the member states, as well as by the mutual dependence that has always existed in the Schengen system. Given the free movement of persons within the EU's borderless Schengen area, any country with a weak system of border control can serve as the entry point to the rest of the area. Therefore, the EU has steadily developed more centralized mechanisms of member state cooperation to help weaker states shore up their border patrols. Nonetheless, the most effective process of border enforcement in Europe remains the internal controls imposed through identity cards and labor market regulations.

With some regularity, the integrity of the Schengen land and sea border is challenged at its weakest points, generally Spain, Greece, and Italy. The Lampedusa crisis in the midst of the Libyan civil war in 2011 demonstrated both the interdependence of the states of the Schengen area, as well as the ability of border states, such as Italy to pressure other EU member states. Between December 2010 and April 2011, more than twenty thousand migrants (mostly Tunisians) arrived on the small Italian island of Lampedusa. Italian authorities then moved large numbers of migrants to camps on the mainland, from which many then went on to France with papers provided by the Italian authorities. When French authorities then sent some of these back to Italy, and the Italians retaliated by reducing security at the camps even further, the interior ministries of both countries agreed to enhance cooperation to reduce the flow of migrants across the Mediterranean (Donadio 2011).

The incident also opened an opportunity for France to push for what was termed stronger *political governance* at the EU level of Schengen cooperation. By December 2011, the European Council (Justice and Home Affairs [JHA]) had recommended "an effective and reliable monitoring and evaluation system . . . which should be EU-based." It would also involve experts from the member states, as well as the commission and "competent agencies" (Council of the European Union 2011).

By March 2012, the council's JHA adopted a set of conclusions that established that a high-level committee should examine and develop action plans to reinforce the protection of external borders against illegal immigration (Council of the European Union 2012). Although the sanctions of the "safeguard mechanism" were not specified in the EU documents, President Sarkozy was indeed specific in his understanding of what was necessary: "We must be able to sanction, suspend or exclude from Schengen any state that fails [to act], in the same way that we can sanction a state in the euro zone" (Leparmentier and Stroobants 2012).

However, it is not the border that is generally at issue in most parts of Europe, since it is widely conceded that the border was crossed legally in most cases (90 percent, according to the French Ministry of the Interior), but the ability of the state to keep track of immigrants once they are already in Europe. In the US case, the border is clearly at issue. The Pew Hispanic Center estimates that only 40 to 50 percent of those in United States illegally originally entered legally through various ports of entry; they are mostly visa overstayers (Pew Hispanic Center 2006).

In both Europe and the United States, resources devoted to border control, as well internal control of immigrant populations, have increased during the past decade, but US internal efforts have tended to be more sporadic and focused on a series of short-lived operations. Although, as noted above, European border cooperation has grown in important ways, the most effective cooperation has been among police forces that track and round up migrants after they are already in the countries of the EU. The Schengen Information System (now in its second phase) has supported EU-wide tracking and investigation in ways that are far more difficult in the US federal system because of the lack of national identity cards in the United States.

One result is that at least some European countries expel undocumented immigrants at rates that are far higher than those of the United States. During the first three years of the Obama administration, formal removals mounted to about four hundred thousand people a year (these removals had been rising since 2006). This was about 3.6 percent of the estimated undocumented population of about eleven million. However, during this same period, the British expelled, through enforced removals, twenty-five thousand people a year, about 4 to 5 percent of its estimated undocumented population, and the French twenty-five to thirty-two thousand people a year, about 7.5 percent.[10]

Since 2007, the number of successful illegal crossings at the Mexican border has diminished while the number of returns has grown, thus stemming the growth in the population of undocumented immigrants. It is also true that the number of formal removals of undocumented migrants has steadily grown. However, because *voluntary departures* (the primary route through which undocumented immigrants have left the United States until now) have vastly diminished at the same time, in part because the border authorities are more reluctant to offer this alternative, the total number expulsions (formal and informal) since 2005 has steadily declined: from almost two million in 2000 to just over eight hundred thousand in 2010

(US Department of Homeland Security 2011). Thus, if on one hand the slowdown in undocumented border crossing can be taken as an indication the border is more secure, on the other hand there is little possibility that the population of almost eleven million undocumented migrants can be reduced very much more, even with more determined internal operations (Schain 2012). Indeed, recognition of the practical impossibility—and for many critics the unacceptable suffering—of significantly reducing the undocumented population in the United States through deportations is an important reason that a pathway to citizenship for the undocumented features in the immigration reform proposals being considered by the US Congress in 2013.

Conclusion

In general, US immigration policy has been far better defined, more consistent and durable than that of Europe, and has found greater political legitimacy. Neither in mass opinion nor among political elites are Americans deeply divided over entry or integration policies as elaborated above. For Europeans, ill-defined and inconsistent policies on entry and integration have poisoned the political dialogue on these issues and have fed and defined support for the radical right.

For more than thirty years, American policy makers have generally avoided the problems of Europe by developing a broad consensus of support for legal immigration. In 1978, the Select Commission on Immigration and Refugee Policy (the Hesburgh Commission) decoupled strong support for legal immigration from opposition to rapidly increasing undocumented immigration. In general, this decoupling has been successfully maintained and has supported this consensus. However, since 2006, the mounting attempts at the state level in places like Arizona and Alabama to drive out undocumented immigrants pose a challenge for legal immigration as well. In every state in which legislation has been passed to make the lives of undocumented immigrants difficult and miserable, legal immigrants (often in the same family) have been implicated as well. At the same time, these challenges often tend to relate the interests of legal immigrants to those of the undocumented, making it more difficult to maintain the decoupling of these two issues.

On the other hand, Europeans do have something to teach us about dealing with undocumented immigration. Americans are deeply concerned and divided about this intractable problem, which has festered for many years. The tools used in Europe— better controlled labor markets and larger programs of expulsions (proportionate to the undocumented population) combined with periodic amnesties—are politically problematic in the United States, primarily because effective workplace enforcement has been consistently opposed by agribusiness, which finds such federal programs as *E-Verify* not only burdensome and sometimes unreliable, but also a barrier to the cheap labor on which they have depended for most of the past century. At the same time, federal programs for more reliable identity documents (the Real ID Act of 2005 and the Secure Communities program, initiated in 2008) have been opposed by many state governments and local police forces as expensive and ineffective. Just beneath the surface is a broad uneasiness about what looks like a national ID program that would apply to all Americans, and not just undocumented immigrants. Nevertheless, in some ways, the immigration legislation that has now been proposed, combined with existing programs of E-Verify and Secure Communities, could move the United States closer to a European model of border and internal enforcement, combined some form of amnesty.

Thus, while the militarization of the border appears to be relatively ineffective, the alternatives suggested by the European experience appear to be gaining some ground. The United States has successfully avoided the pitfalls associated with failed policies in Europe. The question is whether it can avoid the pitfalls associated with failed frontier policies in the United States.

Endnotes

1. In fact, the category of family unification is more complicated. In France, for example, most family migrants are not admitted under family unification rules but under a category of private and family life. This category of admission was created in 1998. It usually involves temporary admission for foreign members of French families who do not easily fit the category of family unification (Insee 2005).
2. The sharp movement toward consensus and away from multiculturalism is summarized and analyzed in three recent articles in *Le Monde*, February 26, 2011, under the rubric, "Le multiculturalisme, entre modèle et crise."
3. This pessimistic position was also supported by the normally pro-multiculturalist Council of Europe (Hollinger 2011).
4. There is also a striking difference between the priorities of mass publics for immigrant integration and the declared priorities of governments. Governments in Europe are far more insistent on sharing cultural values than are mass publics, and congruence is more evident in the United States than in Europe. See German Marshall Fund of the United States 2010, p. 31.
5. Support for expressions of Islam, such as the construction of mosques, is low and in the middle of a "debate" on identity in France at the end of 2009 seemed to be declining. If 31 percent of those surveyed supported the construction of mosques just after September 11, 2001, this percentage declined to a mere 19 percent in December 2009. See Enquête IFOP 2009.
6. The legislation that authorizes the prohibition against the collection of ethnic data is the Loi No. 78—17 du 6 janvier 1978 relative à l'informatique, aux fi chiers et aux libertés. However, this law was modified in 2004, and the National Commission on Computers and Liberty lists seven criteria that could be used to measure diversity. See www. Cnil.fr/index.php?.id=1844 (last accessed June 7, 2008).

7. Quoted in Michael Benton, *Promoting Racial Harmony* (Cambridge: Cambridge University Press, 1985), p. 71.

8. The original text reads, "Un immigré en situation régulière peut tomber dans la clandestinité du jour au lendemain. Pour de nombreux immigrés, la situation d'illégalité peut représenter une phase temporaire du cycle migratoire avant l'obtention d'un titre de séjour" (Tapinos 1999). Translation by author.

9. The French estimate was given by the minister of the interior in an interview in the *Figaro,* May 11, 2005; the British figures were quoted by Professor John Salt in *The Sunday Times* as estimates that he did for the Home Office on April 17, 2005; these figures have been confirmed by *Clandestino* reports. The American figure is from the most recent Pew reports cited in Table 7. In each case, the government has argued that there has been an increase; in the US case, this is double the number cited by Tapinos in 1999. In general, the comparison among France, Britain, and the United States—if not the exact figures—is confirmed in a massive report by the French Sénat in April 2006 (Sénat, 2006). The report also deals with the complex problem of estimating the population of "irregular immigrants." In particular, see the testimony of François Héran in Volume II and cited on p. 47 of Volume I. He also cites the United States as one of the countries where the informal labor market is most important. The data cited by the report (Vol. I, 47), indicates that no country in Europe has a lower rate of irregular immigration than France.

10. These percentages are based on the estimates of undocumented immigrants made in the Clandestino reports, and the removal and expulsion reports published by the US Department of Homeland Security, the UK Home Office, and the French Ministry of the Interior.

References

Adam, N. "Southern Europeans flock to Germany." *The Wall Street Journal.* http://online.wsj.com/article/SB10001424127887323372504578468360472635932.html (May 7, 2013).

Adida, C., D. Laitin, and M. A. Valfort. *"Les Français musulmans sont-ils discriminés dans leur propre pays ? Une étude expérimentale sur le marché du travail."* Paris: French-American Foundation and Presses de Sciences Po, 2010.

Baumard, M. "Ecole: l'échec du modèle français d'égalité des chances." *Le Monde* (February 11, 2010). http://www.lemonde.fr/societe/article/2010/02/11/ecole-l-echec-du-modele-francais-d-egalite-des-chances_1304257_3224.html.

Brouard, S., and V. Tiberj. *Français comme les autres? Enquête sur les citoyens d'origine maghrébine, africaine et turque.* Paris: Presses de Sciences Po, 2005.

Caldwell, C. *Reflections of the revolution in Europe: Immigration, Islam and the West.* New York: Doubleday, 2009.

Council of the European Union. *Implementing the principle of equal treatment between persons irrespective of racial or ethnic origin.* 2000/43/EC of 29 June 2000. Brussels: European Union, 2000.

———. *European Pact on Immigration and Asylum.* Council Doc. 13440/08. Brussels: European Union, September 24, 2008.

———. *Council conclusions on the follow-up of the European Pact on Immigration and Asylum.* Brussels: European Union, June 3, 2010. http://www.consilium.europa.eu/uedocs/cms_data/docs/pressdata/en/jha/114881.pdf.

———. *Amended proposal for a regulation of the European Parliament and of the Council on the establishment of an evaluation and monitoring mechanism to verify the application of the Schengen acquis.* 18196/1/11, REV 1. Brussels: European Union, December 9, 2011.

———. *Council conclusions regarding guidelines for the strengthening of political governance in the Schengen cooperation.* Brussels: European Union, March 8, 2012.

DeSipio, L., and R. O. de la Garza. "Forever seen as new: Latino participation in American elections." In *Latinos Remaking America,* edited by M. M. Suarez and M. M. Paez, 398–430. Berkeley: University of California Press, 2009.

Donadio, R. "France to help Italy block Tunisian migrants." *New York Times.* http://www.nytimes.com/2011/04/09/world/europe/09italy.html?_r=0 (April 8, 2011).

Dubet, F. *Les Places et les chances.* Paris: Ed. su Seuil, 2010.

Enquête IFOP. "Les Français et la construction des mosquées et des minarets en France." *Le Figaro.* http://www.lefigaro.fr/assets/pdf/Sondage-minaret.pdf (December 2, 2009).

Eurostat. *Migration and migrant population statistics.* Brussels: European Union, 2010. http://epp.eurostat.ec.europa.eu/statistics_explained/index.php/Migration_and_migrant_population_statistics.

Fassin, E. "L'Invention française de la discrimination." *Revue française de science politique* 52, no. 4 (2002): 403–23.

———. "Nicolas Sarkozy en marche vers le 'monoculturalisme'." *Le Monde.* http://www.lemonde.fr/idees/article/2011/02/25/nicolas-sarkozy-en-marche-vers-le-monoculturalisme_1485122_3232.html (February 25, 2011).

German Marshall Fund of the United States. *Transatlantic trends: Immigration.* Washington, DC: German Marshall Fund, 2011.

HALDE. *Annual report 2008.* Paris: HALDE, 2008. http://www.halde.fr/IMG/pdf/RA_UK_version_integrale.pdf.

Herm, A. "Recent migration trends: Citizens of EU-27 member states become ever more mobile while EU remains attractive to non-EU citizens." *Eurostat Statistics in Focus,* 98/2008 (2008). http://epp.eurostat.ec.europa.eu/cache/ITY_OFFPUB/KS-SF-08-098/EN/KS-SF-08-098-EN.PDF.

Hollinger, P. "Council of Europe warns on multiculturalism." *Financial Times.* http://www.ft.com/cms/s/0/72c02d9a-39c6-11e0-8dba-00144feabdc0.html#axzz2YUfSHago (February 16, 2011).

Huntington, S. P. *Who are we: The challenges to America's national identity.* New York: Simon and Schuster, 2005.

Insee. *Les immigrés en France.* Paris: Insee, 2005.

Klausen, J. *The Islamic challenge: Politics and religion in western Europe.* Oxford: Oxford University Press, 2005.

Langan, E. "Assimilation and affirmative action in French education systems." *European Education* 40, no. 3 (2008): 49–64.

Leparmentier, A., and J. P. Stroobants. "Le candidat Sarkozy instrumentalise l'Europe." *Le Monde.* http://www.lemonde.fr/politique/article/2012/03/12/le-candidat-sarkozy-instrumentalise-l-europe_1656488_823448.html (March 12, 2012).

Martin, S. F. *Unauthorized migration: US policy responses in comparative perspective.* Paper for presentation at the 2007 Annual Conference of the International Studies Association, Chicago, Illinois, March 2, 2007.

Mayer, N., G. Michelet, and V. Tiberg. "Montée de l'intérêt polarisation anti-islam." In *Rapport racism de 2012,* edited by Commission Nationale Consultative des Droits de L'homme. Paris: CNCDH, 2013.

Nana, C. K. *With strict policies in place, Dutch discourse on integration becomes more inclusive.* Washington, DC: Migration Policy Institute, 2007.

Pew Hispanic Center. *Modes of entry for the unauthorized migrant population.* Fact Sheet. Washington, DC: Pew Hispanic Center. http://pewhispanic.org/files/factsheets/19.pdf (May 22, 2006).

Preston, J. "Despite opposition, immigration agency to expand fingerprint program." *New York Times.* http://www.nytimes.com/2012/05/12/us/ice-to-expand-secure-communities-program-in-mass-and-ny.html (May 12, 2012).

Salins, P. *Assimilation American style.* New York: Harper Collins, 1997.

Schain, M. *The politics of immigration in France, Britain, and the United States.* 2nd ed. New York: Palgrave, 2012.

Scheffer, P. *Immigrant nations.* Cambridge, UK: Polity Press, 2011.

Schlessinger, A. M., Jr. *The disuniting of America: Reflections on a multicultural society.* New York: W. W. Norton, 1998.

Schneider, J. "Memory test: A history of the U.S. Citizen Education Examination." *Teachers College Records* 112, no. 9 (2010): 2379–404.

Schnepf, S. *How different are immigrants? A cross-country and cross survey analysis of educational achievement.* Discussion Paper #1398. Bonn: IZA, 2004.

Sénat. *Rapport de la commission d'enquête sur l'immigration clandestine, créée en vertu d'une résolution adoptée par le Sénat le 27 octobre 2005* (2 volumes). Published in the Official Journal on April 7, 2006.

Spiegel Online. "Merkel's rhetoric in integration debate is 'inexcusable.'" *Speigel Online.* http://www.spiegel.de/international/germany/the-world-from-berlin-merkel-s-rhetoric-in-integration-debate-is-inexcusable-a-723702.html (October 18, 2010).

Stepnick, A., and C. D. Stepnick. "Power and identity: Miami Cubans." In *Latinos Remaking America,* edited by M. M. Suarez and M. M. Paez, 75–93. Berkeley: University of California Press, 2009.

Swann, B. M. S. *Education for all: The report of the Committee of Inquiry into the Education of Children from Ethnic Minority Groups.* Vol. 9453. London: HMSO, 1985.

Tapinos, G. "Immigration et marché du travail." *L'Observateur de OCDE* 219 (1999). http://observateurocde.org/news/archivestory.php/aid/85/Immigration_et_march_E9_du_travail.html.

Tichenor, D. *Dividing lines.* Princeton, NJ: Princeton University Press, 2002.

Triandafyllidou, A. *Clandestino Project: Undocumented migration: Counting the uncountable. Data and trends across Europe.* Final Report, 23 November 2009. Prepared for the European Commission. Athens: Clandestino, 2009. http://clandestino.eliamep.gr.

Tribalat, M. *Faire France.* Paris: Découverte, 1995.

Van Eeckhout, L. "Le Conseil constitutionnel invalide les statistiques ethniques." *Le Monde.* http://www.lemonde.fr/politique/article/2007/11/16/le-conseil-constitutionnel-invalide-les-statistiques-ethniques_979200_823448.html (November 16, 2007).

Williamson, H. "EU six consider introduction of 'integration contracts' for immigrants." *Financial Times.* http://www.ft.com/intl/cms/s/0/8f0fc44e-bada-11da-980d-0000779e2340.html (March 24, 2006).

US Department of Homeland Security. *2010 yearbook of immigration statistics.* Washington, DC: US Government Printing Office, 2011.

CHAPTER 7

Climate Change Policy: Progress and Persistence

Frank J. Convery

The first modern intimation that human activity can have consequences for global health came with the challenge of ozone depletion. Scientists concluded that chlorofluorocarbons (CFCs) manufactured as refrigerants were depleting the ozone layer that surrounds the earth and shields us from ultraviolet radiation. The response was to limit and, over time, come close to eliminating the production and use of CFCs. The second human impact of global import to receive attention is climate change. Again, scientists were the first to identify this potential,[1] and climate change then became part of the public debate and policy decisions. Most scientists who have studied the evidence in detail have concluded that global warming is happening, that human activity is almost certainly a significant contributor to the phenomenon, and that, if action to limit greenhouse gas emissions (GHG) is not taken, the consequences for well-being will be very negative, with the burden born mainly by the poorest residents of our planet (Richardson, Steffen, and Liverman 2011).[2] Carbon dioxide (CO_2), produced mainly by burning of coal, oil, natural gas, and wood accounts for most of the greenhouse gas emissions produced by human activity. Emissions have risen from 22.7 billion metric tons in 1990 to 34 billion metric tons in 2011 (Olivier, Janssens-Maenhout, and Peters 2012). It would be great if the skeptics are right, but if they are, our efforts to address climate change will not be wasted; they will reduce our dependence on volatile sources, find us new ways of reducing our consumption and our energy bills, and create a new wave of enterprise.

Efforts to reach a global agreement have been mediated through the United Nations, culminating in the Kyoto Protocol, which for developed countries sets quantified greenhouse gas emission reduction obligations to be achieved by 2012 and creates mechanisms to support reductions in developing countries. While the

United States refused to ratify the Kyoto Protocol, the European Union (EU) was a strong proponent of the agreement. The EU ratified the protocol and agreed to achieve an 8 percent reduction from 1990 emission levels by 2012.

The EU put in place a number of policies in the 1990s and 2000s designed to reduce greenhouse gas emissions, including energy efficiency measures and, from 2005, an ambitious emissions trading system that would create a market for tradable CO_2 emissions permits (what Americans would call a *cap-and-trade* system).[3] Today, it is clear that the EU's Kyoto commitments will be achieved (see Table 7.1).

In December 2008, the EU agreed to a new set of binding legislation—the climate and energy package—to guide EU climate change policy in the post-Kyoto (i.e., after 2012) period. The climate and energy package establishes the so-called *20-20-20 strategy*, setting out the EU's goals and strategy for climate change policy through 2020. Though the Kyoto commitment period ended in 2012 and talks on a new, binding international climate agreement have yet to succeed, the EU remains committed to pursuing an ambitious climate change policy even in the absence of an international treaty. However, the Great European Recession is shaping the debate, with increasing reluctance in Europe concerning any climate change policies that may negatively impact economic growth and job creation. Growth in the EU and the United States was comparable over the 2002 to 2008 period. However, since then, net growth in the EU overall is expected to be negative over the 2009 to 2013 period.

The relatively robust growth which coincided with the first trading period (2005) provided comfort that it was possible to sustain economic growth in tandem with relatively high prices for allowances. But on September 15, 2008, Lehman Brothers Bank collapsed in the United States. This lit a destructive fire, which swept through various economies in Europe. The European fiscal and banking policy response was successively too little and too late; before action could be taken, the equivalent of seventeen fire chiefs in the seventeen eurozone countries

TABLE 7.1   Total and Per Capita Greenhouse Gas Emissions EU-27, 1990–2010

	1990	*2010*	*Percentage change*
Greenhouse gas emissions (million metric tons of CO_2 equivalent)	5589	4724	−15.5
Per capita emissions (metric tons of CO_2 per person)	11.8	9.4	−20.5
GHG per unit of GDP (constant 2000 prices)	735	450	

Source: Data from European Environment Agency (2011).

had to meet and agree on a strategy in tandem with the European Central Bank and then implement it. Europe started to slide over this economic cliff just as the climate and energy package was agreed upon. The ensuing economic collapse has had very significant implications for the outcomes associated with the climate and energy package.

The EU's 2008 climate and energy package includes the following provisions:[4]

Greenhouse Gases: The EU is to achieve a reduction of 20 percent in greenhouse gas emissions by 2020 from the 1990 baseline. These reduction targets now have the force of European law and are divided into two categories. The first concerns so-called *nontrading sectors* such as transport, agriculture, heat in buildings and small industry, and waste. This category covers 60 percent of all greenhouse gas emissions. Overall, the nontrading sectors will achieve a 10 percent reduction in emissions compared to 2005, with legally binding differentiated targets across member states (ranging from -20 percent to + 20 percent depending on the gross domestic product [GDP] per capita of the state in question, with wealthier states making greater reductions). Also, there is some scope for emissions trading between member states in this sector. The second category concerns so-called *emissions trading sectors* including power production and heavy industry. These sectors, which cover over 40 percent of all emissions, are subject to an overall cap. The cap for 2020 is 21 percent compared to the 2005 baseline—with power sector allowances auctioned from 2013, emissions from aviation included from 2012, and up to 300 million allowances available up to 2015 for carbon capture and storage and innovative renewable energy technology projects.

As regards aviation, the inclusion of foreign carriers into the European Union Emissions Trading System (EU ETS) encountered resistance internationally. China ordered its carriers to not participate in the EU ETS and to cease purchases of new Airbus aircraft. Similarly, India-flagged carriers refused to report verified 2011 carbon emissions to the EU in March 2012 as required by the EU ETS in accordance with direction from the Indian government. In the United States, the first piece of legislation debated after the November 2012 election was the European Union Emissions Trading Scheme Prohibition Act of 2011, which potentially prohibits any operators of civil aircraft in the United States from participating in the EU ETS. On November 9, 2012, the International Civil Aviation Organization (ICAO) Council announced that it was forming a high-level group to provide near-term recommendations to develop a global market-based mechanism to address greenhouse gas emissions from aircraft. The EU has stopped the clock on the application of EU ETS to flights into and out of the EU pending the emergence of a credible international scheme. It continues to apply to domestic flights within the EU (Labrousse, DeVore, and Hayes 2013).

Renewable Energy: The EU has imposed a legally binding obligation that renewable energy will make up a 20 percent share of final energy consumption across the union by 2020. This overall target is distributed across the twenty-seven (now twenty-eight) member states in the form of individual national targets, with some states committing to renewable energy shares above 20 percent and some below 20 percent.

Energy Efficiency: The EU has adopted Energy Efficiency Directive 2012/27/EU,[5] which if fully implemented would reduce energy consumption by 20 percent by 2020. The directive establishes a common framework for promoting energy efficiency in the EU to ensure the target of 20 percent primary energy savings by 2020 is met and to pave the way for further energy efficiency afterward. It lays down rules designed to remove barriers and overcome some of the market failures that impede efficiency in the supply and use of energy.[6]

Thus, the European Union's strategy addresses all emissions, has set legally binding targets, and has a legally enforceable framework for implementation. To date, the EU has succeeded in reducing greenhouse gas emissions using a variety of policy instruments without suffering economically as a result of these efforts. This chapter begins by outlining some lessons from the European experience with climate change policy—considering both the factors that have been crucial to its success and the factors that constrain its prospects looking forward. Finally, this chapter reflects on the lessons the United States might draw from Europe's experience.

Keys to Success in Europe

A number of factors have contributed to the relative success of European climate change policy over the past two decades. There has been strong political leadership behind the policy, across the political spectrum and across a number of EU member states and EU institutions. The political leadership has, in turn, been underpinned by consistently strong public support for ambitious climate change policies. EU leaders have crafted a coherent, comprehensive strategy and pursued it consistently over the years, while adapting it in the face of changing circumstances. Finally, EU climate change policy has benefited initially to some extent from sheer good luck.

Political Leadership and Commitment

EU climate change policy has benefited from consistent and committed leadership. For over two decades, the leadership in the EU's key power centers—the European Commission, which proposes legislation and enforces it once enacted; the European Parliament, which has power of co-decision on environmentally related legislation; and the EU member states (in the council) who must also approve legislation under qualified majority rules—have all been supportive of effective action. Specifically, key leaders of large member states (France, Germany, and the United Kingdom) and the Nordics have been willing to press both for domestic action in Europe, and for action at G7, G20, and UN fora. The United Kingdom is a notable example; successive prime ministers from both the major parties, Margaret Thatcher, John Major, Tony Blair, Gordon Brown, and now David Cameron, have been active on climate change. They have their counterparts in other member states where there has been a cross-party consensus on the importance of addressing climate change. This cross-party consensus on the need to take aggressive policy actions to reduce greenhouse gas emissions contrasts sharply with the situation in the United States where skepticism about climate change science and about the need to take action to reduce greenhouse gas emissions pervades one of the two main political parties.

At the EU level, leadership by the European Commission goes back to the time of Jacques Delors, who as president of the commission (1985–94), used the sustainable development agenda as a means of reinventing the EU and moving it forward to a new and exciting agenda. Subsequently, the commission has viewed taking a leadership role on climate change as an important way to achieve the EU's aspirations for global leadership. The idea of *soft power* and the ability to be a serious player on the world stage is an ambition of important elements of the European political establishment. The fact that the United States hesitated, and then refused, to take global leadership on climate change provided a gap on the global leadership market, which Europe could and did fill (Kelemen 2010; Scheipers and Sicurelli 2007).

Public Support

The corollary of elite political support has been broad popular support, triggered in part by major weather events including a heat wave in Paris and flooding in Germany that created a wave of popular concern about climate change, which translated into public support. A Eurobarometer poll carried out in June 2011 found the following (European Commission 2011a):

- Of those polled, 68 percent considered climate change a very serious problem (up from 64 percent in 2009). Altogether, 89 percent saw it as a serious problem (either "very serious" or "fairly serious"). On a scale of 1 (least) to 10 (most), the seriousness of climate change was ranked at 7.4, against 7.1 in 2009.

- Overall, climate change was seen as the second most serious problem facing the world, after poverty, hunger, and lack of drinking water (considered as a single issue). One in five people surveyed considered climate change the single most serious problem. Fifty-one percent (up from 47 percent in 2009) said it was either the most or one of the most serious problems, compared with 45 percent who said this about the economic situation.
- Currently, 78 percent agreed that fighting climate change and improving energy efficiency can boost the EU economy and jobs; this is up from 2009 when 63 percent agreed that climate action could boost economy and jobs. In no member state did fewer than two in three support this view.
- Basing taxation to a greater extent on energy use is supported by 68 percent, with a majority in every member state in favor of such a shift.
- The public expects Europe to become a climate-friendly society by 2050, a vision the commission outlined in its roadmap to a competitive low-carbon economy. Eighty-eight percent expect that in 2050, Europe will use more renewable energy, 87 percent that Europe will be more energy efficient, and 73 percent that cars will be powered more efficiently than they are today.

The findings of that 2011 Eurobarometer poll reflect the consistently high levels of public concern over climate change in Europe over the past decade. This widespread and intense public concern over climate change has been crucial to keeping climate change policy high on the political agenda in Europe. By contrast, various public opinion surveys reveal that the percentage of Americans who consider climate change to be a "very serious" problem is consistently far lower than the percentage of Europeans who hold that view (Vogel 2012, 137–38).

Coherent Strategy, Persistence and Adaptability

As noted above, over time, strategy has addressed the key elements covering all domestic emissions. For instance, the EU Emissions Trading Scheme (EU ETS) covered the power sector and heavy industry, including over 40 percent of CO_2 emissions. Emissions from nontrading sectors (agriculture, transport, heat, waste) were reduced by fixing a separate cap for each of the twenty-seven member states. These policies reflect the European preference for deciding how much can be emitted over time—the Kyoto Protocol model—and then putting policy in place to meet this cap, rather than the pledge and review approach, where each country decides what it will take on.

Within the framework of this broad strategy, policy has evolved. After the Sustainable Development Conference in Rio de Janeiro in 1992, the European Commission proposed that a Europe-wide carbon tax be introduced and attempted to do so over the 1992–97 period. But fiscal measures require unanimous approval by EU member states, and this was impossible to achieve, so the commission eventually withdrew the proposal. From this failure came the proposal to introduce a cap-and-trade system, which became the EU Emissions Trading System. The idea was that a price signaling scarcity—that the capacity of the atmosphere to absorb more greenhouse gas emissions without potentially catastrophic implications was limited—was the essential requirement for changing the behavior of emitters. The main lesson here is that when policymakers encountered a political roadblock to a key climate change initiative (the carbon tax), they persisted and adapted to the political circumstances by promoting an alternative policy (emissions trading) that could secure political approval.

The EU ETS itself is an interesting example of adapting to policy dysfunction. The experience is elaborated in detail in Ellerman, Convery, and de Perthuis (2010). *Emissions trading* involves setting a cap on emissions, usually expressed in metric tons of CO_2 or CO_2 equivalent per year. Allowances are allocated to the emitters, and the sum of the allocations equals the cap. Where emitters wish to emit more than their allocation, they can either abate or reduce their emissions, or they can buy allowances to cover their extra emissions, or some combination. It is the trading that produces a price, and the incentives are clear: Emitters for whom it is very cheap to reduce emissions will do so and sell the allowances released to those for whom it is more expensive. Economists say this is a cost-effective solution; the cap is achieved at minimum cost. The price attached to emissions also provides an incentive to innovators, which operates 24 hours a day, 365 days a year. If you can come up with a technology, input, or system that reduces emissions at a cost lower than the price of the allowances, you have a market.

For a variety of good reasons, most economists would support the following propositions to guide the design of any cap-and-trade system: (1) the cap be sufficiently tight to produce a significant allowance price; (2) the scheme covers all emissions; (3) allocation of allowances be done by auction and the revenues accruing be used to reduce other distorting taxes in the economy; (4) the time horizon should be long and allow banking of allowances—those who have surplus allowances can use them in future years—and borrowing—those who are short in one year can borrow from the next years.

The early stage of the EU ETS (2005–7) failed all four of these requirements; the cap was too loose (although this did not become clear until the final phase of the period), the allowances were given away for free, there was no banking and borrowing beyond 2007, and less than half of emissions were covered (Convery 2009a). One result was price collapse in 2007. But there was some abatement and learning by doing. A review was built into the process, with the result that the cap was tightened, banking and borrowing to 2020 was allowed, auctioning of allowances for the power sector is to be introduced from 2013; and coverage has been extended to include aviation from 2012 and other gasses and sectors, but not including transport, agriculture, and heat, which are the big emitters in the non-trading sectors.

The weaknesses noted above were of course well known to European Commission officials. But they also knew that accommodating these weaknesses was a necessary requirement for the support of the member states, especially of Germany, whose industry had a domestic voluntary agreement with government that they did not wish to be superseded by EU ETS. The clever piece of institutional engineering was to corral these weaknesses into a pilot period after which changes could be made. Once the experience of the pilot period made it clear that the weaknesses in the system in terms of the four essential requirements described above had to be addressed, EU officials were able to win the support of the previously reluctant member states to make those changes.

A final illustration of the adaptability of the EU's approach to climate change policy was its willingness to learn from the United States. While this book focuses on lessons from Europe for the United States, in the initial design of the ETS, the lesson drawing moved in the other direction: The EU clearly drew lessons from the US experience with emissions trading. When the European Commission failed to win backing for its initial proposals for a carbon tax, it turned to an emissions trading model that drew on US experience. The fact that the United States had successfully implemented an emissions trading scheme for acid rain, that both the design and achievements had been well documented, and there was very generous willingness on the part of both officials and academics to share the lessons meant that there was evidence that such a scheme could be introduced for carbon (Ellerman et al. 2000). The trading scheme, which started in California in 2013, shows features that are informed in part by lessons from what the EU did not initially do: Its coverage is more complete, accounting for 85 percent of total emissions including transport; auctioning follows free allocation; and a floor price of $10.00 per ton was set.[7]

Luck

Finally, it must be acknowledged that the progress on climate change in Europe benefited from a generally very positive macroeconomic environment in the 1990s and 2000s (Table 7.2). For example, although competitiveness concerns loomed large in the debates on EU ETS, in practice, economic growth was robust and the demand from China for commodities like steel, paper, and cement was such that there was de facto no evidence of any negative impacts of climate policy on the competitiveness of European economies. Also, the serendipity of weather events—heat wave in Paris, flooding in Germany—helped bring along public support. The *dash for gas* by the United Kingdom, whereby carbon intensive coal-fired plants were very rapidly replaced by much lower carbon emitting gas plants,

TABLE 7.2   Real Annual GDP Growth (Percentage) From 2002–2014 in the EU-27 and the United States

Year	EU-27	United States
2002	1.3	1.8
2003	1.5	2.5
2004	2.5	3.5
2005	2.1	3.1
2006	3.3	2.7
2007	3.2	1.9
2008	0.3	−0.3
2009	−4.3	−3.1
2010	2.1	2.4
2011	1.5	1.8
2012	−0.3	2.1
2013 (projection)	0.4	2.3
2014 (projection)	1.6	2.6

Source: Data from Eurostat (2013). http://epp.eurostat.ec.europa.eu/tgm/table.do?tab=table&init=1&plugin=1&language=en&pcode=tec00115.

and the extending of the EU to include twelve new member states, comprised mainly of the formerly communist countries of Central Europe who used energy very inefficiently (with therefore commensurate room for low-cost improvements), meant that it was relatively easy to make progress and meet targets (Yandle and Buck 2002). Finally, the key decisions had already been made before the twelve new member states joined. The fact that their incomes are much lower than the fifteen previous members of the EU, and they have the same concerns of emerging economies about potentially being locked out of growth by constrained use of fossil fuels (Poland being the largest and very coal dependent), means that it is likely that agreement would have been more difficult if they had been full partners at the decision table. Indeed, an article in the *Financial Times* (Chaffin and Clark 2012) documents the fact that Poland blocked the tightening up of the cap on emissions in the EU ETS.

Constraints Facing European Climate Change Policy

So far we have focused on lessons about the keys to success of EU climate change policy. But the European experience also highlights important constraints on effective climate policy—constraints which the United States may encounter as well, if and when it attempts to introduce more ambitious climate change policies.

Limited Ability to Fund Major Investments

First, there is limited ability to invest in climate policy initiatives at the EU level. The EU has a very modest budget. The 2011 budget was €126 billion, which amounted to just over 1 percent of the GDP of the twenty-seven EU member states. Of that amount, €56 billion went to agriculture and rural subsidies and €42 billion to cohesion policy (i.e., transfer payments to poorer regions within the EU).[8] This scale of budget translates into a very limited capacity to directly fund major climate change projects, such as carbon capture and storage, or research and development at the EU level. This stands in sharp contrast with a centralized political system, such as China, which can invest hundreds of billions in climate projects, and, according to the 12th Five Year Plan, is likely to do so.[9]

Given the limitations on the EU's ability to fund climate policy at the EU level, responsibility falls on member state governments. However, tight budget constraints also apply now to member states, most of whom are experiencing problems with budget deficits in the context of the ongoing economic crisis.

As fiscal constraints tighten, member states, including their regions and municipalities, who are the main providers of significant subsidies for renewables and energy efficiency are likely cut back or remove entirely the subsidies for these and other purposes.[10] From 2013, allowances will be auctioned—generating about €4 to €30 billion annually to 2020, the amount depending on allowance price, almost all of which will accrue to member states. This may ease the budgetary constraint, but much of this income is likely to be used to address the debt problem, rather than to subsidize renewables and energy efficiency.

Policy Instrument Overlap and Inconsistency

While the EU has a policy framework that is mutually reinforcing, the negative side of this approach is that there is a lot of overlap and inconsistency between specific climate policies. In 2012, this came to the fore in policy debates about the Emissions Trading Scheme. Because of the depth of the recession, demand for allowances to cover emissions shrank, and this resulted in a drop in allowance price. There are concerns in some quarters that this will inhibit investment in carbon capture and storage and in low-carbon innovations generally. Policies that encourage renewables and energy efficiency further reduce the demand for allowances, and this in turn puts more downward pressure on allowance prices. This is exemplified by the new directive on energy efficiency noted above. An impact assessment prepared by the European Commission (European

TABLE 7.3   Public Debt as a Percentage of GDP, 2012

Rank	Country	Debt as Percentage of GDP
1	Greece	161.3
2	Italy	126.1
3	Portugal	119.7
4	Ireland	118.0
5	Belgium	99.6
6	France	89.9
7	UK	88.7
8	Spain	85.3
9	Germany	81.7
10	Austria	74.6
11	US	73.6
12	Netherlands	68.7

Source: Data from Central Intelligence Agency (CIA), *The World Factbook* (Washington, DC: CIA, 2012). https://www.cia.gov/library/publications/the-world-factbook/rankorder/2186rank.html.

Commission 2011b)[11] provided two estimates of the impact of the directive on allowance price in the EU ETS:

- PRIMES model shows reduction in CO_2 price from €16.5 to €14.2 by 2020
- EE3ME model shows price approaching zero (as a result of higher impact of energy efficiency on CO_2 emissions in the trading sectors)

If the latter model proves to be the correct, and if no adjustments are made in (shrinking) the supply of, or (increasing) demand for allowances, the future of the EU ETS will be problematic. Since this is seen as a flagship of European climate policy, and a likely framework for a global carbon-trading scheme, it has negative implications for progress at global level.

There is also potential for inconsistency and inefficiency stemming from the fact that the EU has left it to each member state to determine how to meet its binding caps on emissions from nontrading sectors by 2020. This flexible approach has the advantage of allowing a flowering of approaches. But it means that the overall reduction is likely to be achieved at higher cost than would be achieved if a centralized approach were followed.

"They Haven't Come"

Looking forward, a final constraint the EU faces comes from the failure of the international community to follow its lead on climate policy. The European climate policy strategy is premised on the notion that, "If we build it, they will come." But while the EU has started to build it by taking a leading role on climate change policy, they—the international community, that is—have not come along. Europe now contributes about 11 percent of total carbon emissions (down from 19 percent in 1990). The EU is simultaneously in danger of become less relevant as its share of the total shrinks and of incurring the costs of leadership, substantial political and administrative effort, and increasing constraints on households and businesses—but still failing to engender global action.

TABLE 7.4   Total CO_2 Emissions, Billion Metric Tons, 1990–2011[12]

Jurisdiction	1990	Percentage of Total	2000	2005	2011	Percentage of Total	Per capita 2010
EU 15	3.33	14.7	3.33	3.43	3.03	8.9	
EU 12 (New member states)	1.02	4.5	0.75	0.78	0.76	2.2	
Total EU	4.35	19.2	4.08	4.21	3.79	11.2	7.5
US	4.99	22.0	5.87	5.93	5.42	16.0	17.3
China	2.51	11.1	3.56	5.85	9.7	28.6	7.2
India	0.66	2.9	1.06	1.29	1.97	5.8	1.6
Total	**22.7**	**100**	**25.5**	**29.3**	**33.9**	**100**	

Source: Data from Jos G. J. Olivier, Greet Janssens-Maenhout, and Jeroen A. H. W. Peters (2012).

Lessons for the United States?

Can the European experience with climate change policy offer lessons for the United States as it considers what policy to pursue on climate change? Any lessons for the United States have to be very tentatively proposed, with due modesty, because the context is so different in the US than in the European Union and the prevailing political drivers are dissimilar. To quote Churchill, commenting (unfairly) on Clement Atlee, "Mr. Atlee is a very modest man. Indeed he has a lot to be modest about." However, there are similarities also between the two jurisdictions. Both are suffering budgetary stress and must find other ways besides spending money to solve problems including climate change. The tea party phenomenon in the United States does not have direct analogues in Europe, but in many member states, parties representing an ambition to withdraw from the European project, with a strong emphasis on eliminating immigration, animated in part by anti-Islamic sentiment, are growing in strength and influence. The Euro crisis is crystallizing this emerging antipathy in some countries. And in Europe, as in the United States, there are signs that there is some climate change skepticism in the air, though it is clear from the 2011 Eurobarometer survey noted above that this view has yet to attract widespread popular support. Some member states are evincing reluctance to support the continuation of the EU's pattern of ambition in regard to climate change policy, particularly Poland with its large coal reserves, which is a sort of European analog to West Virginia in the United States in this context. While differences in political and social context present challenges to lesson drawing, the EU experience with climate change policy may still have a few useful lessons to offer the United States, particularly concerning green growth, emissions trading, dealing with economically diverse jurisdictions, and, finally, the importance of persistence.

The Green Growth Performance and the Competitiveness Implications

Much of European action is predicated on a version of the famous Porter hypothesis that those who embrace demanding environmental regulatory obligations first will also lead in the development of the green technologies and businesses needed by all in a carbon and energy constrained world. Jeffrey Immelt, General Electric's (GE) chief executive, provides some support for this line. He argues that the US government must create policies that foster renewables and address climate change: "America is the leading consumer of energy. However, we are not the technical leader. Europe today is the major force for environmental innovation" (Fairley 2005). Comparisons between economic performance of different countries over time is a complex business,[13] but we can say that there is no evidence that the countries in the EU—including the Nordics (Denmark, Finland, Sweden) and Germany and Austria—that have given particular support to renewable energy and energy conservation have been damaged economically by doing so. It is notable that Germany, with about one-quarter of the population of the United States, has the same level of exports ($1.3 trillion in 2010) and a very positive trade balance with the rest of the world. The recent efforts by China, and its ambitions as outlined in its Five Year Plan (2011–15) to be a leader in renewables and energy efficiency, seem to be predicated on the assumptions that a transformation is essential if society is to be sustained economically, socially, and environmentally and could also yield global leadership in some emerging technologies. The Organisation for Economic Co-operation and Development (OECD) has also accepted that such a transformation is essential and is organizing events and producing books, case studies, and materials to support countries that want to make progress.[14]

Emissions Trading

The trading system guarantees that a given quantitative reduction target—minus 21 percent from 2005 by 2020—will be met, and this is no mean achievement. But it does not guarantee a CO_2 price that will stimulate lots of innovation. Because of the depths of the recent recession, demand for allowances has shrunk, and allowance prices have fallen. If innovation beyond what the market will provide is desired, other complementary policy instruments are needed.

A key lesson from European experience in regard to getting an emissions scheme going is to start modestly, make many compromises to get the system up and running, but build in a pilot and review process that allows the limitations to be addressed over time. This worked very well in that many improvements were effected for the second period (2008–13) based on the experience in the pilot period (Convery 2009b). However, in the EU system, there is not an automatic review process to deal with the force majeure represented by the Great Recession. The recession has resulted in shrinking demand for allowances, which in turn has resulted in a price collapse, and there has been no built-in means of addressing this surprise. The European Commission has proposed to shrink supply by taking some of the supply out of the system up to 2016 and adding it back toward the end of the third period (so-called backloading). This would be associated with setting an ambitious reduction target for 2030. But this involves the considerable challenge of securing agreement of the member states and the European Parliament. The California emissions trading scheme has built in some resilience by setting a minimum allowance price of ten dollars and also providing the facility to supply extra allowances into the system in the event of price escalation. Details concerning the choices being addressed in Europe's Emissions Trading Scheme, their implications and feasibility, and the features of the schemes in the United States, China, Australia, and New Zealand are addressed in Convery and Redmond (2013).

A final lesson from the EU ETS is to keep it flexible, so that sectors (e.g., aviation) and countries (e.g., Norway) can be added over time.

Bringing a Wide Range of Economies and Societies to a Shared View and Policy

Effective climate change policy requires burden sharing among diverse economies. The EU offers useful lessons with regard to internal burden sharing among member states. There is a huge range in per capita GDP (purchasing power parity basis) in the EU, ranging from Luxembourg, where it approaches $85,000, to Bulgaria, where it is less than $13,500. Policy moves forward in Europe by, in effect, having the richer countries make more effort on climate change than the poorer ones; the former are given more demanding targets and obligations, and the latter benefit from the transfer of funds for investment in humans and infrastructure, some of which can be used to advance the climate change agenda. This burden sharing practice is a sort of model for what will be needed at global level, and it may provide a useful model for the United States as well. In the United States, a federal program that had customized policies to help those states and regions that are low in income or especially dependent on fossil fuels might help achieve acceptance. With regard to international burden sharing, the EU view is that national effort by advanced economies is essential if we are to make progress. But this needs to be complemented by a global framework, which brings along the wider community and provides a framework where pledges from the bottom up are complemented by top-down stewardship, and where transfers can play a role in getting buy in and achieving progress.

Persistence

Finally, the European experience highlights the importance of persistence in climate change policy. This may be an important message for frustrated advocates of climate change policy in the United States. Keep at it. The failed European efforts in the 1990s to introduce a carbon tax wasted five years, and it took another eight years (1997 to 2005) before the Emissions Trading Scheme was operational. Inclusion of aviation in the EU ETS is now (2013) stalled (see discussion above); however, the policy has resulted in the International Civil Aviation Organization developing its own proposals for a global scheme. The well-known admonition of Calvin Coolidge (1932) is apropos:

> Nothing in the world can take the place of Persistence. Talent will not; nothing is more common than unsuccessful men with talent. Genius will not; unrewarded genius is almost a proverb. Education will not; the world is full of educated derelicts. Persistence and Determination alone are omnipotent. The slogan "Press On" has solved and always will solve the problems of the human race.

This sentiment applies also in the United States. Advocates of climate change policy in the United States who are frustrated by congressional inaction will need to remain persistent in the years to come if they are to see the United States act on climate change. Eventually, if China and the EU have linked emissions trading schemes, and the United States creates a federal scheme and joins this club, they together will cover roughly 50 percent of global carbon emissions and significant progress may be made.

Conclusion

In the area of climate change, the European experience provides a number of insights that may be helpful for the United States. The European experience shows that it is possible to bring a diversity of member states with different values, priorities, and stages of economic development to a shared view as what to do about climate change, how to do it, and act accordingly. The policy model has been to set EU targets that are legally binding and then to mobilize a number of EU policies (including emissions trading, emissions standards for new cars) and individual member state policies (including binding national caps, met by domestic policies, including regulation and carbon taxes) to meet the targets. This effort was enabled by consistent political leadership over a couple of decades, which was underpinned by strong public support and by a robust economy. There has been persistence and clever adaptation, epitomized by the experience with the European Union Emissions Trading Scheme where the pilot period failed many tests but was adapted over time to correct for these limitations. In terms of impact on competitiveness, it is notable that the countries that have been most aggressive in pursuing ambitious climate objectives—including the Nordics (Denmark, Finland, Sweden), Germany, and Austria—have also been among the most successful economically.

There are big challenges ahead. The economic recession in the EU has been of unprecedented duration and depth. This has led to a dramatic fall in the CO_2 allowance price, which in turn has animated a lively debate about what combination of policies, if any, should be mobilized to stabilise and increase the price. The recession has also meant that economic policy dominates all others, including climate policy. Also, the widening of EU membership since 2004 to include Poland and other more coal-dependent countries has brought to the decision-making table new interests that are at present less ambitious in terms of climate than the earlier EU 15 members. But it is unlikely that the EU will give up—persistence and adaptability will continue to be its defining characteristics as regards climate change policy.

Endnotes

1. In the mid-1800s, the Irish born physicist John Tyndall explained the heat in the earth's atmosphere in terms of the capacities of the various gases in the air to absorb radiant heat; he was the first to correctly measure the relative infrared absorptive powers of the gases nitrogen, oxygen, water vapor (the strongest absorber of radiant heat), carbon dioxide (CO_2), ozone, methane, and so forth. He was the first to prove that the earth's

atmosphere has a greenhouse effect. The Swedish chemist Svante Arrhenius in 1896 was the first to formalize the proposition that human action—the large scale burning of coal and release to the atmosphere of CO_2—could lead to global warming.

2. Author and Executive Director James Powell of the National Physical Science Consortium searched the Web of Science for peer-reviewed scientific articles published between January 1, 1991 and November 9, 2012 that had the keyword phrases *global warming* or *global climate change*. The search produced 13,950 articles. He found that 24 of the 13,950 articles, 0.17 percent or 1 in 581, clearly reject human-caused global warming or endorse a cause other than CO_2 emissions for observed warming. The articles have a total of 33,690 individual authors (rounded to 33,700 in the figure). The 24 rejecting papers have a total of 34 authors, about 1 in 1,000 (see http://www.jamespowell.org). Powell (2012) and Nordhaus (2012) provide careful refutations of the skeptic' view.

3. For an overview of the development of EU climate change policy in the 1990s and early 2000s, see Jordan and Rayner 2010.

4. For details on European Union climate policies, see: http://ec.europa.eu/dgs/clima/mission/index_en.htm.

5. Directive 2012/27/EU on energy efficiency, amending Directives 2009/125/EC and 2010/30/EU and repealing Directives 2004/8/EC and 2006/32/EC [OJ L315 p.1].

6. Policy instruments to be mobilized by the Energy Efficiency Directive would include the following steps:

Improve the timeliness and flow of *information* (individual meters, inventory of installations, assess energy efficiency of existing and new installations, promote the energy services market).

Impose requirements (*regulation)* concerning the purchase of high energy-efficiency products and services by public authorities, retrofitting of 3 percent per annum of total floor area owned by local authorities, obligation scheme (annual savings of 1.5 percent) for all for energy distribution and sales companies, waste heat recovery, priority dispatch for electricity from high-efficiency cogeneration.

Remove regulatory and nonregulatory *barriers* to energy efficiency, including split incentives (landlord vs. tenant).

Network tariffs and regulations to provide *incentives* for grid operators to network users to permit them to implement energy efficiency improvements.

Require each member state to prepare and implement an *energy efficiency plan* designed in aggregate to achieve a 20 percent reduction in final energy consumption in the EU by 2020.

7. Further information on the California cap-and-trade program is available from the California Environmental Protection Agency's Air Resources Board at http://www.arb.ca.gov/cc/capandtrade/capandtrade.htm (last accessed June 20, 2013).

8. For EU budget data, see the European Commission website at http://ec.europa.eu/budget/figures/2011/2011_en.cfm (last accessed June 20, 2013).

The huge share of agriculture in the EU budget reflects the view of Pliny the Elder: "The agricultural population, says Cato, produces the bravest men, the most valiant soldiers, and a class of citizens the least given of all to evil designs."

9. Chapter 21, summary available at: http://cbi.typepad.com/china_direct/2011/05/chinas-twelfth-five-new-plan-the-full-english-version.html, p. 29.

10. For a summary of changes (mostly reductions) to renewable energy subsidies enacted or proposed for Germany, Spain, France, and the UK, see Goodman, 2011.

11. For other documentation concerning the EU's Energy Efficiency Directive, see the European Commission's website at http://ec.europa.eu/energy/efficiency/eed/eed_en.htm (last accessed June 20, 2013).

12. The total stock of CO_2 in the atmosphere in 2006 was estimated to be 1.8 trillion (1,800 billion) metric tons of CO_2, so the annual addition of 33 billion metric tons in 2011 added 1.89 percent to the stock (see Richardson, Steffen, and Liverman 2011, 210). What is not known is whether there is a tipping point where the stock triggers dramatic (and probably irreversible) climate change, and if so, what this level is.

13. http://www.thenewfederalist.eu/Europe-vs-USA-Whose-Economy-Wins.

14. http://www.oecd.org/document/10/0,3746,en_2649_37465_44076170_1_1_1_37465,00.html.

References

Chaffin, J., and P. Clark. "Poland warns EU on climate policy." Financial Times. http://www.ft.com/intl/cms/s/0/4422e92c-6883-11e1-b803-00144feabdc0.html#axzz1uNWrh72o (March 7, 2012).

Convery, F. J. "Origins and development of EU ETS." *Environmental Resource Economics* 43 (2009a): 391–412.

———. "Reflections: The emerging literature on emissions trading in Europe." *Review of Environmental Economic Policy* 3, no. 1 (2009b): 121–37.

Convery, F. J., and L. Redmond. "The European Union Emissions Trading Scheme: Issues in allowance price and linkage." *Annual Review of Resource Economics* 5 (forthcoming 2013).

Ellerman, D. A., F. J. Convery, and C. de Perthuis. *Pricing carbon: The European Union Emissions Trading Scheme.* Cambridge: Cambridge University Press, 2010.

Ellerman, D. A., P. L. Joskow, R. Schmalensee, J. P. Montero, and E. M. Bailey. *Markets for clean air: The U.S. acid rain program.* New York: Cambridge University Press, 2000.

European Commission. *Impact assessment: Accompanying Directive on energy efficiency and amending and subsequently repealing Directives 2004/8/EC and 2006/32/EC.* SEC (2011) 779 final. Brussels: European Commission, 2011b.

———. *Special Eurobarometer 372: Climate change.* Brussels: European Commission, 2011a. http://ec.europa.eu/clima/news/articles/news_2011100702_en.htm.

European Environment Agency. *Greenhouse gas emission trends and projections in Europe 2011: Tracking progress towards Kyoto and 2020 targets.* EEA Report No 4/2011. http://www.eea.europa.eu/publications/ghg-trends-and-projections-2011 (2011).

Fairley, P. "The greening of GE." *IEEE Spectrum* 42, no. 7 (2005): 28. http://spectrum.ieee.org/energy/environment/the-greening-of-ge.

Goodman, R. "European renewables: Discussing capping or removal of subsidies." *Infrastructure Journal* (March 22, 2012). http://www.ijonline.

Jordan, A., and T. Rayner. "The evolution of climate policy in the European Union." In *Climate change policy in the European Union,* edited by A. Jordan, D. Huitema, H. van Asselt, T. Rayner, and F. Berkhout, 52–80. Cambridge: Cambridge University Press, 2010.

Kelemen, R. D. "Globalizing European Union environmental policy." *Journal of European Public Policy* 17, no. 3 (2010): 335–49.

Labrousse, F., J. DeVore, and J. Hayes. "European Union: Aviation and the EU ETS: What's next?" *Jones Day.* http://www.mondaq.com/unitedstates/x/223598/Aviation/Aviation+and+the+EU+ETS+Whats+Next (February 26, 2013).

Nordhaus, W. D. "Why the global warming skeptics are wrong." *New York Review of Books.* http://www.nybooks.com/articles/archives/2012/mar/22/why-global-warming-skeptics-are-wrong/?pagination=false&printpage=true#fn-1 (March 22, 2012).

Olivier, J. G. J., G. Janssens-Maenhout, and J. A. H. W. Peters. *Long-term trend in global CO_2 emissions, 2012 report.* The Hague: Netherlands Environmental Assessment Agency and JRC European Commission, 2012. http://edgar.jrc.ec.europa.eu/CO2REPORT2012.pdf.

Powell, J. L. *The inquisition of climate science.* New York: Columbia University Press, 2012.

Richardson, K., W. Steffen, and D. Liverman. *Climate change: Global risks, challenges and decisions.* Cambridge: Cambridge University Press, 2011.

Scheipers, S., and D. Sicurelli. "Normative power Europe." *Journal of Common Market Studies* 45, no. 2 (2007): 435–57.

Vogel, D. *The Politics of precaution: Regulating health, safety, and environmental risks in Europe and the United States.* Princeton, NJ: Princeton University Press, 2012.

Yandle, B., and S. Buck. "Bootleggers, Baptists, and the global warming battle." *Harvard Environmental Law Review* 26 (2002): 177–229.

CHAPTER 8

Urban Transport: Promoting Sustainability in Germany

Ralph Buehler and John Pucher

Since the Second World War, levels of automobile ownership and use have increased greatly, first in North America, then in Western Europe, and in recent decades, throughout the world, but especially in rapidly developing countries such as China and India (Millard-Ball and Schipper 2011; Pucher et al. 2007). The growth in car ownership is closely related to rising per capita incomes so that car ownership almost inevitably rises as a country's per capita income grows.

However, increased reliance on the car has worsened many social and environmental problems: air and water pollution, noise, traffic congestion, greenhouse gas (GHG) emissions, depletion of petroleum and other nonrenewable resources, traffic injuries and fatalities, and reduced accessibility for persons who cannot afford a car or are unable to drive (Transportation Research Board [TRB] 2010; World Health Organization [WHO] 2009). Many national governments as well as nongovernmental organizations (NGOs) have recognized the need to mitigate the negative impacts of car use, especially in cities (European Union [EU] Commission 2009; US Department of Transportation [USDOT] 2009). Even in the United States, which offers perhaps the most glaring example of an unsustainable transport system, federal, state, and local governments have increasingly adopted policies to promote more sustainable travel options (USDOT 2009).

This chapter first provides an overview of differences in levels of motorization and car use in North America and Western Europe, as well as corresponding differences in levels of walking, cycling, and public transport use. The focus of the chapter, however, is on the United States and Germany, countries which are comparable in many ways but contrast sharply in the sustainability of their transport systems. Much of the chapter is devoted to a detailed examination of government policies in the United States and Germany that affect travel behavior and land-use patterns. To provide a local context and specific example, the chapter includes a detailed case study of Freiburg, Germany—considered the most environmentally friendly city in Germany—which has implemented a wide range of innovative measures to promote sustainability. The chapter concludes with lessons that may be useful to other countries in their efforts to enhance the sustainability of their own transport systems.

Car Ownership and Use in North America and Western Europe

The United States leads the world in per-capita levels of car ownership and use. As shown in Figure 8.1, there were 809 cars and light trucks per 1,000 residents in the United States in 2010, about 34 percent higher than the motorization rate in Canada (605) and 37 to 70 percent higher than the rates in the ten Western European countries, ranging from 589 in Germany to 477 in Denmark. The relatively low level of car ownership in Denmark may be due to the high taxes imposed on new car purchases: 105 to 180 percent of the base price, depending on the size and type of car (German Institute for Economic Research [DIW] 2005). By comparison, the tax rate on new car purchases is 19 percent in Germany and averages

FIGURE 8.1   Passenger Cars and Light Trucks per 1,000 Population in Selected North American and European Countries, 2010

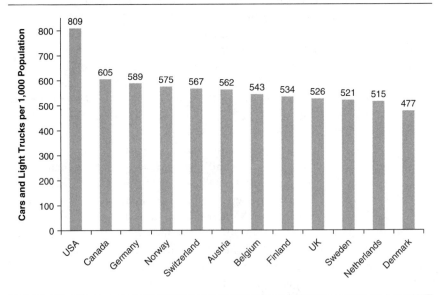

Source: Data from World Bank (2012).

only 4 percent in the United States (but varies from 0 to 7 percent among the fifty states). Since gross domestic product (GDP) per capita in 2010 was much higher in Denmark ($56,245) than in Germany ($40,116) and the United States ($47,153), the lower level of car ownership in Denmark is definitely not due to lower incomes (World Bank 2012).

Corresponding to their higher level of car ownership, Americans also have the world's highest rate of car use. In 2010, Americans drove an average of 21,646 km per capita per year, 46 percent more than Canadians (14,824 km) and 60 to 87 percent more than for the ten western European countries shown in Figure 8.2, ranging from a high of 13,513 km in Finland to 11,561 km in Germany. It is notable that Germany has the lowest level of per capita car use of the ten European countries in Figure 8.2 despite having the highest rate of car ownership. Thus, it is not inevitable that having more cars will result in higher levels of usage. In general, however, car ownership is a prerequisite to car usage, and most broad international studies find that motorization rates are highly correlated with car use per capita.

The most frequently used index of travel behavior is modal split, the percentage distribution of trips by various means of transport. Figure 8.3 highlights the extraordinary dominance of the private car in the United States, where 86 percent

FIGURE 8.2   Passenger Kilometers of Car and Light Truck Travel Per Capita, 2010

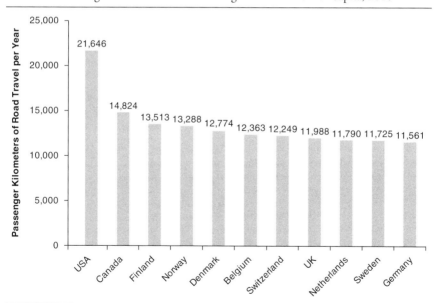

Source: Data from World Bank (2012).

Figure 8.3 Percentage of Daily Trips by Car, Public Transport, Bicycle, and Foot, 2005–2009

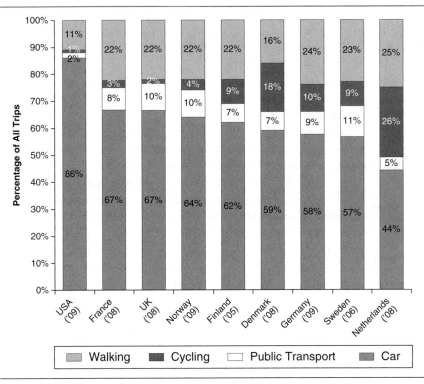

Source: Data collected from national travel surveys in each country.

of all trips are made by car. Far behind are France and the United Kingdom, which are tied for second place at 67 percent of trips by car. Norway and Finland follow closely at 64 percent and 62 percent, respectively. Similar to the pattern of car use shown previously in Figure 8.2, Denmark has a slightly higher car share of trips than Germany (59 percent vs. 58 percent) despite the much higher motorization rate in Germany (589 vs. 477 cars per 1,000 residents). The Netherlands stands out as the least car-dependent country, with only 44 percent of trips by car, roughly half the car share of trips in the United States.

The high levels of walking and cycling in the Netherlands (roughly half of all trips) account for the low share of car trips. Although other European countries have comparable levels of walking (16 percent to 23 percent of trips), no country equals the 26 percent bike share of trips in the Netherlands. Denmark comes closest with 18 percent of trips by bike. Germany, Finland, and Sweden are next at 9 to10 percent of trips by bike. Much further behind are France (3 percent) and the United Kingdom (2 percent), where cycling has become a marginal mode of transport. In last place is the United States, where cycling accounts for only 1 percent of trips. Similarly, the United States comes in last for walking, with only 11 percent of trips by foot, about half of the mode share of walking in the European countries (16 to 25 percent). Since walking and cycling are probably the most sustainable means of travel, the extremely low mode share of walking and cycling in the United States is yet further evidence of the unsustainability of its transport system.

Public transport's mode share also varies widely among countries, from only 2 percent in the United States to 11 percent in Sweden. In most of the European countries, public transport accounts for 7 to 10 percent of trips, about four times the level in the United States. The 5 percent mode share of public transport in the Netherlands is perhaps surprising, but it is because of the extraordinarily high level of cycling in the Netherlands, which often competes with public transport for trips of intermediate distance.

As already suggested earlier, the differences in travel behavior among the countries examined in Figures 8.1 through 8.3 are not mainly attributable to income differences, as all the countries have high per capita incomes, among the highest in the world. One important policy difference is the taxation of car ownership and use. As already noted, the United States has the lowest taxes on car purchases, 4 percent versus a wide range from 19 percent to 180 percent in the other countries (DIW 2005). Perhaps even more important is the gap in taxes on gasoline (petrol). The cost of gasoline is more than twice as high in Europe as in the United States, and almost all the difference in retail price is due to the much higher taxes on gasoline in Europe (International Energy Agency [IEA] 2012)—roughly ten times higher than in the United States (see Figure 8.4). Even Canada has gasoline taxes that are twice as high as in the United States and gasoline prices that are about 50 percent higher. Because fuel expense is the main operating cost of an automobile, this difference in taxation policy is a key explanation for the much higher levels of driving in the United States and the much lower levels of walking, cycling, and public transport use.

Sustainability of Transport Systems in Germany and the United States

Germany and the United States are chosen for detailed comparison in this chapter because of the sharp contrast in the sustainability in their transport systems despite being so similar in many other ways that enable meaningful comparisons of travel behavior. Both Germany and the United States are affluent countries with market economies and federal systems of democratic government. Both countries have vast roadway systems, high rates of car ownership, and roughly the same proportion of licensed drivers. Just as in the United States, most suburban development in

FIGURE 8.4   Premium Unleaded Gasoline Prices and Share of Taxes in 2011 (US $ per Liter; adjusted for PPP)

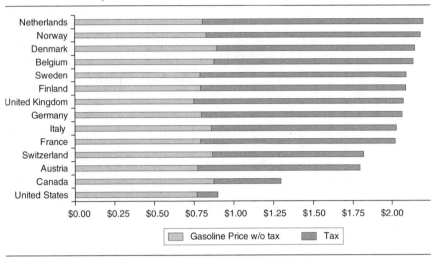

Source: International Energy Agency (2012).

Germany occurred after the Second World War during a period of rapid motorization. These underlying similarities enhance the transferability (or adaptability) of transport policies in Germany to the United States and other affluent countries with high levels of car ownership.

Table 8.1 compares the environmental, economic, and social sustainability of the transport systems of the two countries. Traffic safety is almost twice as high in Germany as in the United States, with less than half as many traffic fatalities per 100,000 residents (5.1 vs. 11.1). That difference is partly attributable to the much higher level of driving per capita in the United States. Even controlling for the amount of car use, the traffic fatality rate per vehicle km driven is 20 percent lower in Germany (5.9 vs. 7.1 fatalities per billion km). Especially striking are the differences in pedestrian and cyclist safety. Pedestrian safety is five times greater in Germany than in the United States (1.9 vs. 9.7 fatalities per 100 million km walked), and cycling safety is more than three times as safe (1.6 vs. 5.5 fatalities per 100 million km cycled) (Buehler and Pucher 2011). The social sustainability of the transport system in Germany exceeds that of the United States not only because of greater safety but also more travel options for everyone. Walking, cycling, and public transport in many parts of the United States are so dangerous, inconvenient, or infeasible that even poor households are forced to buy a car just to get to shopping, employment, education, and medical facilities. Seniors in the United States suffer sharply reduced mobility when they can no longer drive.

TABLE 8.1   Key Indicators for Transport Sustainability in the United States and Germany 2010–2012

		USA	Germany
Social	Traffic fatalities per 100,000 population	11.1	5.1
	Traffic fatalities per 1 billion vehicle kilometers	7.1	5.9
	Cyclist fatalities per 100 million kilometers cycled	5.5	1.6
	Pedestrian fatalities per 100 million kilometers walked	9.7	1.9
	Percent population considered obese (BMI>30; self-reported data)	23.9	12.1
Economic	Share of household expenditures for transportation (percentages)	17.0	14.6
	Annual household expenditures for transportation	$7,677	$5,117
	Ratio of roadway user fees and taxes vs. roadway expenditures by all levels of government	0.58	2.22
	Government subsidy as share of public transportation operating budgets (percentages)	65	25
Environmental	Fuel economy of passenger vehicle fleet (liters per 100 km)	11.4	7.5
	Annual ground passenger transport energy use per person (in gigajoules)	57.6	18.9
	Transportation sector share of CO_2 emissions	32.3	19.6
	Pounds of CO_2 emissions per capita from motor gasoline and diesel combustion	9,112	2,448

Sources: German Federal Ministry of Transportation and Urban Development (BMVBS 1991–2012; International Road Safety and Data Analysis Group (IRTAD) 2012; Organisation for Economic Co-operation and Development (OECD) 2012; USDOT 1990–2012.

Children are almost completely dependent on their parents for mobility. Yet another aspect of social sustainability is overall public health. Some studies show that the extreme dominance of the car in the United States leads to low levels of walking and cycling and low levels of total daily physical activity, contributing to the dangerously high rate of obesity for Americans (23.9 percent of adults vs. 12.1 percent in Germany) (Buehler et al. 2011).

Transport in Germany is also more economically sustainable than in the United States. American households spend an average of 17 percent of their disposable income on transport compared to 14.6 percent in Germany, which amounts to about $2,500 more per year in the United States. For the public sector as well, transport is more economically sustainable in Germany. Federal, state, and local governments combined must subsidize 41 percent of the total operating, maintenance, and construction cost of roadways in the United States. By comparison, the public sector in Germany collects 2.2 times as much revenue from roadway user fees and taxes as the total government expenditures on roadways, yielding surplus funds that are used for a diverse range of other needs, such as education, health, and housing. Just as roadways are more subsidized in the United States than in Germany, American public transport is also more subsidized. As shown in Table 8.1, federal, state, and local governments subsidize 65 percent of the total operating costs of public transport in the United States compared to only 25 percent in Germany, although public transport in Germany is far more extensive and of a much higher quality than in the United States (Buehler and Pucher 2012).

Finally, transport in Germany is more environmentally sustainable than in the United States. In particular, cars and light trucks in Germany are 52 percent more fuel efficient than in the United States (7.5 vs. 11.4 liter per 100 km; 31.4 vs. 20.6 miles per gallon). Combined with the much lower mileage traveled by Germans per year (11,561 km vs. 21,646 km in the US), Germans use only a third as much energy per capita per year for ground transport as Americans (18.9 vs. 57.6 gigajoules). Thanks to the dominance of the car in the American transport system, the long distances traveled on a daily basis, and the relative fuel inefficiency of American cars, the transport sector in the United States accounts for 30 percent of total CO_2 emissions in the country, compared to 20 percent in Germany.

Although there are surely many other possible indicators of sustainability, all available indicators suggest a much higher level of sustainability in Germany along all three major dimensions: social, economic, and environmental. The sections that follow examine the governmental policies in Germany and the United States that help explain the greater sustainability of transport in Germany.

Federal Policies in Germany

The German federal government provides strong incentives for sustainable transport through a wide range of policies. Federal taxes and regulations make car use much more expensive than in the United States, thus encouraging the production and purchase of less polluting and more energy-efficient vehicles. Reinforcing those car-restrictive policies, the federal government provides dedicated funding for public transport investments. Various federal transport funds can be used by states and cities for infrastructure improvements that enhance the safety and convenience of walking and cycling. Federal law requires the cooperation of federal, state, regional, and local levels of government in the land-use planning process, as well as coordination of land-use planning among communities in the same region. The federal government provides strategic leadership and integration of transport and land-use policies within and among all levels of government, starting at the federal level with the consolidated Federal Ministry of Transport, Building and Urban Affairs.

Federal Transport Policies

Federal taxes and regulations make car ownership and use more expensive in Germany than in the United States. In 2011, sales taxes on automobiles were 19 percent, about four times higher than in most US states (ranging from 0 percent to 7 percent, with an average of 4 percent). Similarly, gasoline (petrol) taxes were about nine times higher in Germany ($4.84 vs. $0.53 per gallon) (Buehler, Pucher, and Kunert 2009). The difference in the retail price of gasoline (petrol) in Germany increased significantly from 1999 through 2003 because of a special environmental tax, which incrementally raised the gasoline tax by the equivalent of 70¢ per gallon (US) over five years (Umweltbundesamt [UBA] 2005). Strict EU vehicle regulations, combined with high gasoline taxes and vehicle-registration fees in Germany, favor less polluting and more fuel efficient vehicles. The result is that in 2011, the average fuel economy of German cars and light trucks was 52 percent higher than in the United States (7.5 vs. 11.4 liter per 100 km; 31.4 vs. 20.6 miles per gallon) (BMVBS 1991–2012; USDOT 2000–2012).

Revenues from gasoline taxes and vehicle registration fees in Germany have covered an increasing share of federal, state, and local government expenditures on road construction and maintenance—rising from 92 percent in 1975 to 222 percent in 2010. Thus, roadway user taxes and fees in Germany are more than twice as high as government roadway expenditures. In sharp contrast, roadway users in the United States have covered only 60 to 70 percent of government roadway expenditures (all levels combined) over the same time period. Whereas American federal gasoline tax revenues are earmarked for transport, federal gasoline tax revenues in Germany flow into the general fund, which can be used for any government program.

In both Germany and the United States, the federal government has paid for the construction of limited access highways (the German Autobahn and the US Interstate Highway System). The German federal government, however, has not financed limited access highways within urban areas, only between them and around them (TRB 1998). By comparison, over half the vehicle miles traveled on the US Interstate Highway System (63 percent in 2010) are within urban areas (USDOT 1990–2012). The lack of high-speed urban freeways in Germany, combined with widespread traffic calming of residential neighborhoods, might help explain why the average speed of car travel in German cities is 20 percent slower than in American cities (31km/h vs. 38km/h) (BMVBS 2010; USDOT 2010b).

German state and federal governments jointly develop the Federal Transport Plan, which delineates national transport strategy. Until the early 1970s, this plan focused mainly on automobile travel. Since 1973, however, the plan has included societal goals, such as preserving open space and reducing traffic fatalities, energy use, and vehicle emissions. Since the mid-1970s, the federal government has encouraged the coordination of transport planning across modes and jurisdictional boundaries. For example, the German federal government has provided dedicated matching funds to state and local governments for public transport capital investments—if projects are part of local comprehensive transport plans, comply with land-use plans, and consider the needs of the disabled and the elderly (BMVBS 2005).

The German federal government's role in promoting walking and cycling primarily involves federal traffic laws protecting cyclists and pedestrians and making their safety an integral part of the German driver's license test. Most innovations, however, such as car-free pedestrian zones and integrated, citywide bicycling networks were pioneered and then widely implemented at the local government level. The federal government supported local efforts with technical guidance and flexible funding mechanisms, which allowed municipalities to divert highway funds to nonmotorized modes.

Since the passage of the Intermodal Surface Transportation Efficiency Act (ISTEA) in 1991, the US federal government has also increased funding for public transport, walking, and cycling. However, ISTEA's attempts to promote alternatives to driving were accompanied by simultaneous increases in federal expenditures on roadways. ISTEA required and helped fund regional transport planning and coordination. However, most metropolitan planning organizations (MPOs) do not have any legal authority or political power to enforce regional policy priorities or to alter decisions made by local government jurisdictions or state departments of transport. Moreover, MPOs do not make any specific land-use planning decisions.

Federal Regulation of Land-Use Planning

In Germany, federal, state, regional, and local governments interact in a bottom-up and top-down land-use planning process, which is organized around cooperation and mediation. In general, lower levels of government participate in the preparation of plans at the next higher level of land-use planning. For example, municipalities contribute to plans at the regional level, regional representatives provide input into state plans, and state officials are represented at the federal level. Once plans are made, lower levels of government are bound by the regulations, goals, and objectives outlined in that plan. The lower the level of government, the more detailed the content of the plan. Federal involvement in spatial planning is limited to defining the legal framework for planning, ensuring consistency of planning techniques, and—in collaboration with the states—setting broad strategic goals for spatial development such as sustainability.

Similar to communities in the United States, municipal governments in Germany draw up detailed land-use plans and decide the specific allowable uses of land. Local plans in Germany, however, are restricted by regional and state plans and must be in compliance with federal land use, transport, and environmental laws. At each level of government, land-use planning is explicitly coordinated with housing, transport, and environmental plans. Neighboring jurisdictions are required by law to seek input from each other, forcing states, regions, and municipalities to collaborate with their peers.

The right to develop property is highly circumscribed in Germany. New development is limited by law to areas immediately adjacent to already built-up areas—though exceptions are made on a case-by-case basis. Even in the case of privately owned land, developers and the municipality must convince higher levels of government to permit development of areas not adjacent to already existing settlements.

In sharp contrast, there is no federal land-use planning in the United States, except for federally owned land. Only a few states, such as Maryland and New Jersey, have attempted to develop and enforce state land-use plans. As a result, most land-use planning in the United States is fragmented, uncoordinated, and almost always in the domain of local government jurisdictions.

The federal policies described above establish the framework and provide funding for local policies that make transport more sustainable. The remainder of this chapter focuses on the German city of Freiburg, which introduced many innovative policies that later spread throughout Germany.

Sustainable Transport in Freiburg

Freiburg has 225,000 inhabitants and is the economic, cultural, and political center of the Black Forest region in southwestern Germany. The region has a population of 635,000 and is less than an hour's travel from Switzerland and France. Freiburg's economy is based on tourism, university teaching and research, government and church administration, and a broad range of services provided to the surrounding region (City of Freiburg 2011).

From 1950 to 1970, motorization grew rapidly in Freiburg (from 28 to 248 cars per 1,000 inhabitants) and was higher than for West Germany as a whole (13 in 1950 and 208 in 1970). After the policy reversal in the early 1970s, the automobile ownership rate in Freiburg increased more slowly than the German average. Indeed, from 1990 to 2011, the motorization rate remained stable at 420 per 1,000 inhabitants—30 percent below the German average of 590 in 2011. While motorization levels stagnated, car use decreased in Freiburg. The car share of trips in Freiburg fell from 38 percent to 32 percent between 1982 and 2007, a period when the car's mode share was increasing rapidly almost everywhere else in the world. Over the same period, the bike share of trips in Freiburg almost doubled, from 15 percent to 27 percent, and public transport's share of trips rose from 11 percent to 18 percent.

Freiburg's transport system has become more sustainable in recent decades. From 1990 to 2006, vehicle km of car use per capita in Freiburg declined by 7 percent on all roads and by 13 percent on residential roads. From 1992 to 2005, transport CO_2 emissions per capita in Freiburg fell by 13.4 percent to a level that is 89 percent of the German average and only 29 percent of the American average (Öko-Institut e.V. 2007). Travel is about twice as safe in Freiburg as in Germany as a whole and more than four times as safe as in the United States: 2.6 traffic fatalities per 100,000 inhabitants in Freiburg versus 5.1 in Germany and 11.1 in the United States (Buehler and Pucher 2011). Moreover, social equity is high since all parts of the city are easily accessible by public transport, cycling, and walking. Finally, the financial viability of public transport is high in Freiburg, requiring only 11 percent of its operating costs to be subsidized through government funds, compared to 25 percent for Germany as a whole and 67 percent in the United States (Buehler and Pucher 2012).

The trend away from car use and toward more sustainable transport in Freiburg occurred despite strong population growth, rising incomes, and a booming economy. From 1990 to 2011, Freiburg's population increased nine times faster than the German average (17 percent vs. less than 2 percent). From 1996 to 2010, the number of jobs in Freiburg grew at three times the overall German rate. In 2010, per capita income in Freiburg was 29 percent higher than for Germany as a whole and 16 percent higher than for the United States.

Economic success and widespread political support for sustainability facilitated changes in Freiburg's transport and land-use policies. Since the 1970s, the city has increasingly restricted car use while promoting public transport, cycling, and walking. That combined carrot-and-stick approach has been crucial to generating public and political support for sustainable transport. Perhaps most important, car restrictive measures are not viewed as punitive, since car users are offered safe, convenient, and affordable alternatives.

Integrating Transport and Land-Use Planning in Freiburg

Freiburg's old town was almost completely destroyed in bombing raids during the Second World War. That was the beginning of Freiburg's remarkable history of transport and land-use planning. In 1948, Freiburg's city administration decided to rebuild the city center in its historic compact form. Most of Freiburg's postwar population growth, however, was accommodated in new settlements at the fringe of the existing city. Indeed, similar to many American cities, Freiburg's land-use plan of 1955 endorsed geographic expansion of the city, centered on automobile transport. During this period, old streetcar lines were abandoned and service was cut back, since buses and the automobile were deemed the modes of transport of the future. Land-use plans gave priority to new greenfield developments with wide streets and ample car parking. Even the old town was adapted to the automobile—with new parking lots on historic squares and a direct highway connection from downtown to the Autobahn. During this time, car ownership and use increased, and so did air pollution, traffic fatalities, and traffic congestion (Buehler and Pucher 2011).

Freiburg's second auto-oriented land-use plan of the 1960s was never approved by the city council and was shelved in the early 1970s after long, controversial discussions among the public, council members, and the administration. By then, public opinion had shifted away from supporting automobile centered growth—because of various environmental and social problems caused by the car and the oil crisis of 1973. Over the last forty years, Freiburg has developed a strong tradition of cooperation, negotiation, and consensus among city administration, citizen groups, and local businesses. This cooperation paved the way for a gradual change toward sustainability in Freiburg (Buehler and Pucher 2011).

Freiburg's first integrated transport plan of 1969 had inadvertently laid the foundation for the changes to come. Although still focusing on car use, the plan recommended preserving and potentially expanding the streetcar network, a suggestion the city council adopted in 1972. The early 1970s also saw Freiburg's first integrated bicycling network plan and a new car-free pedestrian zone in the center of old town—the largest pedestrian zone in all of Germany at the time. Citizen groups had successfully lobbied the city administration to restrict car access to downtown, but local business owners at first opposed this idea. The city administration, citizen groups, and local businesses eventually reached a consensus to ban cars from downtown and provide automobile parking garages along a ring road at the fringes of the car-free zone.

Many of the fragmented policies implemented in the 1970s were formalized into official transport and land-use plans beginning in the late 1970s. In 1979, Freiburg's second integrated transport plan focused on environmental protection and sustainable development. The new plan favored public transport, walking, and cycling over the automobile and called for the integration of transport and land-use planning. Priorities for land-use policies shifted accordingly. The land-use plan of 1981 prescribed that new development was to be concentrated along public transport corridors, especially the city's expanding light-rail system.

A. Freiburg's Cathedral Square was used as a car park in the 1960s (above left). During the mid-1970s cars were banned. It is now a lively pedestrian zone with an open air market (above right).

B. In the 1960s, Klarastrasse in Freiburg was dominated by cars, with hardly any room for pedestrians and cyclists (above left). Since traffic calming in the late 1980s, the amount of car traffic has fallen, and also greatly slowed down, transforming Klarastrasse into the safe and quiet neighborhood street it is today (above right).

C. In the 1970s, both lanes of the Wiwili Bridge in Freiburg were reserved for motor vehicles (above left). In the 1990s, the bridge was closed to cars and is now a bicycle bridge providing a key connection between the western residential neighborhoods of Freiburg and the main train station and city center (above right).

Photos provided by the City of Freiburg and Karl-Heinz Raach, Freiburg.

During the 1980s, the city council—encouraged by neighborhood associations—voted to traffic calm all residential neighborhoods to 30 km/hr (19 mph) and to discourage through traffic. The cost of driving was further increased by parking management schemes that limited long-term parking and charged higher fees. The updating of Freiburg's transport plan in 1989 reemphasized the explicit goal of limiting car travel and increasing use of the green modes—walking, cycling, and public transport.

From 1993 to 2011, Freiburg redeveloped two inner suburban neighborhoods around newly extended light-rail lines. Both districts sharply limit car access and parking. All streets are traffic calmed at 30 km/hr (19 mph) or less. Similar to the *woonerf* in the Netherlands and the *home zone* in the United Kingdom, many neighborhood roads are designated as *Spielstrassen*, streets with speed limits set at 7 km/hr (4mph) and traffic priority for pedestrians, cyclists, and playing children. Both communities are compactly laid out and mix residential, commercial, educational, religious, and recreational land uses. They provide a wide range of housing types for low-income as well as affluent households and specifically favor inclusion of women, families, the elderly, and persons with disabilities. Both settlements feature attractive green spaces, low-energy construction methods, solar energy, and rain water reuse (Buehler and Pucher 2011).

Freiburg's most recent land-use and transport plans of 2008 were developed simultaneously and are fully integrated. Both reiterate the earlier goals of reducing car use, but they are more explicit about prohibiting car-dependent developments and actively support car-free neighborhoods. The plans focus on compact

Young families with children in one of the many *Spielstrassen* (home zones) in Freiburg.
Photo: Peter Berkeley

development along light-rail routes, strengthening local neighborhood commercial and service centers, and mixing housing with stores, restaurants, offices, schools, and other nonresidential land uses. Central development is explicitly favored over peripheral development at the suburban fringe. The city has banned all car-dependent, big-box retailers such as home improvement stores, furniture stores, and garden centers, not only because of the car traffic they generate but also because they draw customers away from central city and neighborhood retailers. Moreover, the new land-use plan identifies thirty priority locations for small retail businesses in Freiburg's neighborhood centers, with the goal of keeping trip distances short and assuring local accessibility on foot and by bicycle (City of Freiburg 2008a).

The city coordinated its plans with nineteen neighboring municipalities and twelve special purpose government districts in the region. The plans were developed with extensive citizen participation at every stage and reflect widespread support for environmental protection. Through the political process, Freiburgers have consistently supported restrictions on the overall amount of land available for development outside of already built-up areas. In the Freiburg region, as in most other German regions, large areas of land in and near the city have been explicitly zoned for agriculture (many vineyards and fruit orchards), forest preserves, wildlife sanctuaries, or simply as undeveloped open space. Freiburgers value these undeveloped green corridors throughout the city as important destinations for everyday recreational activities. As documented in the following sections, the complete turnaround in Freiburg's transport policies in the 1970s resulted in dramatic improvements for public transport, bicycling, and walking, while making car use more expensive, slower, and less convenient.

Improvements in Public Transport

After two decades of cutting streetcar services in the 1950s and 1960s, only 14 kilometers of old streetcar lines were still in operation in Freiburg in 1970 (Schröder 2009). Service was slow, infrequent, and outdated; Freiburg's public transport ridership had been continuously declining. Expanding and upgrading the light-rail system was at the center of Freiburg's multifaceted strategy to integrate public transport and land-use planning. Since the opening of the first new light-rail line in 1983, Freiburg has added four new lines with a total extent of 36.4 km in 2010. During the same period, the supply of light-rail service almost tripled. In 2011, 65 percent of Freiburg's residents and 70 percent of all jobs were located within easy walking distance (500 meters) from a light-rail stop (Buehler and Pucher 2011).

Since 1996, Freiburg has improved its regional suburban rail and regional bus system, expanding services from 2.7 billion to 3.5 billion seat kilometers per year

(Zweckverband Regio-Nahverkehr Freiburg [ZRF] 2011). Passenger kilometre of regional rail use rose sixfold between 1997 and 2010, and total public transport demand in the City of Freiburg and the surrounding region increased by more than 70 percent (RVG 2011). Light-rail, regional rail, and bus service timetables are fully integrated in Freiburg. Real-time information is provided by digital displays at rail stations, light-rail stops, and key bus stops. Both light-rail and bus services are faster and more reliable because of traffic signal priority, with lights turning green for oncoming trains and buses at key intersections.

These policies were complemented with an attractively priced, unified ticketing system, which enables riders to use a single ticket for several trip segments and different types of service. In 1984, Freiburg's public transport system offered Germany's first monthly ticket transferable to other users—called the *environmental ticket*. In 1991, the geographic coverage of the environmental ticket was expanded to include the two adjacent counties. These monthly tickets have offered bargain fares for regular public transport users for unlimited travel within the entire region. The percentage of public transport riders using monthly tickets rose from only 39 percent in 1974 to 93 percent in 2011. The environmental ticket introduced in 1984 contributed to the 42 percent increase in ridership between 1984 and 1990. Similarly, the introduction of the regional ticket in 1991 helped increase public transport trips regionwide by more than 70 percent between 1991 and 2010 (Buehler and Pucher 2012).

Pedestrians, bicyclists, and public transport in Freiburg's car-free city center.
Photo: Ralph Buehler

Services, fares, and subsidies for the entire Freiburg region are coordinated by a regional public transport association (ZRF), which serves 635,000 residents in seventy-five towns. ZRF sets the overall public transport policy in the region and develops and updates the regional public transport plan for 17 different bus and rail operators, ninety different lines, and 3,050 km of routes. It is also responsible for receiving funding from federal, state, and local governments and then distributing those funds among public transport operators to cover investment and operating expenses (Buehler and Pucher 2011).

In summary, Freiburg and its surrounding region significantly increased the quantity and quality of public transport services. A higher share of trips by public transport has increased its financial sustainability and reduced CO_2 emissions. Since January 2009, Freiburg's light-rail system has run solely on electricity generated by wind, solar, and water power, thus further decreasing the carbon footprint of transport in Freiburg.

Promoting Bicycling and Walking for Short Trips

The total number of bike trips in Freiburg more than tripled between 1976 and 2010, from 69,500 to 211,000—almost one bike trip per inhabitant per day (City of Freiburg 2011). Between 1982 and 1989, the share of trips by foot in Freiburg fell from 35 percent in 1982 to 23 percent, apparently due to an increase in trip distances and a shift from walking to cycling and public transport. Since 1990, however, the walk share has remained stable in Freiburg, while it has been declining in Germany as a whole.

The decline in walking in the 1980s may have resulted from the city's focus on cycling. Freiburg expanded its network of separate bike paths and lanes from only 29 km in 1972 to 160 km in 2011. Together with 120 km of bike paths through forests and agricultural areas, 400 km of traffic-calmed roads, and 2 km of bicycle streets, Freiburg's cycling facilities have been fully integrated into a 682 km bikeway network. Cyclists can ride on separate facilities and safe, lightly traveled streets between virtually any two points in the city (City of Freiburg 2012).

The city has traffic calmed most residential streets. In 2008, about 90 percent of Freiburgers lived on streets with speed limits of 30 km/hr or less (City of Freiburg 2008b). Speed limits are even further reduced to 7 km/hr in 177 home zones—where cyclists and pedestrians have priority over cars. Traffic-calmed neighborhood streets and home zones encourage more cycling and walking and make them safer. Freiburg allows cyclists to use 70 percent of the city's 125 one-way streets in either direction, while motorists are restricted to one direction—thus shortening bike trips compared to car travel distances (City of Freiburg 2012).

Cyclists on a bicycle path along the Dreisam River in Freiburg.
Photo: City of Freiburg

Over the past three decades, the city has been increasing the supply of bike parking, improving its quality, and integrating it with public transport stops. Between 1987 and 2011, the number of bike parking spaces in downtown almost tripled, rising from 2,200 to 6,040. There are now 1,678 bike parking spots at public transport bike-and-ride facilities. In addition, there is a large bike station at Freiburg's main train station with secure, sheltered parking for 1,000 bikes, bike rental, bike repair, travel advice, and bike shipment to other cities. Not only does the city provide bike parking directly, but it also requires bike parking in all new buildings with two or more apartments, as well as schools, universities, and businesses (City of Freiburg 2012).

Freiburg has encouraged walking primarily through the car-free zone in the center, traffic calming of residential streets, and compact new developments that generate short, walkable trips. Walking in Freiburg's car-free old town has been thriving, with 69 percent of all trips on foot in 2007. For the city as a whole, however, walking levels have stagnated, stabilizing after a long period of decline. In the future, Freiburg plans to improve the connectivity and safety of its citywide walkway network and establish more pedestrian-friendly neighborhood centers.

Restrictions on Car Use

Many of the policies that promote public transport, bicycling, and walking involve restrictions on car use, such as car-free zones and traffic-calmed neighborhoods.

Freiburg's official goal is to reduce car use as much as practical but to selectively accommodate car trips that cannot be made by any other mode. Thus, the city combines disincentives to car use in the town center and residential neighborhoods with improvements of arterials that have been widened to increase their carrying capacity (Buehler and Pucher 2011).

Freiburg's parking policy is designed to make car use less convenient and more expensive. Parking garages are relegated to the periphery of the city center, thus forcing motorists to walk or take public transport to access their cars. In many residential neighborhoods, parking is reserved for residents only and requires a special permit. On-street parking in commercial areas of the city becomes more expensive with proximity to the center. Almost all on-street car parking is limited in duration to prevent long-term parking by commuters. Building codes have reduced parking requirements for cars in new residential developments while increasing parking provisions for bikes (City of Freiburg 2012).

Lessons from Germany

There are many aspects of Freiburg's sustainable transport and land-use policies that could be adapted for use by cities in other countries. For each of the seven lessons listed below, specific examples in the United States that demonstrate the adaptability of Freiburg's approach for use elsewhere are noted. Policies that are feasible in the extremely car-dominated United States are probably transferable to other car-dependent countries like Australia and Canada.

1. *Implement controversial policies in stages.* Freiburg implemented most of its policies in stages, often choosing projects almost everybody agreed upon first. For example, residential traffic calming was initially implemented in neighborhoods whose residents complained most about car travel. Successful implementation in one neighborhood encouraged other areas of the city to request traffic calming as well. Some American cities already use a similar approach. For example, in 2009, New York City closed Broadway to car traffic between Herald Square and Times Square to experiment with a pedestrian plaza. The city has made the change permanent because the trial was successful and won public support (New York City Department of Transportation 2012).

2. *Plans should be flexible and adaptable over time to changing conditions.* Over the last forty years, Freiburg phased in and adjusted its policies and goals gradually over time. The initial decision to keep the remaining streetcar system was made in the late 1960s. In the early 1970s, the city council approved the extension of the system and its upgrading to a modern light-rail system, which finally opened in 1983. Once the expansion had proved successful, more new light-rail lines followed. This phased approach can be found in many American cities, such as the

light-rail extensions in Minneapolis, Minnesota—where the successful Hiawatha Line triggered public demand for a second light-rail line connecting Minneapolis to St. Paul (Metropolitan Council 2009).

3. *Policies must be multimodal and include both incentives and disincentives.* Freiburg has simultaneously made public transport, cycling, and walking viable alternatives to the automobile, while increasing the cost of car travel. Improving quality and level of service of alternative modes of transport made car-restrictive measures politically acceptable. The problem with car-restrictive measures in the United States is that Americans rely on the car for about 90 percent of their trips. Thus, car-restrictive measures are opposed by the vast majority of the population. As cities improve their public transport systems, as well as conditions for walking and bicycling, the political feasibility of restricting car use should increase. For example, as bicycling in Portland, Oregon, increased sixfold between 1990 and 2012, the city transformed hundreds of car parking spaces into bike parking, converted residential roads into traffic-calmed bicycling boulevards, converted car lanes to bike lanes, and changed traffic signals to prioritize bicycles and public transport (City of Portland 2012).

4. *Fully integrate transport and land-use planning.* Policies promoting public transport, cycling, and walking rely on a settlement pattern that keeps trip distances short and residences and workplaces within reach of public transport. There are some successful examples of transit-oriented land use policies in the United States. Since the early 1980s, Arlington County in Virginia developed high-density, mixed-use neighborhoods around four stations of the Washington DC-region's metro system (Transit Cooperative Research Program 2004). A more recent program is the Transit Village Initiative in New Jersey. Since 1999, the state government, in cooperation with New Jersey Transit, has subsidized and facilitated mixed-use, compact development around rail stations in twenty-six cities (New Jersey Department of Transportation 2013).

5. *Citizen involvement must be an integral part of policy development and implementation.* Since the 1970s, citizen participation has been a key aspect of transport and land-use planning in Freiburg. Over time, public opinion in Freiburg has become increasingly supportive of sustainable policies. Portland, Oregon, is probably the best example in the United States, with a history of citizen participation in transport, land-use, and environmental planning. Public involvement has been institutionalized into Portland's transport planning process through a city-funded network of neighborhood associations. Virtually every transport project includes public meetings, citizen advisory boards, focus groups, surveys, and public hearings to ensure citizen participation at every stage (Abbott and Margheim 2008).

6. *Support from higher levels of government is crucial to making local policies work.* Starting in the 1970s, the German federal government reduced funding for

highways and provided more flexible funds for improvements in local transport infrastructure—including public transport, walking, and cycling. Federal government support for public transport, walking, and bicycling has greatly increased in the United States since the early 1990s (USDOT 2010a). The current federal transportation legislation, Moving Ahead for Progress in the 21st Century (MAP-21), is only valid until October 2014, but it considerably reduces federal funding for walking, cycling, and public transport. The future of federal funding for alternatives to the car is uncertain because of political controversy over funding priorities and deficits in the federal transportation trust fund (USDOT 2013).

7.   *Sustainable transport policies must be long term, with policies sustained over time, for lasting impact.* Freiburg started its journey toward more sustainable transport almost forty years ago. Some policies can be implemented quickly, but changes in travel behavior and a more sustainable transport system take much longer. The experience of Portland, Oregon, over the past decades suggests that successful policies there have been self-reinforcing, generating public support and thus enabling even more sustainable policies in successive years (Abbott and Margheim 2008).

Conclusion

Despite many similarities between the United States and Germany in their political and economic systems, Germany's transport system is more sustainable along all three dimensions: social, economic, and environmental. As shown in this chapter, government policies at the federal, state, and local level account for much of the difference in travel behavior and sustainability between the two countries. It is unlikely that German policies could be fully transferred to the extremely car-oriented American context. But as noted in the preceding lessons, many policies have already been adapted at least in part by American cities, thus increasing the overall sustainability of the transport system in the country. The biggest difference is that American cities rarely implement policies that make car use more costly, slower, and less convenient. Incentives for walking, cycling, and public transport can work alone to some extent. However, Germany's example shows that combining incentives for walking, cycling, and public transport with policies that restrict car use has the potential to further increase the sustainability of the transport system.

References

Abbott, C., and J. Margheim. "Imagining Portland's urban growth boundary: Planning regulation as cultural icon." *Journal of the American Planning Association* 74, no. 2 (2008): 196–208.

American Public Transportation Association. *Public transportation factbook 2011.* Washington, DC: American Public Transportation Association, 2012.

Buehler, R., and J. Pucher. "Demand for public transport in Germany and the USA: An analysis of rider characteristics." *Transport Reviews* 32, no. 5 (2012): 541–67.

Buehler, R., and J. Pucher. "Sustainable transport in Freiburg: Lessons from Germany's environmental capital." *International Journal of Sustainable Transportation* 5, no. 1 (2011): 43–70.

Buehler, R., J. Pucher, D. Merom, and A. Bauman. "Active travel in Germany and the USA: Contributions of daily walking and cycling to physical activity." *American Journal of Preventive Medicine* 40, no. 9 (2011): 241–50.

Buehler, R., J. Pucher, and U. Kunert. *Making transportation sustainable: Insights from Germany.* Washington, DC: Brookings Institution, 2009.

City of Freiburg. *Flächennutzungsplan.* Freiburg: City of Freiburg, 2008a.

———. *Verkehrsentwicklungsplan Freiburg Breisgau.* Freiburg: City of Freiburg, 2008b.

———. *FRITZ Daten Online.* Freiburg: City of Freiburg, 2011.

———. *Bicycling in Freiburg.* Freiburg: City of Freiburg, 2012.

City of Portland. *Bicycles.* Portland: City of Portland Bureau of Transportation, 2012.

European Union Commission. *A European vision for sustainable transport.* Brussels: European Commission, 2009.

———. *Bericht fuer das Jahr 2005 ueber die Finanzhilfen des Bundes zur Verbesserung der Verkehrsverhältnisse der Gemeinden nach dem Gemeindeverkehrsfinanzierungsgesetz* [Federal Subsidies for Local Transportation Projects]. Berlin: German Federal Ministry of Transportation and Urban Development, 2005.

German Federal Ministry of Transportation and Urban Development. *Verkehr in Zahlen* [German transport in figures]. Berlin: German Federal Ministry of Transportation and Urban Development, 1991–2012.

———. *Mobilität in Deutschland 2008/2009* [Mobility in Germany 2008/2009]. Bonn: German Federal Ministry of Transportation, 2008.

German Institute for Economic Research. *Die Abgaben auf Kraftfahrzeuge in Europa im Jahr 2005.* Berlin: German Institute for Economic Research, 2005.

International Energy Agency. *Energy prices and taxes.* New York: International Energy Agency, 2012.

International Road Safety and Data Analysis Group. *Traffic safety statistics.* Paris: International Road Safety and Data Analysis Group, Organization for Economic Co-operation and Development, 2012.

Metropolitan Council. *Central corridor light rail transit.* St. Paul, MN: Twin Cities Metropolitan Council, 2009.

Millard-Ball, A., and L. Schipper. "Are we reaching peak travel? Trends in passenger transport in eight industrialized countries." *Transport Reviews* 31, no. 3 (2011): 357–78.

New Jersey Department of Transportation. *Transit villages initiative.* Trenton: New Jersey Department of Transportation, 2013.

New York City Department of Transportation. *Broadway pilot program: Improving traffic flow & safety in the heart of midtown.* New York: New York City Department of Transportation, 2012.

Organization for Economic Cooperation and Development. *OECD Factbook.* Paris: Organization for Economic Cooperation and Development, 2012.

Öko-Institut e.V. *Klimaschutz-Strategie der Stadt Freiburg.* Freiburg: City of Freiburg, 2007. http://www.freiburg.de/pb/site/Freiburg/get/369489/Klimaschutzstrategie%20Szenarien%20und%20Ma%C3%9Fnahmenplan.pdf.

Pucher, J., Z. R. Peng, N. Mittal, Y. Zhu, and N. Korattyswaroopam. "Urban transport trends and policies in China and India: Impacts of rapid economic growth." *Transport Reviews* 27, no. 4 (2007): 379–410.

Regio Verbund Gesellschaft mbh. *Freiburger Verkehrs AG Entwicklung Fahrgäste/Defizit 1980–2010.* Freiburg: Regio Verbund Gesellschaft mbh, 2011.

Schröder, E. J. "Verkehrsentwicklung in der südlichen Euroregion Oberrhein." *Internationales Verkehrswesen* 61, no. 5 (2009): 155–61.

Transit Cooperative Research Program. *Transit-oriented development in the United States: Experiences, challenges, and prospects.* TCRP Report 102. Washington, DC: National Academies, Transportation Research Board, Transit Cooperative Research Program, 2004.

————. *Achieving traffic safety goals in the United States: Lessons from other nations.* TRB Special Report #300. Washington, DC: National Academies, Transportation Research Board, 2010.

Transportation Research Board. *Consequences of the interstate highway system for transit: Summary of findings.* Washington, DC: Transportation Research Board, 1998.

Umweltbundesamt. *Was Bringt die Ökosteuer – Weniger Kraftstoffverbrauch oder Tanktourismus.* Dessau: Umweltbundesamt, 2005.

US Department of Transportation. *Highway statistics.* Washington, DC: US Department of Transportation, Federal Highway Administration, 1990–2012.

————. *Transportation statistics.* Washington, DC: US Department of Transportation, Federal Highway Administration, 2000–2012.

————. *HUD, DOT and EPA partnership: Sustainable communities.* Washington, DC: US Department of Transportation, Federal Highway Administration, 2009.

————. *Federal-aid highway program funding for pedestrian and bicycle facilities and programs—FY 1992–2010.* Washington, DC: US Department of Transportation, Federal Highway Administration, 2010a.

————. *National household travel survey 2008/2009.* Washington, DC: US Department of Transportation, Federal Highway Administration, 2010b.

————. *MAP-21: Moving ahead for progress in the 21ˢᵗ century.* Washington, DC: Department of Transportation, Federal Highway Administration, 2013.

Verband Deutscher Verkehrsunternehmen. *VDV Statistik 2010.* Berlin: Verband Deutscher Verkehrsunternehmen, 2011.

World Health Organization. *Global burden of disease.* New York: World Health Organization, 2009.

World Bank. *World development indicators.* Washington, DC: World Bank, 2012.

Zweckverband Regio-Nahverkehr Freiburg. *Mobilität für die Region.* Freiburg: Zweckverband Regio-Nahverkehr Freiburg, 2011.

CHAPTER 9

Political Democracy: Consensus Building Through Democracy in Europe

Steven Hill

A functioning political democracy is a prerequisite to having an economic system that works for everyone instead of just the better off and the powerful. Most national democracies in Europe are founded on unique political, media, and communication institutions and methods that foster inclusiveness, participation, authentic representation, multiparty democracy, and majoritarian policy based on a consensus of viewpoints. These methods include proportional representation electoral systems, public financing of campaigns, free media time for candidates and parties, universal/automatic voter registration, Question Time, Children's Parliaments, exercises in deliberative democracy, and other methods that foster pluralism, relatively high voter participation, and consensus building. Having multiple parties in their national legislatures has ensured that a broad cross section of viewpoints is at the table of political power, participating in the formation of majoritarian policy. This process has been aided by Europe's various media and communications institutions, which are centered on a well-financed and robust public broadcasting sector (television and radio), a still vibrant newspaper industry, as well as widespread, affordable access to speedy broadband Internet. These in turn have produced one of the most informed publics in the world.

The United States, on the other hand, is plagued by an antiquated, geographic-based, winner-take-all system in which most legislative districts and many states have become one-party fiefdoms with little competition or choice for voters. Voter turnout for national legislative races is one of the lowest in the world among established democracies, generally less than half the number of eligible voters. Women, young people, and other demographics remain vastly underrepresented. Low-population (and usually conservative) states receive far more representation per capita in the US Senate and in presidential elections, even as sensible policy proposals with nationwide support get strangled by Senate filibusters led by senators representing a small proportion of the nation's population. The US corporate media vets which candidates and issues the public will hear about, the newspaper industry is on shaky ground, and public broadcasting is so poorly funded and lacking in visibility or hard-hitting, BBC-like journalism that it cannot act as a counterbalance to the for-profit media corporations. With its political and media institutions unsuited for the challenge of policy formation in the twenty-first century, the American system has become polarized and paralyzed, a barrier to the enactment of new public policies that could address the many serious challenges the country faces.

Most of Europe's democracies, particularly at the national/member state level, are better adapted than America's democracy for the demands of representation, consensus seeking, and policy formation in the twenty-first century. To be sure, European democracies have their share of flaws and they vary in the extent to which they employ the various institutions and practices described in this chapter. Moreover, the global economic crisis tested the resiliency of the world's democracies and, like the United States, various European states exhibited some democratic shortcomings. But even in the midst of the ongoing eurozone challenges, most European national democracies have performed remarkably well (democracy at the continental level, however, is a different story, where the institutions of the European Union are still young and in formation). While recognizing the great diversity across the continent, it is still possible to identify many institutions and practices that are common across most European democracies—and that differ in fundamental ways from US institutions and practices.

Indeed, Europe's thriving, pluralistic, democracies are the most important reason Europeans have been able to harness their capitalist economy to enact a more broadly shared prosperity, universal health care and other supports for families and individuals, and environmental sustainability. In trying to understand Europe's development model—which in other writings I have termed *social capitalism* and the *European Way* (Hill 2010)—Europe's vibrant political democracies have received too little attention. While economy and culture are the twin cores of our daily lives, political democracy is the means for deciding who will sit at the table of power, making policy that affects everything else. In a democracy, the political institutions must shape the economy and mediate the cultural milieu, not the other way around, or vast inequality and political and social polarization will result.

European Democracy's Slow and Patient Rise

Europe's centuries-long evolution of a democratic spirit never was a straightforward path but rather one filled with violence, hypocrisy, and setbacks. As a reaction to their blood-soaked history, the nations of Europe have forged political institutions that foster inclusiveness, participation, authentic representation, multiparty democracy, and majoritarian policy based on a consensus of viewpoints.

Europe's advanced democracy is evident in fascinating ways, large and small, incorporating macro- and microinstitutions. On the little *d* democracy side, we see microinstitutions such as Question Time in Britain, Sweden, Italy, France, and elsewhere, an often televised weekly grilling of the prime minister and other government officials by the opposition party. In Britain, Question Time provides great political theater, and it is informative as well. A rather simple change like Question Time in the United States might force more transparency as well as public engagement, and even alter the types of people who become candidates since elected leaders would need to be eloquent enough to go toe-to-toe during Question Time.

Europeans have decided to make it easy to vote, whereas we in the United States have erected unnecessary barriers. Most European nations vote on a weekend or a national holiday, making this seminal democratic ritual more revered, as well as more convenient, and providing a greater pool of poll workers for election day (the latter an important consideration, since many US jurisdictions have difficulty finding enough poll workers during a busy work day). European democracies also practice what is known as *universal/automatic voter registration*—all eligible voters *automatically* are registered to vote. It is done proactively, on a rolling basis, with the government taking responsibility to make it happen, and the goal is to have 100 percent registration. A national voter database is maintained and each individual is issued a unique numeric identifier, and when one reaches voting age that person is welcomed automatically into the ranks of the enfranchised.

But in the United States, we have an opt-in system in which it is left to the individual to fill out a form and register with the appropriate authorities. Registration drives often are tied to specific elections, leading to various abuses by the partisans who want to register *their* voters but prevent the other side's voters from participating (Bronner 2012). It is also a difficult system to administer, with election officials being overwhelmed at election time by thousands of new registrants who must be processed quickly. This chaotic process, when combined with partisan shenanigans, has resulted not only in lawsuits and elections decided by the courts but also in nearly a third of eligible US voters—about seventy million people—being unregistered to vote, a situation unheard of in Europe. Some states have nearly as many unregistered eligible voters as people who actually vote. For instance, in California there were nine million voters in 2006 compared with seven million eligible voters who were unregistered.

What becomes obvious in observing voter registration and other practices is that European democracies value enfranchisement and participation much more than does the American system. This can be seen not only in practices that affect the entire population but also in the voting rights accorded to prisoners. Most

European democracies allow prisoners to vote because voting is considered a human right as well as an essential part of a prisoner's rehabilitation.[1] But in the United States, only Maine and Vermont allow prisoners to vote, and most states have created byzantine procedures for restoring ex-felons' voting rights, clearly designed more to discourage it instead of facilitating it.[2] Some states actually permanently ban felons from voting even after they have served their time and finished parole. These practices are a legacy of American racism, with a disproportionate number of ex-prisoners being racial minorities.

Representative Democracy, Version 2.0

When you visit the chamber of the US House of Representatives, left and right are plain to see—Democrats on one side, Republicans on the other—with an aisle, a dividing line, down the middle. With only two viable electoral choices, the free marketplace apparently has spread everywhere except to American politics. The US House of Representatives—the *People's House*, as it is called—is hardly "representative" of the American people, with our vast array of ethnicities, religions, languages, geographic regions, and political philosophies.

The People's House actually doesn't look very much like "the people," since those who fill the chairs are 80.5 percent white and 82 percent male in a country that is 67 percent white and majority female. Also, most of the seats are filled by lawyers and businessmen, with nearly a majority being millionaires (Center for Responsive Politics 2013). The average age is fifty-seven, and on the whole, the People's House hardly looks or thinks like the American people. The Senate is even worse in this regard. Of one hundred senators, only six are racial minority (with one African American, who was appointed to fill a vacancy), only twenty are women, and the average age is sixty-two; and even greater income disparities exist between the senators and their voters than in the House (Manning 2013). Two hundred years into our history, the US Congress is still a fairly patrician body, more closely resembling the ancient Roman Senate than a New England town meeting.

But in Germany's Bundestag, one can observe several aisles and numerous sections, a different one for each political party. Germany is a multiparty democracy, with five to six parties usually winning representation in the national parliament. Seeing a visual display of it is a shocking reminder of how lacking in actual representation the US House of Representatives is. The Social Democrats and the Christian Democrats are the two main parties, one center-left and the other center-right; they are joined by the Green Party, the Free Democratic Party, the Christian Social Union, and the Left Party, a broad spectrum of public opinion occupying the chairs of the national legislature (and in four state legislatures, the new Pirate Party has managed to win some seats). In addition to this broad ideological representation, following federal elections in 2009, 32 percent of Germany's national representatives were newcomers and 33 percent were women (nearly twice as many as in the US House), including the country's first ever female head of government, Chancellor Angela Merkel. A handful of Turkish-descended parliamentarians sat with their peers and three parliamentarians were Muslim. The average age of representatives was fifty, and even a twenty-three-year-old was elected on the strength of votes from young Germans (in recent years, a nineteen-year-old also has been elected) (Deutsche Welle 2002; AP 2007). These representatives were from broad backgrounds, experiences, and political perspectives, with more than one hundred occupations represented in the Bundestag—not only lawyers and businesspeople but also pastors, doctors, teachers, engineers, housewives, bricklayers, cooks, goldsmiths and artists (German Bundestag 2011, 4–5).

It is difficult for a nation, especially one as diverse as the United States, to reach a consensus on the pressing issues of our times when so much of the nation is not seated at the table of political power. The comprehensive supports for families and workers available in Germany and other European democracies hardly even receive a debate in the US Congress (ironically though, as members of Congress, they have given themselves and their families European-level benefits). And Europe's proactive policies to tackle global climate change have been approached timidly throughout this decade, even by Democrats and President Barack Obama. Without a multiparty democracy in which all significant points of view are represented, including centrist perspectives in an increasingly polarized Congress as well as in many state legislatures, political debate in the United States has become stunted along increasingly narrow lines in which the best interests of the vast majority of the American people are poorly represented.

Why does Europe enjoy multiparty democracy while the United States does not? The answer is simple: Europe uses more modern political institutions than the United States does, including proportional representation electoral systems; universal/automatic voter registration; public financing of campaigns; free media time for candidates and parties; and a robust, well-funded public broadcasting sector that balances the corporate media. The United States has none of these, instead relying on antiquated political institutions that for the most part are still rooted in their eighteenth-century origins and on a public broadcasting sector that is too poorly funded to balance the corporate sector and too worried about maintaining its funding from Congress and major corporations to engage in penetrating, incisive, BBC-like journalism.

Winner-Take-All Elections Make Everyone a Loser

The United States is one of the last advanced democracies to use a geographic-based political system that elects state and federal representatives one seat at a time, district by district, and the only democracy to elect its chief executive in a hodgepodge of individual state contests that turns a national election into one dominated by a handful of battleground states. In the modern era, this winner-take-all system, as it is called, has produced a stark landscape of legislative districts—indeed, entire states—that are little more than one-party fiefdoms. As a result, unequal treatment based on where one lives is a recurring theme in America's antiquated political system, playing out in numerous ways that increasingly is undermining majority rule, contributing to political paralysis, and presenting major challenges for a nation as diverse as the United States in the twenty-first century.

Despite the excitement of the 2008 and 2012 presidential elections, the fact is, most elections in the United States are predictable snooze-fests. From election to election, typically three-fourths of races for the House of Representatives are won by lopsided landslide margins and over 90 percent by noncompetitive ten-point margins. In 2012, incumbency protection and lack of competition ruled; even in the 2010 races for the House of Representatives, in which the House swung from Democratic to Republican control, only 12 percent of incumbents lost in November. For the vast majority of seats, political analysts can easily predict not only which candidate is going to win but even the margin of victory, because the districts are so predictable. State legislative races are worse yet. In 2012, 40 percent of the races had no candidate from one of the two major parties because the districts were so lopsided that it was a waste of time for one of the parties to contest the general election (McGlennon and Mahoney 2012). Most statewide contests for the Senate, governor, or the Electoral College vote for president were just as noncompetitive as the House or state legislative races. The winner-take-all system has rendered whole states as partisan strongholds, where one side wins most or even all the representation, and other points of view go unrepresented—that is why it is called *winner-take-all*. For most voters, the choice offered where they live is not that of a two-party system but whether to ratify the candidate of the lone party that dominates their district or state.

Most American voters have been rendered superfluous but not as a result of partisan redistricting or incumbents drawing their own legislative district lines or even campaign finance inequities, the usual reasons cited. Recent research shows that in most states, liberals and conservatives live in their own demographic clusters, with liberals dominating in cities and along the coasts and conservatives dominating in rural areas and many suburbs. When those demographics cast votes via the single-seat, winner-take-all system, the vast majority of districts are branded either Republican red or Democratic blue before the partisan-line drawers even sit down at their computers and draw their squiggly district lines. And of course for statewide elections there are no district lines yet similar dynamics play out. That means election results mostly are by-products of partisan residential patterns (i.e., where people live), combined with the winner-take-all system. Redistricting reforms and campaign finance reform, while having their merits, will not greatly affect these fundamental challenges caused by America's eighteenth-century political system based on exclusively geographic representation.

Making matters worse, the winner-take-all electoral system exaggerates the adversarial nature of American politics, making the achievement of a national consensus on the most pressing issues more difficult. Winner-take-all breeds an adversarial "If I win, you lose" clash of opposing forces amid efforts by the winners to take all from the losers. *Purple America*—neither red nor blue—is smothered by the winner-take-all nature of the US system. With one side dominating whole regions and states, political monocultures have resulted where debate and discussion of innovative ideas have virtually ceased, leaving the two sides bunkered down in their regions like combatants in a political and cultural war that has become increasingly polarized and bitter.

Given America's winner-take-all dynamics, multiparty democracy is impossible, and that has additional repercussions. A broad spectrum of voters living in the same district and holding widely divergent views are expected to share a single representative, an increasingly impossible task in a modern pluralistic world. Without authentic representation, many people don't bother voting, so it is hardly surprising that voter turnout in the United States is one of the lowest in the world among established democracies. For the tens of millions of "orphaned voters" living in the opposite party's lopsided districts and states, there is literally nothing to vote for, even during exciting 2008 and 2012 presidential elections, or in the 2010 House races in which the majority was up for grabs. Only 39 percent of eligible adults voted in the 2006 House elections, which improved to about 57.5 percent in 2008 with the draw of a presidential election. Then turnout in House races declined again to about 40 percent in the 2010 midterm congressional elections, only to increase to 55 percent in the 2012 presidential election.[3] That is very low compared to other democratic nations; the United States is ranked no better than 140th in the world in voter turnout, trailing India, South Africa, Uganda, and Estonia in the world's rankings for national legislative elections.[4]

But it's not just elections to the US Congress that are hurting American democracy. Our presidential elections suffer from problems similar to those of the House and Senate; that is, the system is geography based, resulting in a stark lack of competition in nearly all states and regional balkanization. The vast majority of voters live in locked-up states, which, as we saw in 2000 and 2004, produced a presidential election decided by small swathes of undecided swing voters in a handful of battleground states such as Florida and Ohio. The 2008 presidential election, occurring during a time of economic crisis and to replace an unpopular Republican president, saw a few more states in play, as did the 2012 presidential election when about ten states were swing. But the vast majority of states were still Democratic or Republican strongholds. In most states, the candidates don't actively campaign or spend any of their billion-dollar war chests since everyone knows well in advance who will win there.

Differential treatment based on where one lives plays out in alarming ways in both the Senate and the Electoral College. Both are structured to give low-population, predominantly rural states more representation per capita than higher-population states (in the Senate, each state has two Senators regardless of population; in the Electoral College, each state has a number of electors equal to its number of Senators and House members). Political scientists Frances Lee and Bruce Oppenheimer have shown that electing two senators from each state, regardless of population—a legacy of the deal struck by the constitutional founders so that the slave-owning states would join the fledgling nation—has had the effect of disproportionately favoring the low-population states when it comes to representation of interests, policy, federal spending, and even leadership positions in the Senate (Lee and Oppenheimer 1999). And because these states tend to be the most conservative in the country, that representation quota has allowed for the Republican Party's overrepresentation in the Senate in most elections since 1958 (Lee and Oppenheimer 1999; Winger 2007a). It's like having a foot race in which one side starts ten yards ahead of the other. During the federal appropriations process, that has resulted in Democratic blue states, such as California, New York, New Jersey, and Illinois, heavily subsidizing GOP red states, such as Alabama, Mississippi, Alaska, and North Dakota. Billions in blue-state tax dollars end up in red-state pockets. It turns out that the most conservative states benefit from the types of redistributive government programs that American conservatives usually disdain (Tax Foundation 2005).[5]

But it is not just federal spending that is affected by the malapportioned Senate and its antimajoritarian tendencies. In recent years, conservative senators from low-population states representing a small segment of the nation have thwarted or slowed down many policies despite a healthy majority of Americans supporting those positions: health care reform, financial industry reform, gun control, campaign finance reform, global warming, labor law, paid parental and sick leave, the pullout of troops from Iraq and restrictions on war funding, huge subsidies for oil companies, and raising automobile mileage standards to a level long ago reached in Europe and Japan. One of the increasingly severe roadblocks in the unrepresentative Senate is its use of various arcane rules that further undermine majority rule. None of these is more arcane than what is known as the *filibuster*, which requires sixty out of a hundred senators to agree to stop endless debate on a particular piece of legislation before the full Senate may vote. The filibuster allows a mere forty-one senators representing a fraction of the nation's population to stymie what the majority wants.

The filibuster used to be a tactic used sparingly—a half-dozen times per year during the tumultuous 1960s—but since President Obama's election, the Republican minority in the Senate has used the filibuster as a regular tactic, and when the Republicans had a Senate majority in the early 2000s, the Democratic minority similarly escalated the use of the filibuster. Perversely, the 41 Republican senators regularly mounting filibusters represent barely a third of the nation's populace yet through the filibuster have been able to strangle any legislation favored by senators representing the other two-thirds. The resulting paralysis and gridlock has undermined both majority rule and the Senate's credibility (Smith 2009). These antimajoritarian tendencies of the Senate have plagued the United States for a long time; in fact, they are widely blamed for perpetuating slavery for decades (Dahl 2002; Weingast 1998). Two of America's most influential and important founders, James Madison and Alexander Hamilton, opposed the creation of the Senate because of its antidemocratic tendencies and its "unjustifiable limit on national majorities" (Dahl 2002).

The situation with the Electoral College is similar. Low-population states, which usually are conservative, have more electoral votes per capita than the mid-size and high-population states, which in turn gives an edge to election of Republican or conservative presidential candidates. And because the president appoints and the Senate confirms nominees to the US Supreme Court and to lower federal courts, this conservative bias is built into American courtrooms as well. Republican Supreme Court justices have had a solid majority for years on the high court, despite the nation not being majority Republican.[6]

Thus, a *representation subsidy* for low-population, conservative states is hard-wired into all three branches of government. Overrepresented conservatives long have led the country in directions that are unsupported by a majority of Americans. The US political system, originally created for a sparsely populated, eighteenth-century agrarian society led by wealthy slaveholders, with voters numbering no more than two hundred thousand propertied white males, is inadequate for a diverse, sprawling, free-trading, high-tech nation of 300 million people in a twenty-first-century world. Without a major overhaul of its most basic constitutional structures, the American political system may be unable to effectively address many of the major policy challenges facing the country.

Democracy, European-Style

In Europe, on the other hand, proportional representation electoral systems have produced better representation, more electoral competition, and much higher voter participation rates because more voters actually have viable political choices representing a range of views that appeal to them. Political parties from across the political spectrum are able to compete for voters' sympathies and win their proportionate share of seats in the legislatures. There are few safe seats or locked-up regions; everywhere is competitive, and even minority points of view can win representation in parliament. That's because under PR, as *proportional representation* is sometimes called, a political party receiving 10 percent of the popular vote wins 10 percent of the legislative seats instead of nothing, and another political party winning 60 percent of the vote wins 60 percent of the seats instead of everything.[7] Representatives are elected from multiseat districts instead of one-seat districts, making it possible for conservatives to win seats in liberal to progressive areas (like cities) and for liberals and progressives to win representation in conservative areas. This substantially reduces regional balkanization and partisan polarization. Minor parties and independent candidates can win their fair share of representation, too.

In the United States, minor parties are discriminated against with byzantine ballot access laws and various dirty tricks played by the two major parties. But Europe's PR systems allow minor parties to compete on a more level playing field, and minor parties are valued for the constructive role they can play in a robust and confident democracy. These small parties often act as the laboratories for new ideas, challenging and stimulating voters, the media, and the major parties to think outside the conventional political box. Multiparty democracy creates dialogue between the political center and the margins, which in the short run can sound noisy and untidy but in the medium and long terms allows a much fuller airing of the issues and an inching toward national consensus.

European democracies recognize the importance of this dynamic, so minor parties are encouraged, just like the major parties, with public financing of campaigns, free media time for campaigning, and inclusion in televised debates. But only the use of proportional representation allows smaller parties to win their fair share of seats. As the French political scientist Maurice Duverger observed half a century ago, the US-style, winner-take-all electoral system using one-seat districts and plurality voting tends to result in a two-choice–two-party political system and is notorious for preventing minor parties and independent candidates from winning (Duverger 1954). So, not surprisingly, minor party and independent candidates in the United States are hardly ever elected at any level of politics. Out of 535 seats in the Congress, minor parties held none and independents held two following the 2012 elections; with more than 7,300 seats in state legislatures, minor parties held only seven seats (six of them by the Progressive Party in Vermont) and independents held 22 seats, for a total of 29 non-major two party officeholders following the 2012 elections.[8] That was the highest number since 1942, yet as FairVote executive director Rob Richie has commented, "Lightning strikes more often than that."

With a much fuller marketplace of political parties and their ideas to generate voter interest, and with no balkanized, one-party districts and regions where only one party prevails, it is not surprising that Europe's multiparty democracies lead the world in voter turnout. Some nations have double the turnout of the United States, with Malta (93 percent), Luxembourg (90 percent), Belgium (89 percent), Denmark (88 percent), Sweden (85 percent), Austria (82 percent), Norway (76 percent), Netherlands (75 percent), Italy (75 percent), Germany (71 percent), Ireland (70 percent), Spain (69 percent), Finland (67 percent), United Kingdom (66 percent), and Slovenia (65 percent) leading the way (Institute for Democracy and Electoral Assistance 2013). Multiparty hustle and bustle have fostered more spirited debate and increased voter engagement to a degree that has been impossible in the United States.

PR also tends to elect a far greater percentage of women to legislatures. The major reason for this is that women are more likely to run and voters are more likely to vote for them when there is more than one seat to fill. In US state legislative elections, for example, women tend to win seats in significantly higher percentages in multiseat districts than in one seat districts (Tremblay 2007). In addition, PR systems, especially list systems, give women additional leverage to demand that political parties add more females to their lists of candidates. Greater representation of women is important not only from a fair representation standpoint; various studies have shown a strong correlation between profamily policies enacted by legislatures and the number of women elected to those legislatures (Lijphart 1999). In Europe, the presence of more female legislators has brought more focus on family policies, as well as contributed to a distinctly European outlook that forms the core of its social capitalist values. With women's representation in the US House still stuck at 18 percent and 20 percent in the Senate—seventy-eighth in the world—Sweden leads the way with 45 percent of seats held by women in its national parliament, followed by Finland (42.5 percent), Norway (40 percent), Denmark and the Netherlands (39 percent), Belgium (38 percent), and Spain (36 percent).[9]

Germany presents an interesting laboratory for measuring the impact of electoral systems on women's representation, since it uses both a US-style district-based, winner-take-all method to elect half of its parliamentarians and a PR method to elect the other half.[10] The result: Women win about 13 percent of the winner-take-all seats—about the same as in the United States—and about 46 percent of the PR seats, for an overall total of 33 percent. Other nations using this *mixed member* system, such as New Zealand, Italy, Russia, and Japan, also see two to three times as many women elected to the PR seats as to the winner-take-all seats.

European democracies also have led the way in electing young people to national parliaments. In addition to Germany, Sweden has also elected a nineteen-year-old in recent years. In Europe's PR democracies, many countries have seen twenty-somethings from both the left and the right elected to their national parliaments. Political parties have incentive to broaden their appeal by including young people on their lists of candidates, who then reach out to and mobilize youthful voters. But in the United States we are missing out on opportunities to incorporate young people with their distinctive and refreshing perspectives into the fabric of American politics; electing one seat at a time doesn't lend itself to including young people as candidates.

The groups that so far have had unimpressive political representation in Europe have been ethnic and racial minorities. Racial and ethnic representation has lagged not only because of discriminatory attitudes but also because historically, European countries have had small racial and ethnic minority populations. As these populations have increased, they have begun making electoral inroads by winning representation in federal and state parliaments in Germany, the United Kingdom, Sweden, the Netherlands, Denmark, Switzerland, and elsewhere. While America has elected a lot more minority representatives than European nations have, the 19.5 percent of House members and 6 percent of Senators that are racial and ethnic minority are for a national population that is *one-third* minority, compared with minority populations in Europe of around 10 percent or less. So while at first glance the United States seems to be a much better example of fairer multiracial representation, in fact America has as large a gap in the ratio of ethnic and racial representatives to population as do most European democracies.

Europe's diversity of representation—in partisanship, gender, age, and increasingly ethnicity—only has been possible because of the use of proportional voting methods. Europe's democracies have a much greater ability to field a broader range of candidates who have a real chance of being elected and who talk about a greater breadth of issues. Those features attract more voters to the polls. But in America's archaic winner-take-all democracy, the connection between voters and candidates largely has been severed because most candidates are still older white males who run in lopsided partisan districts where they don't even need to campaign to win reelection. However much the American people may yearn for more choices on election day, America's winner-take-all duopoly prevents the rise of new political parties and new types of leaders that can fill this void.

Europe's use of proportional voting systems ensures that all significant points of view win a seat at the table. Moreover, voters win representation on the basis of what they *think*, not where they *live*, an increasingly valuable foundation for representation in this modern, mobile, pluralistic world. In the antiquated US-style winner-take-all democracy, next-door neighbors can have opposite political opinions, but only one of them can win representation, fostering "If I win, you lose" adversarial politics. But in Europe's multiparty democracies, the goal is to give everyone representation, no matter where they live, and bring all sides to the table, where they can hash out a consensus.

Impact of Europe's Democracy on Policy: Consensus Versus Exclusion

It is not just in better representation and more robust political discourse that Europe's multiparty democracies outshine America's two-party duopoly.

Research also has demonstrated that proportional voting systems produce legislative policy that is more responsive to the desires of the populace than winner-take-all systems.

Professor Arend Lijphart from the University of California, San Diego, reviewed performances of thirty-six countries, classifying them into *majoritarian* and *consensus* democracies, proxies for winner-take-all and proportional democracies, respectively. He concluded, "The consensual democracies clearly outperform the majoritarian democracies with regard to the quality of the democracy and democratic representation." They also are more likely to have enacted comprehensive supports for families and individuals, have a better record on the environment, on macroeconomic management, and on controlling violence and putting fewer people in prison (Lijphart 1999). When political scientists John Huber and G. Bingham Powell compared nearly two dozen western democracies that used either a proportional or a winner-take-all electoral system, they found that policy passed by governments elected by PR were more responsive to the desires of the populace (Huber and Powell 1994; Powell 2000).

Some US defenders have criticized European democracies as being too paralyzed by attempts to achieve this consensus. But Europe, with its social capitalism founded on the bedrock of a pluralistic representative democracy, has pulled even with and even surpassed the United States in many health care, social, economic, energy, and transportation categories. Yes, European governments have clear problems and faults and sometimes resemble debating societies. And unquestionably, the big challenge facing Europe today of how much its various member states should unite into a federalist state on the continental level has tested their political systems. But even in the midst of that challenge, most of Europe's national democracies have continued working remarkably well.

Not surprisingly, given the considerable defects of the peculiar, antiquated US political system, few of the world's democracies have copied it. Not many countries have adopted our district-based, winner-take-all system to elect their legislatures, and no countries have copied our malapportioned Senate or our flawed Electoral College method for electing the president. For those not steeped in the mythologies of the American system, the defects of the geographic-based political system and its outdated eighteenth-century practices are too large to ignore. Instead, most new democracies have copied the political institutions of western Europe and created multiparty democracies.[11]

The Infrastructure of Political Communication

Besides multiparty democracy founded on the bedrock of proportional representation, another crucial component to consensus building and a thriving democracy is the means by which average citizens and voters receive information and news. In the modern age, four types of communication infrastructure are necessary to foster a vigorous democracy and robust political debate: a healthy public broadcasting sector that acts as a balance to the profit-driven corporate media, free media time for candidates and parties, some degree of public financing of campaigns, and affordable and widespread access to high-speed broadband Internet. Most European democracies outstrip the United States in all of these areas.

Nearly all European democracies award public financing of campaigns to all political parties that achieve a minimum threshold of the vote, typically 1 percent or so. Giving public money to a party with so few votes is completely alien to the American way of thinking, but in Europe a dramatic difference in philosophy exists. European democracies try to encourage political debate and a free marketplace of ideas as part of its consensus-seeking process. By publicly financing campaigns, European democracies provide all candidates and parties with sufficient resources to communicate with voters. That allows lesser-funded candidates and parties to challenge ones that are better-funded and to raise issues that stir real debate, which spurs voter engagement.

In addition to giving public money to candidates and political parties, another essential component of a flourishing multiparty democracy is the generous provision of free radio and television airtime for political parties and candidates. Broadcast media are the greatest expense of any candidate or party's campaign, especially in the biggest and most important races, so this is a valuable contribution to the quest for leveling the playing field and fomenting robust political debate and consensus seeking. Free media time on both TV and radio is awarded to all political parties that achieve a minimum threshold of the popular vote, typically 1 percent or less, with the bigger parties awarded more airtime. Ad slots last from five to ten minutes in length, considerably longer than the thirty-second sound bites in US political ads. This permits a more substantive presentation of the party's issues and positions.

But in the United States, the Democrats and Republicans enjoy a duopoly that they wish to preserve. So the two major parties go out of their way to prevent voters from hearing other points of view. Not only is public financing of campaigns rare on the American political landscape, but free media time for candidates and parties is virtually non-existent and the state bureaucracies controlled by the two major parties discriminate against and even harass minor parties with draconian ballot access laws and other tactics.[12] This loss of political debate and stifling of new ideas is one of the most insidious downsides to America's privately financed campaigns and two-party duopoly. In the absence of public financing or free airtime, running for public office in the United States is extremely expensive, a situation that has allowed wealthy interests as well as the corporate media to become gatekeepers of candidates' viability. Particularly for the bigger races like president, governor, and US Senate, broadcasters maintain a de facto *boardroom primary* in which successful candidates are vetted by media gatekeepers, as well as by big campaign donors. The media gatekeepers also have a veto over which issues will be discussed during the electoral season (Hill 2012).

Moreover, various studies have demonstrated that corporate broadcasters have developed a habit of severely restricting political coverage (Falk and Aday 2000; Campaign Legal Center 2000) and shortened the length of the political sound bite heard on the news to eight seconds (Ruskin 2000). This severely cramps the parameters of political debate.

Various media institutions in Europe also differ substantially from those in the United States, with dramatic consequences. European democracies also have corporate broadcasters, but they also have many more politically diverse media and communication outlets that have fostered a flowering of public opinion, debate, and analysis. In particular, Europe enjoys the benefits of more robust public television and radio networks, as well as a cornucopia of numerous daily newspapers with editorial slants from the right, left, center, center-right, center-left, far left, and back again. Europe's public broadcasting sector is more omnipresent and influential, and for a very simple reason—it is more generously funded. Public broadcasters such as the British Broadcasting Corporation (BBC), France's TFI, Germany's ARD, and Italy's RAI benefit from an annual budget of fifty to ninety dollars per capita, compared to only three dollars per capita for American public broadcasting (McKinsey and Company 2004).

Nearly as important as the level of funding is the *mechanism* of public funding. In the United States, public broadcasting is funded primarily by budget allocations from Congress and donations from corporations. Public broadcasting must be careful not to bite the hands that feed it. But in Europe, many of the public broadcasters are funded by mandatory public subscription fees, with all households required to pay a monthly fee of approximately fifteen dollars (about $180.00 per year). This gives these media outlets their own funding base, which is mostly independent of the government's mood swings. That in turn allows them to display a level of journalistic independence that American public broadcasting can only dream about.

Finally, in the Information Age in which an informed citizenry is enhanced by its access to the democratizing aspects of the Internet, broadband access and penetration in Europe remains much greater than in the United States. Europe's high-speed connections are about half as expensive as America's and lightning fast in comparison, which is ironic since the United States used to lead the world in this category (Luce 2013). When combined with a more robust public broadcasting sector, these diverse information and media sources in Europe play an integral role in the political and cultural landscape. They establish a tone and quality that the corporate broadcasters have to compete with. Enacting European-style publicly financed campaigns, free media time, better-funded public broadcasting and more affordable and faster Internet service would greatly open up American democracy to new voices and new ideas that would engage more voters.

Civic Literacy: Making Democracy Work

The robust and comprehensive nature of European media and communications institutions, when combined with public financing, free media time for campaigns and parties, universal/automatic voter registration, and proportional representation electoral systems, contribute to a greater degree of what political scientist Henry Milner has called "civic literacy"—the knowledge and capacity of citizens to make sense of their political world. Societies with high degrees of civic literacy are ones in which the people show an ability not only to be conversant in the politics and issues of the day but also to identify the impacts that specific policy options will have upon their own interests and those of their community. Milner's thesis is built on Robert Putnam's widely discussed *social capital*, but Milner went beyond Putnam to draw greater attention to the impact of political institutions and the media and to show how civic literacy underpins effective democracies, economic performance, and social justice (Milner 2002; Putnam 2000). Various studies have demonstrated that the peoples of Europe are among the most educated and informed in the world, not only about their own domestic politics, but also about international affairs. Americans, on the other hand, consistently perform near the bottom of these measurements.[13] Europe's greater level of civic literacy compared to the United States is greatly enhanced by its better-equipped political and media institutions.

Challenges to European Democracy

While the European democracies are well equipped for consensus building and policy formation, unquestionably a continent of half a billion people has significant challenges to deal with in the years ahead—all the more so in the wake of the recent economic crisis, which magnified the shortcomings of European democracies and forced issues of greater political and economic integration onto the table. Not all the European nations always live up to the high standards described above. In France, the print media are known for being too cozy with the power structure, and some of the most powerful media groups had links to the administration of President Nicolas Sarkozy (Scalbert 2007). Major political parties in France have been wracked by scandals over campaign finance and tax evasion in recent years. As their economies struggle to recover from the eurozone crisis, some political parties in Spain and Greece have become mired in corruption and tax evasion scandals. Italy's longtime prime minister Silvio Berlusconi remains a glaring affront to democratic standards. Media magnate Berlusconi had gobbled up nearly all the private television media in Italy and then used that resource as a stepping-stone to a successful political career. Then, as prime minister, Berlusconi also oversaw the Italian public broadcasting sector, giving him unprecedented influence over nearly all televised media in Italy. That is not how civil society is supposed to work in a representative democracy. In the face of such crises and the inability of many European governments to get their economies growing again in the aftermath of the Great Recession, it is not surprising that citizens across much of southern and eastern Europe are expressing dissatisfaction with the functioning of their national democracies (Eurobarometer 2012, 52–53).

But despite these shortcomings, Europe's democracies are far from broken. Consider Italy, which has long been treated by US critics as the poster child of struggling European democracy. The constantly collapsing coalition governments in Italy in the post–World War II period have provided steady fodder for finger-wagging lectures from the *New York Times,* the *Washington Post,* and the like. But it is rarely noted that Italy has enjoyed enough stability within its instability to have the eighth-largest national economy in the world and a high standard of living. Other nations occasionally have had difficulties forming coalition governments, with Belgium taking a record 541 days to swear in a government following the June 2010 elections. Nevertheless, any political turmoil in most of the European multiparty democracies has not prevented them from prospering or enacting Europe's unique brand of social capitalism and workfare supports for families and individuals, which, on the whole, have continued to work remarkably well, even during a time of economic crisis. Most of the criticisms leveled at European democracies—"they lead to weak coalition governments" or "they elect fascists and neo-Nazis" or "they produce weak welfare states in which nobody works" and, paradoxically, "everyone pays high taxes"—turn out to be overhyped exaggerations and stereotypes.

While it is true that proportional representation can provide far-right or far-left parties an opportunity to enter parliament, it is little recognized that the US winner-take-all system allows small slices of the most zealous parts of the electorate (the *base*) to acquire exaggerated power. A handful of these voters can determine which party wins the presidency or the US House if they tilt the results in even one battleground state, such as Florida or Ohio, or in a handful of close House districts. Forty-one senators representing as little as a third of the nation have been able to stonewall legislation via constant filibusters; and the small Tea Party wing of the Republican Party has been able to bring the nation to the brink of default on the national debt. So the US-style winner-take-all system often is—in its own ways—bedeviled by minority rule and extremists. Besides, PR systems have a fail-safe: They can handle political extremists by raising the *threshold of victory* (the percentage of the vote needed to win a seat) to a suitably high level that limits the extremists' political impact. Proportional systems and multiparty democracy are used by most of the established democracies in the world, all of them establishing different victory thresholds to fine-tune their democracies and make them as representative—or as exclusive—as they need them to be. Among the many PR democracies in the world today, very few have had the problems of Italy, Israel, or Germany's Weimar Republic in the early 1930s, the most frequently criticized examples of PR.

In fact, Germany's political system demonstrates the possibility of creating interesting hybrids, which the United States could learn a lot from. The German electoral system combines US-style, single-seat, winner-take-all districts with proportional representation, offering the benefits of both. New Zealand, Italy, and Japan also use this mixed member system. Bicameral state legislatures in the United States provide an easy opening for such a mixed system. States could use geographic-based representation via winner-take-all districts in one chamber of the legislature and proportional representation in which voters win representation based on what they think in the other.

One important European institution where the functioning of democracy has been subject to sharp criticism is the European Union (EU). The EU, through its institutions, including the European Parliament, the Council of Ministers, and the European Commission, on the whole has capably tackled the difficult task of representing twenty-eight nations, dozens of languages, and half a billion people located across a sprawling continent. Nevertheless, it is seen by many Europeans as a distant, meddling bureaucracy, issuing directives from on high, including the enforcement of its eighty thousand pages of regulations that touch everything from air travel to household chemicals and the recipes for cheese and French bread. While the European Parliament is directly elected, it is not allowed to introduce legislation. The European Commission is the only EU body allowed to initiate legislative proposals, even though it is not directly elected by the broader European public. Consequently, the European Union is seen as being too removed from electoral controls, too complex for citizens of the member states to comprehend, and generally unaccountable to its citizens.

Complicating matters further still, while the current structures have been adequate for a loose confederation of member states, the eurozone crisis has revealed that they are inadequate for a monetary, fiscal, and transfer union, which the eurozone core of seventeen member states appears to be evolving into (Latvia will become the eighteenth member state using the euro beginning in January 2014). Europeans certainly have the expertise to design a continent-wide democratic system, but what is lacking is a continent-wide consensus over how united and federalized their union should be. Outstanding questions remain over how much sovereignty each nation should cede to the supranational body and whether they should join together to become a United States of Europe. The economic collapse in 2008 and subsequent aftershocks to the eurozone exacerbated these questions over continental unity, as individual nations had to decide how much they should pool their resources and help bail each other out.

Unquestionably, the European Union's democratic institutions have a ways to go before they match those of Europe's national democracies, but the EU is a work in progress. It is instructive to recall that a full seventy years after its first government, the United States fought a bloody civil war over states' rights (and the related issue of slavery), which at its core was a violent disagreement over the powers of central government and member states' sovereignty. It took many decades for America to settle some of its most divisive regional differences. Similarly, the European Union will take many years to construct.

Conclusion

The United States has a much older democracy, and just like an old computer it doesn't have the latest operating system or other flashy features that a new computer has; America's older democracy is missing some of the innovations of Europe's newer democracies. However, we have to be careful about projecting what lessons the United States can learn from Europe because the context is so different across the Atlantic, and institutions often are path dependent as they are embedded in specific histories and culture. Moreover, special interests often jealously guard their perks and privileges within the existing order, making far-reaching reforms difficult or impossible to enact. Certainly, two special interests in the United States that frequently resist fundamental political reform are the Democratic and Republican parties.

Still, there are many European innovations that the United States could implement that don't threaten the two-party system, and these are likely to have the best chance of succeeding in the short run. These include universal/automatic voter registration, Question Time, free media time for candidates, and a more robust public broadcasting sector. Another possible reform that might gain some legs is direct election of the president via a national popular vote plan, which takes advantage of the fact that state legislatures decide how to award presidential electors. If a number of states that in aggregate hold a majority of electoral votes enter into a compact in which all signatories award their state's electoral votes to the winner of the national popular vote, the presidential race would become a de facto national direct election without passing a constitutional amendment. This National Popular Vote plan was launched only a few years ago and already has enough participating states with 136 electoral votes, which is more than half of the 270 electoral votes needed to activate the compact.[14]

But when it comes to more profound reforms, such as proportional representation and public financing of campaigns, the hostility of the duopoly to opening up the political system is deeply rooted and will be a formidable obstacle. Electoral system reforms are most likely to happen at the local and state levels before the federal level. Yet with the controversies swirling around voting rights lawsuits, which increasingly pit representation of racial minorities against the electoral success of the Democratic Party, as well as the insider cronyism that infects the decennial redistricting process, proportional voting methods may gain more viability as the best method to liberate state and local elections from these inherent contradictions of the winner-take-all system where only one side wins and everyone else loses. Indeed, the use of a proportional voting system would go a long way toward electing more minorities without having to gerrymander race-conscious districts and also electing more women and young people; it also could do a lot to decrease the ongoing partisan polarization by giving representation to the full breadth of the political spectrum, including moderates who often act as the bridge builders in legislatures and yet have become an increasingly endangered species there. The goal of decreasing balkanization and coming closer to "representation for all" by changing the electoral system could quickly rise in popularity as Americans grow more and more frustrated with a polarized, do-nothing Congress.

An overhaul of the US Senate so that it is more representative and less biased toward white, rural America will be even more difficult since it will require a constitutional amendment. But even that may eventually reach a viability point as the United States gallops forward demographically, becoming more and more a Rainbow America even as the Senate remains stuck in a nineteenth-century time warp that favors white, rural America.

Despite their many shortcomings, Europe's pluralistic, consensus-seeking democratic political institutions, particularly at the national/member state level, are better adapted than America's democracy for the demands of representation and policy formation in the twenty-first century. These institutions have been crucial for the enactment of policies that support broadly shared prosperity and more family-friendly societies, and they will be crucial as Europeans confront the policy challenges of the twenty-first century. Ironically, just as at one time the torch of democracy was passed to the young breakaway American republic, which exhibited a popular "tumult" of political activity observed by the French aristocrat Alexis de Tocqueville in his seminal work *Democracy in America* (1956), today it can be said that the torch has passed back across the Atlantic. It is in Europe that representative democracy is better equipped to foster broad consensus among diverse populations, stakeholders, and interests about the best policies necessary for the twenty-first century.

Endnotes

1. In October 2005, the European Court of Human Rights ruled that Britain's banning of prisoners from voting had breached the basic right to free elections, writing, "[The] removal of the vote . . . runs counter to the rehabilitation of the offender as a law-abiding member of the community" (BBC News 2005).

2. For summaries of state felon voting laws see Sentencing Project (2007) and ProCon.org, "State Felon Voting Laws," http://felonvoting.procon.org/view.resource.php?resourceID=286 (last accessed June 20, 2013).

3. Voter turnout is derived by the author from the election statistics kept by the clerk of the US House of Representatives, comparing the clerk's turnout information (as the

numerator) to the "voter eligible population" (as the denominator) compiled by the United States Election Project. See "Election Statistics," Clerk of the US House of Representatives, http://history.house.gov/Institution/Election-Statistics/Election-Statistics (last accessed June 19, 2013); and "Voter Turnout," United States Election Project, http://elections.gmu.edu/voter_turnout.htm (last accessed June 19, 2013).

4. This measurement is for the Voting Age Population (VAP) in the 2012 presidential election year, but for the 2010 nonpresidential year the United States was ranked even lower, 169th. See Institute for Democracy and Electoral Assistance (IDEA), Voter Turnout Database, http://www.idea.int/vt/viewdata.cfm# (last accessed June 20, 2013).

5. In 2005, Alaskans received from the federal government $1.84 for every dollar they pay in federal taxes, Mississippians received $2.02, and North Dakotans $1.68. California and New York, with large urban areas and some of the neediest of residents, received only $0.79; Illinois received even less, a mere $0.75; and New Jersey only $0.61.

6. For a full exploration of how "unrepresentative" the US Supreme Court is of the views of most Americans, see Hill, 2012, chapter 9.

7. In PR systems, the percentage of vote it takes to win one seat is dependent on the "victory threshold" of representation, which is derived by making each contested seat in a multiseat district equal to the same proportion of votes. That is, if ten seats are being elected at once from a multiseat district, each seat will be worth 10 percent of the vote in that ten-seat district. Winning 30 percent of the vote will gain three out of the ten seats, 60 percent of the vote will gain six out of the ten seats, and so on. By adjusting the victory threshold, you can fine-tune your democracy and decide how inclusive or exclusive you want it to be. Some of these European democracies have constructed the electoral rules to allow a multiplicity of political parties (some say too many parties); others, such as Germany, use electoral rules that effectively limit the number political parties that are able to win seats in parliament to five or six. See the website of FairVote (www.fairvote.org) for additional resources about proportional representation.

8. Data based on National Conference of State Legislatures (2013) and personal correspondence with Richard Winger, editor-in-chief of *Ballot Access News*, http://www.ballot-access.org.

9. See statistics on women's representation worldwide, published by the Inter-parliamentary Union, http://www.ipu.org/wmn-e/classif.htm. A notable laggard in Europe is the United Kingdom at only 22.5 percent, but even that is still higher than in the United States.

10. Germany's system is "compensatory," meaning the overall partisan balance of seats reflects the PR vote, not the winner-take-all vote.

11. Even America's own progenitor, Great Britain, from whom American founders adopted many of their eighteenth-century practices, is midstream in a remarkable political transformation, having adopted PR for electing representatives to the European Parliament, the London City Council, the Scottish and Wales regional assemblies, and Scottish local councils.

12. Presidential candidate Ralph Nader filed numerous lawsuits against the Democratic National Committee for mounting what Richard Winger (2007b), editor of *Ballot*

Access News, called an unprecedented and massive legal effort to remove Nader from the ballot in the 2004 presidential election. (Also see Amato 2009).

13. Participants in these tests typically are asked questions to see if they can find Iraq on a map of the Middle East, or if they can identify the name of the UN secretary general, or if they know the name of the president or prime minister and other high government officials (Milner, 55–65).

14. See http://www.NationalPopularVote.com (last accessed May 24, 2013).

References

Amato, T. *Grand illusion: The myth of voter choice in a two-party tyranny.* New York: New Press, 2009.

Associated Press. "A numeric profile of the new congress." *Fox News.* http://www.foxnews.com/story/0,2933,241441,00.html (January 4, 2007).

British Broadcasting Corporation. "Q&A: UK prisoners' right to vote." *BBC News.* http://news.bbc.co.uk/2/hi/uk_news/4316148.stm (October 6, 2005).

Bronner, E. "Partisan rifts hinder efforts to improve U.S. voting system." *New York Times.* http://www.nytimes.com/2012/08/01/us/voting-systems-plagues-go-far-beyond-identification.html (July 31, 2012).

Campaign Legal Center. "Networks skimped on candidate, issue coverage during campaign, study finds." *Political Standard* 3, no. 9 (2000).

Center for Responsive Politics. "Millionaire freshmen make Congress even wealthier." *OpenSecrets Blog.* http://www.opensecrets.org/news/2013/01/new-congress-new-and-more-wealth.html (January 16, 2013).

Dahl, R. *How democratic is the American Constitution?* New Haven, CT: Yale University Press, 2002.

Deutsche Welle. "German parliament sports young face." http://www.dw-world.de/english/0,3367,1430_A_642760_1_A,00.html (September 24, 2002).

Duverger, M. *Political parties: Their organization and activity in the modern state.* New York: Wiley, 1954.

Eurobarometer. "Public opinion in the European Union." *Standard Eurobarometer* 78. http://ec.europa.eu/public_opinion/index_en.htm (2012).

Falk, E., and S. Aday. "Are voluntary standards working? Candidate discourse on network evening news programs." *Annenberg Public Policy Center of the University of Pennsylvania.* http://www.appcpenn.org (December 20, 2000).

German Bundestag. *Facts: the Bundestag at a glance.* Berlin: German Bundestag, Public Relations Division. https://www.btg-bestellservice.de/pdf/80140000.pdf (2011).

Hill, S. *Europe's promise: Why the European way is the best hope in an insecure age.* Berkeley: University of California Press, 2010.

———. *10 steps to repair American democracy: 2012 election edition.* Boulder, CO: Paradigm Publishers, 2012.

Huber, J. D., and G. B. Powell, Jr. "Congruence between citizens and policymakers in two visions of liberal democracy." *World Politics* 46, no. 3 (1994): 291–326.

Institute for Democracy and Electoral Assistance. *Voter turnout database.* Stockholm: Institute for Democracy and Electoral Assistance, 2013. http://www.idea.int/vt/viewdata.cfm#.

Lijphart, A. *Patterns of democracy: Government forms and performance in 36 countries.* New Haven, CT: Yale University Press, 1999.

Luce, E. "Corporate tie binds US to a slow Internet." *Financial Times* http://www.ft.com/intl/cms/s/0/98e2a5fc-7c54-11e2-99f0-00144feabdc0.html (February 24, 2013).

Manning, J. "Membership of the 113th Congress: A profile." *Congressional Research Service Report for Congress,* July 1, 2013.

McGlennon, J., and I. Mahoney. *State legislative competition in 2012: Redistricting and party polarization drive decrease in competition.* College of William and Mary, Thomas Jefferson Program in Public Policy. Working Paper. http://www.wm.edu/as/publicpolicy/documents/st_leg_comp_2012_final.pdf (2012).

McKinsey and Company. *Review of public service broadcasting around the world.* http://www.ofcom
.org.uk/consult/condocs/psb2/psb2/psbwp/wp3mck.pdf (2004).

Milner, H. *Civic literacy: How informed citizens make democracy work.* Medford, MA: Tufts University
Press, 2002.

National Conference of State Legislatures. "Party composition of state legislatures." *State Legislatures
Magazine.* http://www.ncsl.org/legislatures-elections/elections/statevote-charts.aspx (2013).

Powell, G. B., Jr. *Elections as instruments of democracy: Majoritarian and proportional visions.* New
Haven, CT: Yale University Press, 2000.

Putnam, R. *Bowling alone: The collapse and revival of American community.* New York: Simon &
Schuster, 2000.

Ruskin, G. "Disgusted by politics on TV? Turn it off." *Fort Worth Star Telegram,* October 29, 2000.

Scalbert, A. "Who controls the media in Europe?" *Rue 89.* http://www.rue89.com/2007/11/05/qui-
controle-les-medias-en-europe (November 5, 2007).

Sentencing Project. *Felony disenfranchisement laws in the United States.* http://www.sentencingproject
.org/Admin/Documents/publications/fd_bs_fdlawsinus.pdf (2007).

Smith, J. E. "Filibusters: The Senate's self-inflicted wound." *New York Times 100 Days Blog.*
http://100days.blogs.nytimes.com/2009/03/01/filibusters-the-senates-self-inflicted-wound
(March 1, 2009).

Tax Foundation. *Federal spending received per dollar of taxes paid by state, 2005.* http://www.taxfoundation
.org/taxdata/show/266.html (2005).

Tocqueville, A. de. *Democracy in America.* New York: New American Library, 1956.

Tremblay, M. "Democracy, representation, and women: A worldwide comparative analysis."
Democratization 14, no. 4 (2007): 533–53.

Weingast, B. R. "Political stability and civil war: Institutions, commitment, and American democracy."
In *Analytic Narratives,* edited by R. H. Bates, A. Greif, M. Levi, J. L. Rosenthal, and B. R. Weingast
(148–93). Princeton, NJ: Princeton University Press, 1998.

Winger, Richard. "2006 vote for U.S. Senate." *Ballot Access News* 22, no. 9 (2007a): 4.

———. "Nader sues Dems." *Ballot Access News* 23, no.8 (2007b): 3.

———. "2010 was best mid-term election for minor party and independent candidates in over 75
years." *Ballot Access News* 26, no. 8 (2010): 1.

Chapter 10

Transatlantic Lesson Drawing: Utopia, Road to Ruin, or Source of Practical Advice?

R. Kent Weaver

The chapters in this volume have provided a wealth of information about policy choices made in Europe in a variety of policy sectors, ranging from Europe-wide actions to combat climate change to diverse national actions to make public pension systems more sustainable and local actions to promote more a livable and sustainable urban environment in Freiburg, Germany. In some cases, the authors have argued that European experience provides positive lessons about policies that should be copied or adapted by the United States; in other cases (e.g., immigration policy) the lessons are more about mistakes to be avoided. In the case of policies to promote child development and work–life balance, there are both suggestions about societal gains associated with emulating European experience and some cautionary notes about potential effects on the employment of women.

This concluding chapter will consider how policymakers and policy entrepreneurs (e.g., interest groups, civic activists, and others who do not currently hold public office) can make use of this information to affect public policy in the United States.[1] Drawing on existing literatures on how policy learning occurs across national and even continental boundaries as well as the case studies in this volume, both the broad empirical question—"*Can* the United States learn from European policy experience?"—and the normative question—"*Should* the United States try to learn from European policy experience?" will be discussed. The answer to both questions, it is argued, is a qualified "Yes."

More important, however, is the argument that these questions need to be reframed. There are many potential sources of European policy lessons and many pathways to influencing US policymaking. Both the plausibility of specific sources of policy lessons and pathways to policy impact may vary across sectors. Thus, more precise questions need to be addressed in any analysis of transatlantic lesson drawing. First, from whom can and should lessons be drawn? Second, who can effectively use these lessons to achieve their objectives, and what are the factors that make policy-specific European experience more or less relevant to policymaking in the United States? Third, can lessons be utilized at the subnational level in the United States as well as the national level? Finally, if specific policies *are* adapted and applied in the United States, what concerns should Americans have about their effectiveness in practice?

Multiple European Sources of Lessons

A first issue that arises is which European experiences US policymakers and policy advocates should draw upon. Except in those sectors where European Union directives impose substantial unity in policy outputs (e.g., competition policy), European policy remains very diverse both in terms of outputs and outcomes, and it differs both across countries and over time. That very diversity should be seen as one of the benefits of looking to European policy experience: If the fifty American states offer great variety of what Louis Brandeis called "laboratories of democracy," the twenty-seven member states of the European Union (EU), plus other non-EU members like Switzerland and Norway, offer even greater variety not just of policy options, but of social and economic characteristics that shape the eventual outputs and outcomes when those options are implemented under varying conditions. Subnational governments in Europe also offer potential policy lessons in many sectors (Betskill and Bulkely 2004; Marsden et al. 2011). Rather than thinking about *a* European policy lesson for the United States, those hoping to draw such lessons should analyze *which sources and which lessons* are most appropriate and why.

Types of Lessons

Those who hope to use policy lessons from Europe should also recognize that lessons can be of several types and be utilized in several ways. A first distinction is between *substantive* policy lessons and *strategic* lessons. Substantive lessons relate primarily to the content of the policy, such as eligibility rules, administrative structures, and patterns of financing, for example. Strategic lessons relate primarily to how supporters of a policy option attempt to build and maintain political support for that option over time—such as in the ways that they frame a problem in public debates and mobilize support among interest groups and political parties. As will be discussed further below, strategic lessons may be particularly difficult to translate from a European to a US environment because of differences in political institutions, value preferences, and partisan alignments. But this difficulty is likely to be much greater in policy sectors with a very high political salience and profile, and concentrated stakes for well-organized interests, such as climate change, health care, immigration, and pension policy. It may be less of a problem in other sectors, such as urban transportation.

A second lesson-drawing distinction is between *positive lessons* about practices to be emulated and *negative lessons* about things to be avoided (as well as lessons that are more ambiguous). In many policy sectors, the diversity of European experience allows both types of lessons to be drawn. In the pensions sector, for example, Europe offers positive lessons from Sweden about efficient ways to structure a system of mandatory individual retirement savings accounts, negative lessons from Italy and Greece about the risks of unsustainably high pension commitments, and cautions from Hungary about the political vulnerability of individual account tiers when countries face severe fiscal stress. In the area of climate change policy, European experience with carbon markets offers both evidence of the potential pitfalls of poor institutional design and lessons about how to avoid and correct initial mistakes. In short, in most policy sectors, Europe offers examples of both very good practices and very bad ones from a variety of sources rather than just a single "lesson from European experience." One should be careful not to assume that the experiences reviewed in this volume—which generally oversample positive experiences—are replicable even within all member countries of the European Union, let alone in the United States.

A final set of distinctions relates to how closely a foreign model is copied. Even within the realm of positive lesson drawing about policy substance, Richard Rose has noted that simply copying a single policy or program "more or less intact" is only one possible form of lesson drawing. Creating a "hybrid" from two different models or a "synthesis" from several different models, or simply taking one or more foreign models as an "inspiration," or "intellectual stimulus to develop a novel program" are also important forms of lesson drawing (Rose 1993, 30; see also James and Lodge 2003, 180). Indeed, copying is probably not the most promising form of lesson drawing, given constraints on adoption and implementation discussed below.

Looking to European models for concrete, specific lessons on particular policy issues is likely to be a more fruitful form of drawing lessons from Europe than wholesale copying or adaptation of European practice. Comprehensive reorientation of city planning and intermodal transportation systems on the model of Freiburg, Germany, is unlikely to be feasible in many US cities in the short term, for example. On the other hand, concrete lessons on the design of a system of bicycle lanes and urban bike-sharing practices may be much more feasible. Indeed, stressing the European source of a policy lesson may sometimes be counterproductive, given the negative connotations attached to European policy within conservative political circles in the United States that Daniel Kelemen notes in the introductory chapter to this volume. Moreover, scholars have noted that even *within* Europe, policy ideas are often transformed and adapted to different national environments as they cross national boundaries (Pedersen 2007). Policy practices are also altered in implementation, as will be discussed further below. In short, Europe should be looked to for policy lessons that are substantive more than strategic, negative (what to avoid) as well as positive (what to do), and concrete and substantive—with a focus on synthesis rather than direct copying.

Lesson Drawing How and by Whom? The US Policymaking Process

The existing literature on policy diffusion suggests important lessons related to the barriers and opportunities likely to be encountered in cross-national policy lesson drawing, both to how such lessons can get on *policy agendas* and whether or not they are eventually *adopted.* Rather than a simple uniform lesson-drawing process, that process can involve multiple actors and multiple pathways to policy impact. Dolowitz and Marsh (1996, 2000), for example, discuss nine broad sets of actors who may be involved in lesson drawing: elected officials, political parties, bureaucrats, pressure groups, policy entrepreneurs and experts, transnational corporations, think tanks, supranational governmental and nongovernmental institutions, and consultants.

These actors bring a variety of roles and motivations to the policymaking process—and of course, many of these categories of actors are themselves internally heterogeneous. To make sense of this diversity, John Kingdon's (1995) analysis of agenda setting offers a particularly useful framework for thinking both about the potential for lesson drawing in the United States and lesson drawing from Europe in particular. Kingdon argues that policies are likely to move onto the agenda when there is a "coupling" of developments in three separate "streams"—the problem, policy, and political streams. These streams frequently operate with separate but partially overlapping sets of actors and political logics. Important factors that facilitate or constrain US lesson drawing from European experience in each of the policy streams are summarized in Table 10.1.

The *problem stream* relates to how particular issues are perceived by the public—notably their salience, who is to blame for an unsatisfactory situation, and whether the sector is perceived as an appropriate arena of responsibility for government. Several distinctive sorts of developments in the problem stream may put an issue on government's agenda. What Kingdon calls *focusing events*—for example school shootings, food safety crises, or perceived security breakdowns leading to terrorist attacks—are one factor that may put issues on the agenda and change public perceptions. In such cases, politicians may feel intense political pressure to

TABLE 10.1   Policy Streams and Policy Learning

Policymaking Stream	Conditions Facilitating (+) and Inhibiting (−) Policy Learning From Europe	Potential Applications to US Learning From Europe
Problem stream	+ Similar levels of economic development facilitating common perceptions of problems, their relative importance, and acceptability of costs of addressing them	Environmental and urban congestion problems and demographic aging challenges roughly comparable in Western Europe and United States; widespread post-materialist values in both regions
	− Differing perceptions of (1) causes of social phenomena or (2) whether "problems" are amenable to government solutions	Inequality, labor market and social inclusion policies, family support policies, climate change policies
Policy stream	− Labor and environmental interests having more privileged access to government in many European countries than in United States	Center-left social protection and environmental policies generally more likely to make it to agendas in Europe than the United States
	+ Rich array of think tanks and other policy-focused organizations in United States focused on seeking policy solutions and making them accessible to policymakers.	Large number of policy organizations in United States seeking to influence policy increases the range of alternatives considered
	− Negative information weighted more heavily than positive information in weighing alternatives	Costs associated with foreign lessons in any policy sector are likely to be weighted more than gains
	− Widespread suspicion in United States of policies that reduce income inequality or can be portrayed as infringing on individual freedom or disincentivizing work	Inequality, labor market and social inclusion policies, family support policies, climate change policy options are likely to be constrained

(Continued)

TABLE 10.1   (Continued)

Policymaking Stream	Conditions Facilitating (+) and Inhibiting (−) Policy Learning From Europe	Potential Applications to US Learning From Europe
	− Feedback from current policies that create concentrated winners who would be worse off if policy alternatives were adopted	Options constrained in climate change policy, health and pension policy, and other sectors where companies or groups have strong stake in the status quo
	− Financial constraints in era of slow growth	Any policy option that requires commitment of new financial resources unlikely to be considered or adopted
Politics Stream	− Political institutions with multiple veto points inhibiting any changes from the status quo in the United States, especially during periods of divided government and high polarization	Any policy changes requiring national legislation difficult in the United States, but especially policy sectors with high partisan polarization
	+ Career incentives leading politicians in United States to seek credit for policy innovations that provide benefits to voters; access to policy agenda relatively porous	US politicians may incur search costs of looking for foreign-inspired policy options

act quickly, which may lead to a truncated search process for responses (e.g., failing to fully explore the implications of copying a foreign policy model) and thus to suboptimal outcomes (Dolowitz and Marsh 2000, 8). Fiscal strain—felt especially in the pensions and health care sectors—can also prompt searches for foreign lessons that may help relieve that strain (Marmor, Freeman, and Okma 2005).

Other developments in the problem stream that may help to put an issue on the agenda include statistical indicators that show a rise in unemployment, crime rates, home foreclosures, or HIV infection rates, and evidence that costs of a program are rising rapidly and unexpectedly. Comparative indicators from Europe, notably on the outsized share of gross domestic product (GDP) consumed by health care in the United States, despite relatively poor US rankings on longevity and other health care indicators, are already widely cited in US health care debates (see for example Muennig and Glied 2010; Reinhardt, Hussey, and Anderson 2004).

In theory, the fact Western Europe and the United States are at similar levels of economic development should lead to a high degree of parallelism in the problem streams of the two countries. In Inglehart's (1995) classic formulation, wealthy countries should have similarities both in many of the types of problems that they confront (e.g., air and water pollution, urban congestion) and public willingness to address those problems because greater societal affluence leads to higher levels of post-materialist willingness to forgo personal consumption to pursue social goods like a clean environment (for a contrasting view, see Fairbrother, forthcoming). But there are important differences in values between the two regions that affect how problems are perceived. For example, Americans are less likely to believe that the poor are trapped in poverty and more likely to believe that the poverty is due to a lack of effort (Alesina and Glaeser 2004, chap. 7), even though intergenerational social mobility is lower in the United States than in many European countries (Organisation for Economic Co-operation and Development 2010).

The process of problem definition is not one in which political actors, including politicians and policy entrepreneurs outside of government, are passive bystanders confronted by objective facts about policy problems, moreover. As Deborah Stone (1989, 282) has noted, political actors "do not simply accept causal models," rather they select and interpret facts, creating images and composing "stories that describe harms and difficulties, [and] attribute them to actions of other individuals or organizations." Important differences in the problem stream can arise through these processes. Climate skeptics in the United States, including many with close linkages to well-funded conservative think tanks, often deny either whether global warming is occurring or whether it is caused by human activity (Jacques, Dunlap, and Freeman 2008). As Schulze-Cleven notes in his chapter in this volume, European labor market institutions are often portrayed in US debates as rigid and stifling—the source of problems rather than a potential solution. US critics who seek to discredit the accuracy of indicators of US–European health differentials cannot simply dismiss superior health outcomes in most west European countries out of hand, but they argue that poor US health outcomes are the result of differences in income inequality and lifestyle choices rather than differences in the efficiency of health care systems (see for example Frech, Parente, and Hoff 2012); that is, they attempt to change the definition of the problem. Indeed, David Vogel (2012) argues that one of the major reasons for the stronger emergence in Europe of a "precautionary principle" in guiding environmental and consumer safety regulation than in the United States was not a greater frequency of "alarm bell events" (e.g., oil spills and food safety disasters) but rather stronger voices in the United States disputing the meaning and the policy implications of those alarm bells. Moreover, even if perceptions of a particular harm are shared between Americans and Europeans, the American system of checks and balances may foster a greater skepticism among Americans that a harm is susceptible to government solutions (Kingdon 1999). In short, while the objective problems faced by governments in the two regions have strong overlaps, there is less overlap in how those problems are perceived and the kinds of strategic problem framings that advocates of a particular problem framing can use to try to promote policy action.

The *policy stream* consists of the supply of policy options that are available to policymakers to address those problems. In many sectors, there are sets of policy entrepreneurs who are already committed to a particular solution (e.g., green transportation alternatives) who try to attach that policy solution to various policy problems (e.g., climate change, energy supply disruptions) as they rise in salience. Kingdon argues that policy options are likely to be seriously considered by policy-makers, however, only when they are perceived to be technically and administra-tively feasible, consistent with societal values, and affordable. But these search processes are not neutral: Policy entrepreneurs are likely to be biased both in the foreign models they consider and those that that they choose to devote scarce resources into pushing. Moreover, the identity of policy entrepreneurs and their leverage in the policymaking process has significant differences between most west European countries and the United States. Most European countries have stronger labor unions than in United States and linked social democratic or labor political parties that give them privileged access when their party partners are in govern-ment. In addition, green parties play a stronger role in several European countries, especially in countries such as Germany that have a high degree of proportionality in their electoral systems. These features are also likely to provide privileged access to policy options that might not gain serious consideration in the United States. In the United States, health care providers were historically intransigent in fighting national health insurance rather than compromising because they believed they could win and, therefore, did not need to compromise to ensure that they had a voice in negotiations over health care reform, while those pushing for health care reform limited the options they put on the table as well as how they were framed. But the United States does have a rich array of think tanks and other policy-focused institutions of diverse ideological persuasions that are active in national policy debates, drawing ideas from multiple sources and translating them into terms that are accessible to policymakers (Stone 2000).

Several additional factors are also likely to inhibit lesson drawing about specific policy options pioneered or tested in Europe. One factor is a general one suggested by prospect theory: Negative information (i.e., information about costs) is gener-ally weighed more than positive information, and individuals tend to be loss averse (see for example Kahneman and Tversky 1979). Thus, even if a policy option has strong overall net benefits, it may provoke substantial resistance from those who would be worse off. This is especially true if those who would suffer net costs from adopting a particular option are concentrated and politically resourceful, have good access to the media and substantial resources with which to influence public opinion, and are able to tap into and frame their arguments in terms of broadly shared American values (e.g., support for individual liberties, suspicion of government regulations). For example, a recent study of utilization of policy experiences from other countries in health care debates finds they are characterized by a high degree of "[u]nwarranted inferences, rhetorical distortion, and caricatures" (Marmor, Freeman, and Okma 2005; see also Marmor 1993). Nor is this a new development, as Jacob Hacker (1998, 100–11) notes: Around the end of World War I, opponents of the American League for Labor Legislation's proposals for comprehensive health insurance in the United States simultaneously labeled them "pro-Bolshevik" and "pro-German."

A focus on the political attitudes of policy elites, the mass public, or both should not be carried too far. Simplistic notions that *American exceptionalism* in values constrains policy choices is captured by ideas like "Americans want less government," "Americans mistrust government," and "Americans believe in equality of opportunity, not equality of outcomes" (see for example King 1973). Research suggests that the reality is more complex, as Graham Wilson (2009, 465) has noted: "Americans are believers in small government in theory, but they support most government programs in practice . . . Americans are ideological conservatives and programmatic liberals." Americans also exhibit substantial diversity in their attitudes toward government.

Nevertheless, widely held values in the United States do privilege issue framings that question a more activist role for government and redistributive policymaking. This can be a critical resource for opponents of those types of policies (Kingdon 1999). And what Sniderman and Piazza (1995) have referred to as the "scar of race" inhibits the adoption of equity-enhancing changes in programs that have a racialized image, such as Temporary Assistance for Needy Families, Medicaid, and child care (see also Alesina and Glaeser 2004; Gilens 1999).

Several literatures suggest additional constraints on cross-national lesson drawing in the policy stream. The literature on policy feedback and path dependence (see for example Hacker 2004; Pierson 1993, 2000) provides especially useful supplements to Kingdon's framework. First, it suggests that policy change may require substantial transition costs. To take a particularly obvious example, moving from a system of driving on the right-hand to the left-hand side of the road would involve a huge cost to change traffic lights, road alignments, signage, and so forth, plus the costs of changing the stock of motor vehicles—not to mention the learning and coordination costs as drivers have to adjust their behavior. In the case of pension policy, moving from a pay-as-you-go public pension system (in which today's workers pay for current retirees) to a system where each generation saves for its own retirement means that some generation must pay both for their retirement and that of the preceding generation, although these costs can be spread out over more generations by borrowing to pay the transition costs.

Resource constraints are another policy feedback that constrains policy change. As Paul Pierson (1998, 2001) and others have noted, a series of economic and demographic trends in recent decades has made it more difficult to find resources for expansionary budget initiatives. Slower improvements in productivity and overall economic growth have meant that the resources available for allocation by politicians are shrinking. Income tax indexation and flattening of income tax structures in many countries have eroded the fiscal dividend that inflation produced in many countries. In addition, population aging and the maturation of many welfare state program commitments have resulted in higher pension and health care costs that put enormous pressure on existing budgetary commitments, let alone leaving room for new budgetary initiatives.

The *political stream* concerns the structure of political institutions and micro-level incentives that create and limit the opportunities of groups to form and influence policymaking or implementation and for politicians to anticipate, shape, and respond to problems (see for example Tarrow 1996). The political stream can also vary over time as a result of factors such as a new party or leader in power that has come into office with a campaign commitment to a particular initiative, a national mood shift (e.g., increased environmental concern after 1970), or a crisis or focusing event.

Several distinctive features of US politics that relate primarily to the politics stream constrain the applicability of potential lessons from Europe to the United States. At the national level, political institutions make *any* policy change difficult as a result of multiple veto points (e.g., checks and balances between the executive and legislature). These constraints have been reinforced by the high prevalence of divided government over the past forty-five years.

Some features of US institutions do create potential opportunities for drawing policy lessons from Europe. In particular, politicians in the United States are heavily dependent on their own records to win reelection and advance their careers, and they may see responsibility for sponsoring a policy innovation (without necessarily stressing its geographic origins) as an opportunity to claim credit with voters. Moreover, access to the policy agenda is relatively porous rather than dominated by parties and government bureaucracies. But recent changes in American political parties and the electorate have led to a period of increasingly homogeneous, programmatic, national, and relatively evenly balanced and polarized parties. In particular, many Republican legislators are now concerned with primary challenges from the Tea Party wing of the party rather than the general election, making it difficult for their leaders to agree to compromises across partisan lines (see for example Mann and Ornstein 2012). These changes pose another critical constraint on lesson drawing from Europe on many issues discussed in this volume. In climate change policy, denial (or at least skepticism) on the role of humans in causing global warning has become a virtual litmus test among Republican political leaders. This makes even weak action difficult in a period of divided party control of national governmental institutions in the United States. The very strong social conservative movement in the United States, closely allied with the Republican Party, also has implications for many social policies, notably with respect to women's employment, child care, and early childhood education.

As the agenda-setting literature pioneered by Kingdon suggests, having good policy solutions is not enough—the solutions must be framed in ways that are attractive to politicians, build coalitions among multiple constituencies, and are able to survive the American institutional system of multiple veto points. That is no mean set of feats, particularly in an era of divided government, polarized parties, and internal dynamics of the Republican Party that make it difficult for them to compromise.

The Kingdon "streams and windows" framework also provides a very useful conceptual basis for identifying factors that can affect whether a window of opportunity for drawing policy lessons from Europe is likely to open up. Kingdon stresses that the opening of a window usually requires that developments in two or all three policy streams converge—for example when a crisis leads to a problem being perceived as particularly salient (problem stream), a policy response that policy entrepreneurs have long pushed for appears to offer a viable solution to the problem (policy stream), and politicians sympathetic to that option come to power after an election (politics stream).

Policy windows can also close unexpectedly. In the problem stream, the public may lose interest in a focusing event that appeared to pose a serious threat, especially if it is not repeated (e.g., Hurricane Katrina), or a new crisis in another sector may cause politicians and the public to shift their attention to that sector. Politicians may create the perception that a patchwork response has addressed the problem even when it has not. The public may simply become inured to or bored with a problem, such as crime or gun violence, viewing it as insoluble by government (Downs 1972; Pralle 2009). In the policy stream, no available alternative may emerge, or a test of an initially plausible policy option at the state level may produce discouraging results about its effectiveness that causes that alternative to be discredited. In the politics stream, another change in personnel or party controlling government may lead to an initiative being abandoned, or politicians may try and fail to get action and decide not to invest further time and resources in what they have come to perceive as a lost cause.

Kingdon's analysis, combined with the specific arguments about US capacity for lesson drawing from Europe outlined above, suggests that the coupling necessary for substantive policy lessons from Europe to have an impact on US policy debates may in fact occur through several distinct ways that can differ across policy sectors.

Much cross-national policy learning occurs through what can be called an *expert-dominated* path, especially on issues that have relatively low political visibility, weak ideological divisions, and limited conflict among resourceful interest groups. In sectors with these characteristics, policy problem are likely to be perceived and framed similarly by experts in the United States and Europe; moreover, highly technical policy substance can lead to deference to perceived experts. Technical experts frequently have well-developed, sector-specific international policy networks that effectively diffuse information about potential policy options (the policy stream) and their effectiveness. In many sectors, such as the urban transportation sector, providers trying to sell their own products are another source of policy learning that operates across national and continental boundaries (Marsden et al. 2011), as are consulting firms operating transnationally. Low issue salience and lack of concentrated interests lead to lack of political conflict.

A second, more indirect, potential pathway for policy lessons to move from Europe to the United States is through international consensus, often embodied in international treaties that impose obligations on signatory countries. Kelemen and Vogel (2010, 428) have shown that the European Union has replaced the United States as "the strongest proponent of the expansion of international environmental law" in recent decades. However, the United States has shown its unwillingness to ratify, let alone implement, very broadly shared agreements—for example, the Framework Convention on Tobacco Control and the Kyoto Protocol on climate change. In these cases, the most important blockage to US ratification occurred in the political stream: The international consensus pathway to policy learning can be successful only when there is weak or non-existent interest group and partisan opposition to a policy proposal.

A third potential pathway to European policy influence on US policymaking is what can be called the *ideological partisan* path. In this model, there are substantial agreements on the nature of policy problems and the range of acceptable options between specific governing parties in a European country and the United States that facilitate the flow of policy ideas in both directions. This flow of ideas may be either through direct contact or through ideological networks and institutions (e.g., think tanks) that are shared across national boundaries (Stone 2000). Observers have noted patterns of two-way policy options between the Thatcher and Reagan (and G.W. Bush) and the Clinton and Blair governments. The reliance of the G.W. Bush administration on pension privatization proposals pioneered in part by Thatcher's government is an example. But the pension privatization example also illustrates that ideological affinity is not enough for policy options to move from the policy agenda to actual ratification: The latter is most likely to occur when there is unified party control of Congress and the presidency in the United States. As noted above, that has become increasingly uncommon in the United States.

While all of these pathways are plausible and have served as conduits for the flow of policy ideas, the first, the expert-dominated path, is probably the most important, though least visible. It is of continuing importance because it does not rely on episodic ideological agreement between governments, as the ideological–partisan pathway does. It depends instead on ongoing professional networks and flows of information and trust that are fostered by shared professional understandings and expertise.

Subnational Lesson Drawing

Given the multiple veto points, partisan polarization, and prevalence of divided government in the national government of the United States, using policy lessons from Europe—indeed, any effort to enact major change in national policy in the United States—is extremely difficult. In some cases, lesson drawing and ensuing policy change may be easier at the state or even local level in the United States than at the national level. But this is not uniformly true across policy sectors, because federalism can affect policy dynamics in several different ways (Weaver 2009). As outlined in Table 10.2, which federalism dynamic is dominant—and thus whether it makes sense for advocates for a particular policy option to focus on adoption by subnational governments—depends on several facilitating and inhibiting conditions, notably which level of government has the legal *authority* over a specific policy sector, whether a particular government has the *capacity* to innovate, whether politicians have the *motivation* to innovate, and whether there are strong *communication flows* across subnational units. These four factors can vary across policy sectors and over time as well as across countries.

One possibility is that federalism may lead to a policy dynamic driven by the *internal determinants* of individual states, such as the ideology of the voting public in that state, state per capita income (which influences state fiscal capacity to launch innovations that are costly), legislative and executive professionalism, as well as differences in interest group pressure, partisan balance in the legislature, and the severity of particular problems (see for example Matisoff 2008; Wiener and Koontz 2010). The public finance literature, similarly, suggests that federalism may lead to heterogeneity across states or localities if those units choose to specialize in providing particular packages of public goods (e.g., better public transportation versus better schools or lower taxes) that attract different residents and firms with distinctive policy preferences. Even when policy lessons from Europe are blocked at the national level in the United States by ideological opposition or institutional gridlock, opportunities might exist for policy innovation at the state level, especially among states that are outliers in terms of ideological balance, fiscal capacity, or some other variable. Thus, some European policy ideas might be more likely to be deployed in certain states—e.g., EU environment policies might be

TABLE 10.2 Policy Dynamics of Federalism and Policy Learning

Policy Dynamic	Facilitating Conditions				Likely Policy Result
	Jurisdiction/ Authority	Resources Required	Politicians' Motivations for Innovation	Communications Flows Across States	
Internal determinants	States have exclusive jurisdiction.	Resource requirements are substantial; states vary in capacity and central government does not redistribute resources.	Responding to voter preferences that are heterogeneous across states	Limited	Policy outputs are heterogeneous across states over time.
"Laboratories of democracy"	States have exclusive or shared jurisdiction.	Resource requirements are limited.	Competition among state politicians to show issue leadership and attract investment	Strong	Policy outputs become more heterogeneous in initial stages of innovation then more homogeneous as innovation is broadly diffused and successful innovations are widely copied by other states.

Facilitating Conditions

Policy Dynamic	Jurisdiction/ Authority	Resources Required	Politicians' Motivations for Innovation	Communications Flows Across States	Likely Policy Result
Preemption/ Supplantation	States have shared jurisdiction, but national government has preemption authority.	Resource requirements are limited.	Responding to (1) voter preferences that are relatively homogeneous across states, and/or (2) business preferences for uniform regulatory regime	Strong	Policy outputs become more heterogeneous in initial stages of innovation, then more homogeneous as uniform federal policy supplants state choices.
"Race to the bottom"	States have exclusive or shared jurisdiction.	Resource requirements are high.	Fear of competitive effects on mobile factors of production	Strong	Policy outputs are homogeneous across states at low level of intervention.
Mutual buck-passing	States and central government have unclear or shared jurisdiction.	Resource requirements are high.	Opponents of policy intervention powerful and concentrated	Strong	Policy outputs are homogeneous across states at low level of intervention.

deployed in states like California where environmental groups and values are strong, and European transport policy ideas might be adopted in states or localities with dense populations similar to many European jurisdictions. Indeed, David Vogel (2012) has noted that California has often been an entry point for European-style and European-influenced regulations into the United States.

A large literature also suggests, however, that policy adoptions in states are not entirely independent: Policy adoptions in one state may affect outcomes in other states through learning, competition, or some combination of the two. Moreover, the specific policy dynamics of policy innovation and whether or not innovations spread among states may vary across sectors. On the optimistic side, federalism may provide an opportunity to experiment ("laboratory of democracy") with policy ideas, including those with European origins, that have not yet (and may never) gained broad national acceptance. As evidence from state-level experiments emerges, successful innovations in one or a few states may be observed by policymakers in other states and eventually diffused quite broadly, or even adopted as national policy by the federal government (Gray 1973; Karch 2007). Federalism is most likely to lead to this learning-based diffusion of innovation over time when (1) subnational units have at least shared jurisdiction over a sector; (2) reforms require modest budgetary and administrative resources or even save money; (3) the policy and the constituency it serves are popular with the public in most states, and political opposition is limited or politically marginal; and (4) channels for transmitting policy lessons between states are strong. In some situations, the federal government may preempt or supplant state actions at some point in the diffusion process. This is most likely when jurisdictional arrangements explicitly permit federal preemption of state action and a strong constituency wants a uniform set of rules across states rather than a patchwork of inconsistent state policies. Business interests seeking to avoid aggressive policies in some states are especially likely to promote preemption, or at least "ceiling preemptions" that prevent lower level governments from exceeding a particular standard (see Pertschuk et al. 2013).

Federalism may also have perverse competitive consequences, however. Federalism may lead to competition between subnational units to attract business or discourage residence by those who are high consumers of public services, resulting in a *race to the bottom*—or at least to a provision of goods, services, or transfers less generous than would be the case if such competition was absent (Harrison 2006; Konisky 2007; Peterson and Rom 1990). Because of an interest in keeping their tax rates down, states might provide lower levels of transfers and services than they would otherwise prefer for fear that their policy efforts may encourage in-migration (and discourage out-migration) by persons who are likely to be high consumers of transfers and other government services if the states are more generous than neighboring political jurisdictions (see for example Berry,

Fording, and Hanson 2003)—a situation that Baybeck, Berry, and Seigel (2011) refer to as "defensive behavior." A race to the bottom is especially likely where states have discretion (or complete control) over program standards, the costs of policy are substantial and resource differences across states is high, and the policy or clientele served is unpopular. Finally, federalism may even lead to a mutual buck-passing by both levels of government—and thus to governmental inaction—especially in situations where it is unclear which government has legal authority over a policy sector, budgetary costs to government opposition are high, and there is concentrated opposition to government action from some societal interests that makes taking an initiative seem costly to politicians at both levels (Harrison 1996).

This review of evidence on the policy dynamics of federalism suggest that there is substantial variation across the sectoral cases discussed in this volume in the potential for subnational policy reform in the United States that draws on European experience. State ability to innovate in immigration policy is quite limited in the United States, although states have been pushing the boundaries in recent years. States have no role with respect to what criteria are used in setting rules for immigrant entry—indeed immigration is an exclusive jurisdiction of the federal government. However, a number of states have begun to take more assertive roles in border and illegal immigration enforcement, some of which have been upheld by the courts.

Opportunities for subnational reform are also quite limited in the public-pension sector, because of the dominant role of the Social Security program, the high costs of pension initiatives, and state fears of increasing costs through payroll taxes that would put them at a competitive disadvantage relative to other states. State initiatives are limited largely to small state supplements to the means-tested federal Supplemental Security Income program, and lesson drawing from Europe about minimum pension levels appears to be essentially non-existent. In short, effective (though not de jure) preemption has already taken place through federal legislation and is unlikely to be reversed.

In the health care sector, there are some opportunities for learning from European experience at the state level given the substantial roles given to the states by the Obama administration's Affordable Care Act (ACA). But the very limited success of states in moving toward universal coverage on their own (Gray et al. 2010), and the great resistance to implementing the ACA in many states where Republicans dominate state government, suggests that internal determinants (notably ideology and fiscal capacity) and race-to-the-bottom policy dynamics are likely to dominate where states have policymaking discretion in health care.

States also have some opportunities for innovation in climate change policy and have done so in a number of areas, such as policies to promote alternative energy (Matisoff 2008; Rabe 2004; Wiener and Koontz 2010), where many European governments have substantial experience. However efforts to pursue carbon-trading markets at the state level (notably in California) or through inter-state compacts have encountered the same pressures that have blocked them at the national level, specifically intense opposition from affected industries and fear that businesses will flee to other jurisdictions. As Steven Hill notes (see chap. 9), most major institutional reforms, such as a shift in electoral systems and public financing of campaigns, are more likely to occur at the subnational level rather than in Washington DC. But even here, the outlook is bleak, as recent highly partisan state-level battles over redistricting plans and voter-ID laws demonstrate (Savage and Fernandez 2012). In a situation of intense partisan polarization, electoral reforms like proportional representation that either lower the advantages enjoyed by a dominant party or that increase uncertainty are unlikely to be adopted. And given the low esteem in which politicians are held, proportional-representation electoral rules that strengthen the role of party leaders (which in most European systems utilize some form of closed or semi-closed list) are unlikely to gain broad popular support.

Perhaps the greatest opportunity for lesson drawing at the subnational level among the sectors discussed in this volume is the case of urban transportation and land use. As in Germany, these sectors are primarily matters of subnational jurisdiction in the United States. And while many projects in this sector are extremely expensive, others are not. Moreover, some federal funding is available for innovative practices in the United States.

The transportation case offers important strategic lessons as well as substantive ones, notably on sequencing policy changes, with those having the policies with broadest support implemented first and involving citizens in the planning process. There are, nevertheless, important differences that limit direct lesson copying across the Atlantic, especially the much higher reliance of Americans on auto travel and thus greater resistance to auto-restrictive policies. The general lesson here is that concentrating reform efforts that draw on European experience in favorable subnational venues may be the best strategy in a few policy sectors, but reform advocates should not assume that this strategy can be pursued in most policy sectors.

Potential Pitfalls in Policy Implementation and Sustainability

The barriers to adopting policy lessons from Europe are formidable, as the discussion above suggests. Even if a government does adopt substantive and administrative aspects of policy from abroad, several problems may arise in the transfer process that undercut the effectiveness of a reform over the short or long term. These can be divided into two categories: *policy implementation* problems and *political sustainability* problems. Implementation problems include poor coordination across multiple agencies and levels of government, resistance from front-line workers, and failure of the targets of public policy to adjust their behavior in ways sought by policymakers—for example, resistance by commuters to leaving their cars, or resistance by workers to extending their working lives and saving more for retirement (Weaver, forthcoming). As Dolowitz and Marsh (2000; see also James and Lodge 2003) have noted, policymakers in the "learning" country may lack adequate information about the requisites for successful copying or adaptation of that reform. If the US political environment is characterized by, for instance, higher levels of coordination problems among agencies than in a policy's country of origin, the benefits associated with that policy might not be realized to the same extent.

For many policies, European experience can provide empirically rich lessons about problems that may arise in the policy implementation process. Even where policies are formally the same within the EU, differences in policy implementation as a result of variations in governmental capacity, political will of governing leaders, and civil society pressures can lead to differing policy outputs and outcomes (Falkner, 2010; Falkner and Treib 2008). This is both good news and bad news for potential US lesson drawers: On the positive side, looking at a variety of European experiences can help to give a deeper understanding of what constraints might lead to different outcomes on this side of the Atlantic. On the negative side, looking at multiple European experiences raises learning costs, which are already likely to be high. Thus, there is a risk that learning may draw on an unrepresentative sample of countries: those that have had a successful experience and are touting their success but that may not have the same set of underlying conditions found in the United States.

The political sustainability of borrowed reforms must also be considered. Over time, programmatic changes tend to create new interest and constituencies that frequently bolster those policies by creating a constituency against change (Pierson 2000). But a self-reinforcing political dynamic is not always present. Eric Patashnik (2003, 2008) has argued that even after major policy reforms are adopted, they are subject both to outright reversal or to erosion—modifications that alter and may undercut the intended purposes of reform without gutting it entirely. In the United States, temporary majorities (e.g., during periods of united party control of the national government) may enact policies that are later subject to attempts at reversal (e.g., the Obama health care plan) or which are increasingly captured by attentive constituencies, contrary to the intentions of those who originated the proposal. Thus a thorough analysis of proposals to adapt European policies for the United States must include an understanding of potential second-order effects on postreform agendas, participants, and bargaining leverage.

Strategic Lessons for Promoting Policy Change

The analysis above and the case study chapters in this volume make it clear that even where specific European policy experience offers potentially transferable substantive policy lessons for the United States, there is no guarantee that such lessons will be adopted. Nor is there a single strategic template available to policy-makers and advocates seeking to shift US policy in a direction informed by European experience. Instead, strategies must be adapted to the distinctive political and institutional dynamics that characterize individual policy sectors. Different sectors are conducive to different pathways to policy transfer, each with their distinctive ways of coupling the problem, policy, and political streams. Several strategic lessons are in order for those who seek to apply European policy experience to the United States.

First, framing the rationale for policy reform as "this policy works in Europe" should not be the main framing of any effort to sell a policy reform. Rather the main rationale should be that a reform can help to address a specific, concrete problem for the United States. Indeed, saying that it works in Europe might be political poison. In many cases, policies of European origin can be reframed in a way that is both workable and politically sellable in a US context. But proponents of such reforms should also be prepared to defend against efforts to frame their proposals as "inappropriate" European imports by those who do not want change from the status quo.

Second, Kingdon's analysis of policy windows suggests some important practical implications for advocates of particular policy approaches both inside and outside government. Reform advocates should be both persistent and prepared to mobilize resources quickly, given the unpredictable nature of opening and closing of policy windows.

Third, the presence of multiple veto points in US political institutions also suggests that advocates of policy change should take partial victories where they can win rather than engaging in "strategic disagreement" (Gilmour 1995) and holding out for a more complete victory later on. It is often difficult to know which policy compromise is the "camel's nose" that can be expanded on in later initiatives and which is a dead end that will stall reforms by giving rise to perceived policy failures or leading to a political backlash. But the structure of American political institutions and the current state of American politics suggest that a small but certain victory now is generally preferable to an uncertain hope for a bigger victory in the future.

Endnote

1. The existing literature frequently distinguishes between policy transfers that occur voluntarily on the part of the recipient country (often characterized as *lesson drawing*) and those that involve some degree of coercion on the part of another government or

a supranational institution—for example, *conditionality* attached to loans from international financial institutions (see for example Dolowitz and Marsh 1996). The boundaries between the two are not always clear in practice: for example, competitive pressures can result in indirect coercion to lower corporate tax rates or environmental standards, and heavy dependence on a single external national market can create pressures to adhere to the product standards of that market. The focus here will be solely on lesson drawing that is largely *voluntary*.

References

Alesina, A., and E. L. Glaeser. *Fighting poverty in the US and Europe: A world of difference.* Oxford: Oxford University Press, 2004.

Baybeck, B., W. D. Berry, and D. A. Siegel. "A strategic theory of policy diffusion via intergovernmental competition." *Journal of Politics* 73, no. 1 (2011): 232–47.

Berry, W. D., R. C. Fording, and R. L. Hanson. "Reassessing the 'race to the bottom' in state welfare policy." *Journal of Politics* 65, no. 2 (2003): 327–49.

Betsill, M. M., and H. Bulkeley. "Transnational networks and global environmental governance: The cities for climate protection program." *International Studies Quarterly* 48, no. 2 (2004): 471–93.

Dobbin, F., B. Simmons, and G. Garrett. "The global diffusion of public policies: Social construction, coercion, competition, or learning?" *Annual Review of Sociology* 33 (2007): 449–72.

Dolowitz, D. P., and D. Marsh. "Learning from abroad: The role of policy transfer in contemporary policymaking." *Governance* 13, no. 1 (2000): 5–23.

———. "Who learns what from whom: A review of the policy transfer literature." *Political Studies* 44, no. 2 (1996): 343–57.

Downs, A. "Up and down with ecology: The issue attention cycle." *Public Interest* 28, no. 1 (1972): 38–50.

Fairbrother, M. "Rich people, poor people, and environmental concern: Evidence across nations and time." *European Sociological Review,* forthcoming.

Falkner, G. "Institutional performance and compliance with EU law: Czech Republic, Hungary, Slovakia and Slovenia." *Journal of Public Policy* 30, no. 1 (2010): 101–16.

Falkner, G., and O. Treib. "Three worlds of compliance or four? The EU-15 compared to new member states." *Journal of Common Market Studies* 46, no. 2 (2008): 293–313.

Frech, H. E., III, S. T. Parente, and J. Hoff. *US health care: A reality check on cross-country comparisons.* Health Policy Outlook No. 3. Washington, DC: American Enterprise Institute, July 2012. http://www.aei.org/files/2012/07/11/-us-health-care-a-reality-check-on-crosscountry-comparisons_10021827743.pdf.

Gilens, M. *Why Americans hate welfare: Race, media, and the politics of antipoverty policy.* Chicago: University of Chicago Press, 2009.

Gilmour, J. B. *Strategic disagreement: Stalemate in American politics.* Pittsburgh: University of Pittsburgh Press, 1995.

Goodman, J. D. "Bike lanes proliferate, and protest gets louder." *New York Times,* November 23, 2010: A26.

Gornick, J., and M. Meyers. "More alike than different: Revisiting the long-term prospects for developing 'European-style' work/family policies in the United States." *Journal of Comparative Policy Analysis: Research and Practice* 6, no. 3 (2004): 251–73.

Gray, V. "Innovation in the states: A diffusion study." *The American Political Science Review* 67, no. 4 (1973): 1174–85.

Gray, V., D. Lowery, J. Monogan, and E. K. Godwin. "Incrementing toward nowhere: Universal health care coverage in the states." *Publius: The Journal of Federalism* 40, no. 1 (2010): 82–113.

Grynbaum, M. M., and M. Connelly. "Bicycle lanes draw wide support among New Yorkers, survey says." *New York Times,* August 22, 2012: A20.

Hacker, J. S. "The historical logic of national health insurance: Structure and sequence in the development of British, Canadian, and US medical policy." *Studies in American Political Development* 12, no. 1 (1998): 57–130.

———. "Privatizing risk without privatizing the welfare state: The hidden politics of social policy retrenchment in the United States." *American Political Science Review* 98, no. 2 (2004): 243–60.

Harrison, K. *Passing the buck: Federalism and Canadian environmental policy*. Vancouver: University of British Columbia Press, 1996.

Harrison, K., ed. *Racing to the bottom? Provincial interdependence in the Canadian federation*. Vancouver: University of British Columbia Press, 2006.

Inglehart, R. "Public support for environmental protection: Objective problems and subjective values in 43 societies." *Political Science and Politics* 28, no. 1 (1995): 57–72.

Jacobs, A., and R. K. Weaver. *Policy feedbacks and policy change*. Paper presented at the 2010 annual meeting of the American Political Science Association, Washington, DC, September 2010.

Jacques, P. J., R. E. Dunlap, and M. Freeman. "The organisation of denial: Conservative think tanks and environmental scepticism." *Environmental Politics* 17, no. 3 (2008): 349–85.

James, O., and M. Lodge. "The limitations of 'policy transfer' and 'lesson drawing' for public policy research." *Political Studies Review* 1, no. 2 (2003): 179–93.

Karch, A. *Democratic laboratories: Policy diffusion among the American states*. Ann Arbor: University of Michigan Press, 2007.

Kahneman, D., and A. Tversky. "Prospect theory: An analysis of decision under risk." *Econometrica: Journal of the Econometric Society* 47, no. 2 (1979): 263–91.

Kelemen, R. D., and D. Vogel. "Trading places: The role of the United States and the European Union in international environmental politics." *Comparative Political Studies* 43, no. 4 (2010): 427–56.

King, A. "Ideas, institutions and the policies of governments: A comparative analysis: Parts I and II." *British Journal of Political Science* 3, no. 3 (1973): 291–313.

Kingdon, J. W. *Agendas, alternatives, and public policies*. 2nd edition. New York: HarperCollins, 1995.

———. *America the unusual*. New York: Bedford St. Martins, 1999.

Konisky, D. M. "Regulatory competition and environmental enforcement: Is there a race to the bottom?" *American Journal of Political Science* 51, no. 4 (2007): 853–72.

Mann, T. E., and N. J. Ornstein. *It's even worse than it looks: How the American constitutional system collided with the new politics of extremism*. New York: Basic Books, 2012.

Marmor, T. R. "Health care reform in the United States: Patterns of fact and fiction in the use of Canadian experience." *American Review of Canadian Studies* 23, no. 1 (1993): 47–64.

Marmor, T. R., R. Freeman, and K. Okma. "Comparative perspectives and policy learning in the world of health care." *Journal of Comparative Policy Analysis* 7, no. 4 (2005): 331–48.

Marsden, G., K. T. Frick, A. D. May, and E. Deakin. "How do cities approach policy innovation and policy learning? A study of 30 policies in Northern Europe and North America." *Transport Policy* 18, no. 3 (2011): 501–12.

Matisoff, D. C. "The adoption of state climate change policies and renewable portfolio standards: Regional diffusion or internal determinants?" *Review of Policy Research* 25, no. 6 (2008): 527–46.

Mintrom, M., and S. Vergari. "Advocacy coalitions, policy entrepreneurs, and policy change." *Policy Studies Journal* 24, no. 3 (1996): 420–34.

Muennig, P. A., and S. A. Glied. "What changes in survival rates tell us about US health care." *Health Affairs* 29, no. 11 (2010): 2105–13.

Organisation for Economic Co-operation and Development. *Economic Policy Reforms 2010: Going for Growth*. Paris: Organisation for Economic Co-operation and Development, 2010.

Patashnik, E. "After the public interest prevails: The political sustainability of policy reform." *Governance* 16, no. 2 (2003): 203–34.

———. *Reforms at risk: What happens after major policy changes are enacted*. Princeton, NJ: Princeton University Press, 2008.

Pedersen, L. H. "Ideas are transformed as they transfer: A comparative study of eco-taxation in Scandinavia." *Journal of European Public Policy* 14, no. 1 (2007): 59–77.

Pertschuk, M., J. L. Pomeranz, J. R. Aoki, M. A. Larkin, and M. Paloma. "Assessing the impact of federal and state preemption in public health: A framework for decision makers." *Journal of Public Health Management and Practice* 19, no. 3 (2013): 213–19.

Peterson, E., and M. C. Rom. *Welfare magnets: A new case for a national standard.* Washington, DC: Brookings Institution, 1990.

Pierson, P. "When effect becomes cause: Policy feedback and political change." *World Politics* 45, no. 4 (1993): 595–628.

———. "Irresistible forces, immovable objects: Post-industrial welfare states confront permanent austerity." *Journal of European Public Policy* 5, no. 4 (1998): 539–60.

———. "Increasing returns, path dependence, and the study of politics." *The American Political Science Review* 94, no. 2 (2000): 251–67.

———. "Coping with permanent austerity: Welfare state restructuring in affluent democracies." In *The new politics of the welfare state,* edited by P. Pierson (410–56). Oxford: Oxford University Press, 2001.

Pralle, S. B. "Agenda-setting and climate change." *Environmental Politics* 18, no. 5 (2009): 781–99.

Reinhardt, U. E., P. S. Hussey, and G. F. Anderson. "US health care spending in an international context." *Health Affairs* 23, no. 3 (2004): 10–25.

Rose, R. *Lesson-drawing in public policy.* Chatham, England: Chatham House, 1993.

Savage, C., and M. Fernandez. "Court points to discrimination in halting Texas voter ID law." *New York Times*, August 31, 2012: A11.

Sniderman, P. M., and T. Piazza. *The scar of race.* Cambridge, MA: Belknap Press, 1995.

Stone, D. A. "Causal stories and the formation of policy agendas." *Political Science Quarterly* 104, no. 2 (1989): 281–300.

Stone, Diane. "Non-governmental policy transfer: The strategies of independent policy institutes." *Governance* 13, no. 1 (2000): 45–70.

Tarrow, S. "States and opportunities: The political structuring of social movements." In *Comparative perspectives on social movements: Political opportunities, mobilizing structures and political framings,* edited by D. McAdam, J. D. McCarthy, and M. N. Zald (41–61). New York: Cambridge University Press, 1996.

Vogel, D. *The politics of precaution: Regulating health, safety, and environmental risks in Europe and the United States.* Princeton, NJ: Princeton University Press, 2012.

Weaver, R. K. "The politics of policy toward low income families." In *Making the work-based safety net work better,* J. K. Scholz and C. Heinrich, (292–338). New York: Russell Sage Foundation, 2009.

———. "Paths and forks or chutes and ladders? Negative feedbacks and policy regime change." *Journal of Public Policy* 30, no. 2 (2010): 137–62.

———. "Compliance regimes and barriers to behavioral change." *Governance,* forthcoming.

Wiener, J. G., and T. M. Koontz. "Shifting winds: Explaining variation in state policies to promote small-scale wind energy." *Policy Studies Journal* 38, no. 4 (2010): 629–51.

Wilson, G. "Exceptionalism in a time of stress." *Harvard Journal of Law and Public Policy* 32, no. 2 (2009): 455–71.

Index

⑤SAGE research**methods**

The essential online tool for researchers from the world's leading methods publisher

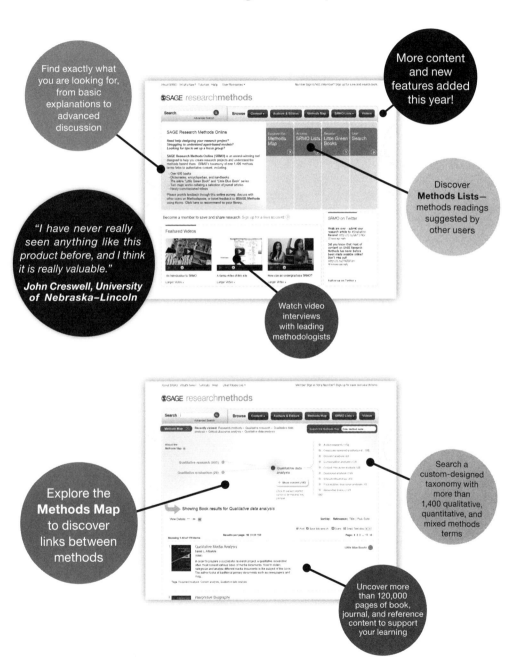

Find exactly what you are looking for, from basic explanations to advanced discussion

More content and new features added this year!

"I have never really seen anything like this product before, and I think it is really valuable."

John Creswell, University of Nebraska–Lincoln

Discover **Methods Lists**— methods readings suggested by other users

Watch video interviews with leading methodologists

Explore the **Methods Map** to discover links between methods

Search a custom-designed taxonomy with more than 1,400 qualitative, quantitative, and mixed methods terms

Uncover more than 120,000 pages of book, journal, and reference content to support your learning

Find out more at
www.sageresearchmethods.com